Bowls, Polls & Tattered Souls

Tackling the Chaos and Controversy That Reign over College Football

STEWART MANDEL

WILEY

John Wiley

Published by John Wiley & Sons, Inc., Hoboken, New Jersey
Published simultaneously in Canada

Design and composition by Navta Associates, Inc.

For general information about our other products and services, please contact our Customer Care Department within the United States at (800) 762-2974, outside the United States at (317) 572-3993, or fax (317) 572-4002.

Wiley also publishes its books in a variety of electronic formats. Some content that appears in print may not be available in electronic books. For more information about Wiley products, visit our web site at www.wiley.com.

Library of Congress Cataloging-in-Publication Data

Mandel, Stewart.
    Bowls, polls, and tattered souls : tackling the chaos and controversy that reign over college football / Stewart Mandel.
        p. cm.
    Rev. ed. of: Bowls, polls & tattered souls. c2007.
    Includes index.
    ISBN 978-0-470-04917-4 (cloth)
    ISBN 978-0-470-37355-2 (pbk.)
    1. Football—United States. 2. College sports—United States. 3. Bowl Championship Series. I. Mandel, Stewart. Bowls, polls & tattered souls. II. Title.
    GV951.M25 2008
    796.332—dc22

                                                                2008017089

Printed in the United States of America

10   9   8   7   6   5   4   3   2   1

CONTENTS

Introduction

What do you do for a living? Me? I deal with confused people. Lots of them. All day. Every day.

It's true I also attend football games, conduct interviews, and write stories. But the confused people—they're the one constant throughout. Their bewildered queries, their pleas for clarity await me nearly every time I check my e-mail, filling my in-box by the hundreds. Their messages often start the same way: "How can you possibly explain . . . ," "Am I missing something here, or . . . ?," "Maybe you can help me figure something out . . . ," or, my personal favorite, "How can you be such an idiot?"

I cover the great sport of college football for SI.com and *Sports Illustrated*. Anyone who's ever spent a Saturday in the Horseshoe (Ohio State) or the Swamp (Florida), the Big House (Michigan) or Death Valley (LSU), knows well that what makes college football so special is not necessarily the action on the field but the collective energy of the ninety thousand diehards in the stadium surrounding it. The depth of passion among college football fans is unlike that of any other American sport, surpassed in intensity perhaps only by that of other countries' soccer fans. Though many college football fans are certifiably nutty, fortunately, they've yet to reach the point of assassinating a quarterback. (Riots, on the other hand, are not out of the question.)

Since 2003, I've been interacting with these fans on a weekly basis, thanks to the Mailbag column I pen for SI.com. The idea of the Mailbag is to answer several reader-submitted questions, usually pertaining to particular events in the news that week. Most readers, understandably, are primarily concerned about their own favorite teams and are seeking my opinion about something. Do I think they'll win this weekend? Do I think their coach is the right guy for the job? Do I think their star running back has a chance at the Heisman? And, of course, the obligatory, "Why don't you give my team more respect?" College football fans seek validation for their teams from the national media the way a two-year-old seeks attention from his mommy. They can't help it—they're an extremely proud bunch.

They're also, as I've found out, an extremely confused bunch, and to be honest, I can't say I blame them. If you stop and think about it, not much about college football makes a lot of logical sense, from the way its champion is determined to the schedules the teams play to the fact the coaches can make $4 million a year while the players scrap for laundry money. Truth be told, the entire sport is basically a season-long exercise in chaos, which is why, when I filter through several hundred Mailbag submissions each week, there are a host of recurring questions that continually come up. Like, say, why is college football the lone remaining sport on the planet without a playoff? And while we're at it, why the need for thirty-two bowl games? Why does the Big Ten have eleven teams? How does recruiting work? Who exactly votes for the Heisman Trophy? And why do so many Heisman winners flop in the NFL? Why is it that a team like undefeated Boise State does not even get the chance to play for the national championship? Why does Notre Dame get its own TV contract?

And, oh yeah—tell me again why we don't have a playoff?

I occasionally take stabs at these and other similar topics in the Mailbag, but the reality is, most are extremely complicated issues that cannot possibly be summed up in a couple of paragraphs. And that's why I wrote this book. I figured it was long past time that somebody with firsthand knowledge of the situation sat down and took the time to explain, in detailed yet still (I hope) easy-to-understand terms, why exactly college football is the way it is. Each chapter of *Bowls, Polls & Tattered Souls* tackles a different hot-button issue that I know from reading all those e-mails is a source of much consternation, confusion, and, in some cases, even anger and resentment among fans from Miami to Minnesota, Cal to Clemson. The much-despised BCS is obviously the most pervasive and divisive of all college football topics, which is why it's also first on the list of chapters, but in truth, there's almost no element of the sport that does not generate its own share of controversy.

Before we get into the meat and potatoes, I think it's important to understand one underlying truth about college football that digs to the heart of the sport's prevailing sense of chaos. And that is: Nobody's in charge. I'm serious. There is no commissioner in college football like there is in professional sports. There isn't even one central office or organization that oversees the sport. You might think it's the NCAA, but that's not true. While all of the schools that participate in football are NCAA members that abide by its rules and participate in its championships for every other sport, football is the one sport that has managed to basically remain a free-for-all.

Think about it. At the start of the year, Major League Baseball draws up the season schedule for all thirty teams, which all play an equal number of home and away games. In college football, each conference constructs its schedule differently depending on the number of teams, and each school decides for itself whether to play a hard or easy non-conference slate. Some teams open against Texas A&M and Clemson, others against Texas State and the Citadel. There's no confusion in the NFL as to how the playoffs work—the owners of all thirty-two teams agree to the rules and the league office administers them. The BCS, on the other hand, is basically run by the six richest conferences, much to the chagrin of the other five. When a brawl breaks out during a Knicks game at Madison Square Garden, it's NBA commissioner David Stern who levies the suspensions. When a brawl breaks out during the Miami-Florida International game, it's left to the two teams and their conference to decide what's a fair punishment, and one side's assessment may be completely different from the other's.

Complete chaos, I tell you.

The most glaring recent example of college football's decentralized nature one could possibly imagine occurred on September 16, 2006. It was a much-anticipated Saturday that included seven games between ranked opponents, including Nebraska at USC, Michigan at Notre Dame, and Florida at Tennessee, but one, number 15 Oklahoma at number 18 Oregon, wound up overshadowing all others because of a truly bizarre and unfortunate ending. After scoring a touchdown with 1:12 remaining to cut the Sooners' lead to 33–27, the Ducks lined up for an onside kick, their last remaining hope of winning the game contingent on recovering it, which they did—at least according to the officials. Since 2005, the NCAA has allowed conferences to employ an instant-replay system, much like the NFL, in which an advisory official in the press box with access to television replay angles can adjust or overrule a call on the field if deemed incorrect. The process usually holds up the game for several minutes. Such was the case with this call. As sixty thousand spectators at Autzen Stadium waited for the decision, viewers watching at home on ABC were treated to twelve different replays of the kick from five different angles—all of which showed quite clearly that Oregon player Brian Paysinger had touched the ball within a 10-yard radius, thus invalidating the Ducks' recovery. But that wasn't all—Oregon never had the ball. At least one camera angle showed that while the refs had rushed to the scene of the pileup, the ball itself had scooted out from the scrum and into the hands of nearby Oklahoma player Allen Patrick, who nonchalantly walked off with it.

After 4 minutes of deliberation, however, the replay officials some-how upheld the call. Given new life, Oregon promptly drove down the field for the go-ahead touchdown and Oklahoma missed a long field-goal attempt on the final play. Game over. The ensuing controversy was immediate and immense. Within hours, the clips of the incriminating replay had been plastered all over YouTube. Incensed Oklahoma fans lit up my in-box urging me to treat the game as a Sooners victory when filling out that week's AP ballot. Two days later, the president of the university, David Boren, would write a letter to Big 12 commissioner Kevin Weiberg asking him to push for the game to be eliminated from the record books due to what Boren described as "an outrageous injustice." After reviewing what happened, Pac-10 commissioner Tom Hansen acknowledged an error had been made and responded by suspending the members of the officiating crew for one game and issuing an apology to Oklahoma.

Over the next few days, however, further details about the incident emerged—and they weren't pretty. First, it was revealed that the Pac-10 had a rule in place requiring its schools to use Pac-10 officials for home nonconference games, and that the replay official who ultimately made the decision, Gordon Riese, was a Portland, Oregon, native. Charges of home cooking were plentiful, and Riese received threatening phone calls and at least one death threat. Furthermore, it would eventually come out that due to a technical error, Riese had not been able to view all the different camera angles that fans had seen at home. And while other conferences, including the Big Ten and the SEC, had plunked down extra money for the high-end DVSport replay system, which uses the same touch-screen technology as the NFL, the Pac-10 was apparently using a cheaper system that is essentially a glorified TiVo. None of these details sat well with Oklahoma fans, who continued to cry foul the rest of the season, never knowing whether their team, which finished the regular season 11–2 and Big 12 champion, could have made a national-title run had the correct call been made and they hadn't lost to Oregon.

So let's review. Only in college football would a team get to choose who officiates its home games. By all accounts, Riese, a twenty-eight-year officiating veteran, was an honest man who was so torn up by what happened that, following a one-game suspension, he took a leave of absence the rest of the season, eventually lost his job, and said he was diagnosed with depression. Still, his role in the home-state team's controversial win didn't exactly give off the greatest appearance. Only in college football would there be no uniform standard across the sport for what type of replay equipment conferences should use. You think the Packers are using DVSport while the Seahawks are using TiVo? Only in college football would the decision of how to treat the game result in the context of the national-championship race be left to the entirely subjective realm of the voters. And, of course, only in college football would the aftermath of such a controversy inspire so much venom as to elicit a passionate, albeit over-the-top letter like the one Boren wrote.

The unfortunate by-product of all this chaos is that it's created an unmistakable case of paranoia among both fans and participants of the sport. Nobody trusts anyone in college football—not the opposing coaches, not the rule-makers, and certainly not the media. After all, theirs is the only sport on the planet where the media has a say in the final outcome. Personally, I've been accused at one time or another of being a Michigan grad with an obvious bias against Ohio State, and an Ohio State grad with a blatant hatred toward Michigan. Some tell me I'm an East Coast snob with a bias against West Coast teams, while others insist I'm a USC homer who hates anyone in the Heartland. In the interest of full disclosure, I should also confess that, according to my readers, I am biased against Florida, Florida State, Miami, Tennessee, Auburn, Georgia, Virginia Tech, Penn State, Oklahoma, Texas, Texas A&M, Texas Tech, Cal, Oregon, Nebraska, Iowa, Wisconsin, Louisville, West Virginia, and Boise State.

Why, might you ask, would all these fans think I have it out for their school? Because, at some time or another, I probably wrote something negative about their team. In most cases, it was probably deserved. In many cases, it was a one-time thing. And in nearly every case, I was probably just trying to get a cheap laugh. But in the profoundly partisan mind of the true college football fan, there can be no gray area. You are either for us or you are against us. You either sing the fight song on Saturdays, or you're the enemy.

The topics in this book, though, are universal to fans of all teams—and every one of them can be traced to the aforementioned lack of a central leader in college football. Nearly every element of the sport is defined by a power struggle of some sort—be it the never-ending fight by bowl games to remain relevant in the twenty-first century or the Darwinian struggle of schools to affiliate with the strongest possible conference; the battle among recruiting analysts to break the news of that next big commitment or the unspoken competition among athletic directors to hire the splashiest coach.

One cannot follow college football on even a casual level without being affected in some way by the chaos and the controversy. I can't say that reading this book will make it any easier to swallow the injustice of seeing your undefeated team get left out of the national championship game. It probably won't make you feel any better about those NCAA sanctions your team just got slapped with while your rival down the road keeps getting off scot-free. And I'm not sure reading this book will make you any more fired up to watch the PapaJohns.com Bowl. Hopefully, however, you'll have a much better understanding of why these things are the way they are. The only thing I ask in return: Please, don't shoot the messenger.

1

One Nation, Under the BCS

Controversy isn't all bad. It keeps people interested in the game, keeps them talking about it.

—Former SEC commissioner Roy Kramer, primary architect of the Bowl Championship Series, 1999

———

The BCS is, simply, the worst idea in sports. . . . Worse than the designated hitter. Worse than the possession arrow. If you could find someone playing indoor soccer, they would agree it's worse than that, too.

—St. Petersburg (Florida) Times, *2004*

E very day, on college campuses all across the country, bright young
scholars and renowned professors work to solve many of society's
greatest dilemmas. America's universities have helped formulate
national and international policy, improve Fortune 500 companies,
decode ancient texts, and cure deadly diseases. Yet these same schools
can't seem to devise a conclusive way to determine which one has the
best football team in a given season.

Since 1998, college football's national champion has been decided
by something called the Bowl Championship Series, or BCS. In order
to properly explain what the BCS is, it is helpful to first clarify what the
BCS is *not*:

1. The BCS is not an actual organization. You cannot walk into some
   skyscraper in New York City or an office park in Topeka, Kansas,
   and ask to "speak to someone with the BCS," because the BCS
   does not physically exist. The phrase "Bowl Championship Series"
   refers solely to a coalition of college football's four most prestigious
   bowl games, the Rose, Orange, Sugar, and Fiesta, which between
   them take turns hosting a fifth game, the BCS National Championship. Technically there is no actual Series, either, just a championship game and four separate, completely unrelated bowls. The
   phrase "Bowl Championship Series" was devised by a former
   ABC exec who figured it would make for catchier promos than,
   "Tune in next week for Some Really Big Bowl Games."

2. Unlike March Madness, the sixty-five-team NCAA tournament
   that concludes each college basketball season, the BCS is *not* an
   NCAA-administered event. The NCAA has never awarded an
   official national championship for its highest level, Division I-A.
   In fact, other than a largely cursory certification process for bowl

games ("Do you have a stadium?" "Yes." "Will you be selling hot dogs?" "Yup, brats and nachos, too." "How about $30 T-shirts?" "Most definitely." "Perfect, you're certified"), the NCAA has almost no authority over college football's Division I-A postseason. Everything pertaining to the BCS and its national championship game, from payouts to entry rules to uniform colors, is determined by administrators from the nation's major conferences (such as the Big Ten and the SEC) and Notre Dame, which, while unable to beat the top teams in those leagues, manages to retain the same level of clout. Imagine for a moment that the World Series was operated not by Major League Baseball, but by the Yankees, Red Sox, Cubs, and Cardinals, and you have the BCS.

3. Finally—and as its rulers would be the first tell you—the BCS is *not*, nor was it ever intended to be, a playoff. The participants in the national title game are the number 1 and 2 teams at the end of the regular season as determined by a convoluted rankings system (more on that in a moment). The winners of the other BCS games do not feed into that game, nor do the other four bowls necessarily match the next-best teams (that is, number 3 vs. number 4, number 5 vs. number 6). They do, however, hand out some very pretty trophies.

"The current structure is designed to match the number 1 and 2 ranked teams, identified through a ranking system, in a bowl game," Big 12 commissioner Kevin Weiberg explained to a congressional panel in 2003. "It is an extension of the bowl system." Unfortunately, no one bothered to ask college football fans beforehand whether they wanted to see the bowl system extended. And thus the most divisive creation in the history of American spectator sports was born.

The BCS was devised in the mid-1990s by the commissioners of the nation's major conferences (and Notre Dame) in response to years of fan frustration over "split national championships," the semiregular occurrences where different teams would finish the season number 1 in the sport's two recognized polls, the Associated Press and coaches, having never had a chance to meet on the field. There have been ten such splits since UPI introduced the coaches' poll in 1950, including three (1990, 1991, and 1997) in the eight seasons immediately prior to the BCS's inception. The idea was to stage the sport's first official number 1 versus number 2 championship game while still preserving the longtime tradition of bowl games. There had been similar attempts in the past, including the Bowl Coalition (1992–94) and Bowl Alliance (1995–1997), but none could guarantee a number 1 versus number 2 game due to the Big Ten and Pac-10's exclusive partnership with the Rose Bowl. This proved particularly exasperating in 1994, when Nebraska and Penn State both finished undefeated. The Huskers swept the number 1 spot in both polls after beating number 3 Miami in the Orange Bowl, while the Nittany Lions could do little to impress voters by routing number 12 Oregon in the Rose Bowl. "It's a shame that the two best teams in the country didn't play each other," said Penn State quarterback Kerry Collins. Apparently others agreed. After years of resistance—and at the strong urging of TV partner ABC—the Big Ten, Pac-10, and Rose Bowl signed on to a so-called Super Alliance (later dubbed the BCS) allowing those leagues' champions to play in a different bowl in years they finished number 1 or 2. ABC paid a reported $296 million for the rights to all four games for four years, beginning with the 1998 season. (The championship game did not become a separate entity until 2006, when the BCS expanded to five games.) "The Rose Bowl was the missing link," then-ACC commissioner Gene Corrigan said in announcing the deal on July 23, 1996. "This is the Super Alliance. This is the ultimate."

As officials across college football took turns patting one another on the back following the announcement, the last Big Ten athletic director to sign off on the deal, Michigan's Joe Roberson, expressed his reservations to the *Los Angeles Times*. "The first thing I don't like about it is that it turns the Rose Bowl, in years it doesn't have the national title game, into a loser's bowl. All the attention and focus will be on that title game," said Roberson. " . . . Another thing I don't like about it is that the first year we have three or four claimants to those first two spots, there will be a lot of complaining, and that will result in more pressure, more demands for an NFL-style playoff."

Joe Roberson resigned from his job a year later, but he could not have been a bigger prophet if he'd predicted the dates of the next ten major earthquakes.

To say the BCS has been "unpopular" since its inception is like saying that Britney Spears's career is starting to suffer. BCS-bashing among fans, newspaper columnists, talk-radio hosts, and even coaches has become almost as common a December tradition as the Army-Navy game, particularly when there is any sort of controversy surrounding the national-title game matchup. "The Bowl Championship Series is a flawed and idiotic way to decide who should be the best and brightest in college football," *St. Louis Post-Dispatch* columnist Bryan Burwell wrote after 12–1 Florida edged 11–1 Michigan for a spot in the 2006 game. "I don't think there is any question that there are flaws in the system," said Wolverines coach Lloyd Carr. "I hope one day we have a system where all the issues are decided on the field."

To defend the BCS for a moment, the bigwigs who devised the thing never claimed their invention would be a foolproof method for crowning a champion. "It's not perfect," said former SEC commissioner Roy Kramer, the BCS's primary architect. "We never said it was." In fact, most of the title-game controversies over the years would have occurred whether there was a BCS in place or not. For instance, in 2004 Auburn fans went ballistic when their 12–0, SEC champions were left out of the title game in favor of fellow undefeated Oklahoma, whom number 1 USC wound up beating 55–19. Prior to the BCS, however, the Trojans would have automatically gone to the Rose Bowl to face Big Ten champion Michigan—ranked just number 13 that season—and both Auburn *and* Oklahoma would have been left in the cold. Furthermore, the two most memorable championship games of the BCS era—Ohio State's double-overtime upset of Miami in the 2002 title game and Texas's last-second 41–38 win over USC in 2005 (which garnered college football's highest TV rating in nineteen years)—involved matchups that would not have been possible before the Rose Bowl came on board. In both cases, the participants were undefeated, consensus number 1 and 2 teams that the nation was eager to see meet. So it's not as if the BCS hasn't been a step forward.

But in a sport where the teams only play twelve or thirteen games, you're inevitably going to have years where the number 1 and 2 teams are not clear-cut. Such ambiguity was part of the sport long before the BCS ever came into existence; it's just that now the disgruntled have a defined target at which to vent. Similarly, taxes were unpopular long before there was an IRS, but guess who gets the hate mail? Plus, much like those Washington bureaucrats, the minds behind the BCS have helped contribute to their image problem by giving the not-so-subtle impression that they're making up the rules as they go along. Nearly every season of the BCS's existence has presented a new, previously unimagined scenario, and with it another tweak to the rules or structure. In just nine years, the BCS has undergone more makeovers than Michael Jackson—and has been the butt of only slightly fewer jokes.

When the standings used to determine the BCS's number 1 and 2 teams first debuted in 1998, they included the AP and coaches' polls, a strength-of-schedule rating, and three computer polls (the *New York Times*, Jeff Sagarin, and the esteemed law firm of Anderson and Hester). This arcane formula, intended to reduce the effect of any human biases in the traditional polls, was the brainchild of Kramer, a former football coach and career athletic administrator with zero qualification as a mathematician. How did he come up with the thing? He had his minions test the formula by applying it to past seasons' results and making sure it spit out the correct two teams each year. Joked then-Florida coach Steve Spurrier, a longtime playoff advocate: "I think Commissioner Kramer's formula is so good that they ought to take it to basketball, baseball, tennis, and golf and make them go through it."

Apparently not convinced that his formula was complex enough, Kramer offered an open invitation the following summer to computer geeks across the country and wound up adding five more computer polls, bringing the total to eight. They included one by some guy named David Rothman. Another, the Dunkel Index, could both rank college football teams and predict the weather. This would be the first of four overhauls of the standings over the next seven years, nearly all of them in response to some previously unforeseen controversy:

1. The first really big ruckus happened in 2000, when Florida State, the number 3 team in both the AP and coaches' polls, reached the title game ahead of number 2 Miami—the one team FSU had lost to during the season.* Whoops. Adding insult to injury, the Seminoles lost 13–2 to Oklahoma in the Orange Bowl, that year's title game, while Miami whipped Florida in the Sugar Bowl. In response, the BCS added a "quality win" component the following season, giving teams a "bonus" for beating top-15 opponents. Had it been in place the previous year, Miami would have finished number 2. I'm sure the Hurricanes were relieved.

2. The next season provided an even bigger head-scratcher when, over Thanksgiving weekend, previously undefeated Nebraska lost its last game of the season 62–36 to 10–2 Colorado—then, over the next two weeks, proceeded to move back up to number 2 in the final standings when four teams above them lost. The Huskers went to the Rose Bowl, site of that year's title game, and got creamed 37–14 by Miami. Because Nebraska had benefited from numerous lopsided victories, the BCS's now-annual formula tweak involved ordering the computer geeks to remove any margin-of-victory factor from their respective rating systems. So, if you're keeping track, the formula now encompassed a team's record, schedule strength—and a bunch of computers that would solely evaluate record and schedule strength.

3. The 2003 season managed to produce the BCS's worst possible nightmare: USC, 11–1 and the number 1 team in both the AP and coaches' polls, managed to finish number 3 in the BCS standings, leaving 12–1 Oklahoma—despite having just lost its conference championship game to Kansas State 35–7—to play 12–1 LSU in the Sugar Bowl. The Tigers beat the Sooners and were promptly crowned national champions by the coaches, who were

---

*And number 4 Washington had beaten number 2 Miami. People didn't seem as sympathetic about the Huskies' exclusion, but Washington fans would kill me if I didn't mention them.

required to vote the winner of the title game number 1 in their final poll. The AP, free of any such obligation, stuck with the Trojans after their Rose Bowl win over Michigan, creating . . . a split national championship. "The fundamental mistake we made was we thought the public would accept a computer-influenced outcome," Big Ten commissioner Jim Delany said in 2005. "They used to rag on the coaches and the writers so much, espousing the various conspiracy theories about favoritism and regional biases. So we introduced computers, and as soon as the computers reorganized the order from what the voters had, suddenly *they* became the bad guys." In the BCS's most drastic overhaul to date, the formula was promptly rejiggered so that the human polls would account for 66 percent of a team's score—up from 25 percent in the past. Somewhere, the now-retired Kramer held a moment of silence for his de-emphasized computers.

4. Wouldn't you know it, just a year after they did that, the pollsters were dealt their own nightmare scenario: three major undefeated teams (USC, Oklahoma, and Auburn) up for two spots in the title game. The Trojans and Sooners had been number 1 and 2 all season, so, not surprisingly, the pollsters kept them that way—but not without some major-league lobbying from Auburn fans, who located voters' e-mail addresses and deluged them with arguments and statistics supporting the Tigers. That 2004 season also saw another controversy when, the last week of the season, voters moved 10–1 Texas ahead of 10–1 Cal for the number 4 position, allowing the Longhorns (whose coach Mack Brown had issued a public plea to the voters) to lock up a Rose Bowl at-large berth that would have gone to the Bears. Though journalists had been in the business of ranking the teams they cover for nearly seventy years, this particular conflict-of-interest crisis was too much for the AP to bear. Within weeks, the wire service's lawyers sent a nasty letter ordering the BCS to "cease and desist" any use of its poll. A simple "we're pulling out" would have sufficed, but it was a damaging image blow nonetheless.

The BCS's consecutive debacles of 2003 and 2004 brought the public's long-mounting frustration with the system to a boiling point, prompting renewed calls for college football to finally join the rest of the civilized world in adopting some sort of playoff. In a December 2003 online survey conducted by New Media Strategies,* a staggering 75 percent of football fans said they'd like to see the BCS scrapped, with 54 percent supporting an NCAA-style tournament. Literally every other NCAA-sponsored sport ends its season with a tournament, including all three of its lower levels (Division I-AA, II, and III) for football. Through the years, fans have taken it upon themselves to e-mail sportswriters, conference commissioners, and university presidents with elaborate proposals for a Division I-A playoff, everything from a two- or four-team mini-tournament to be played after the BCS bowls in January to an extensive eight-, sixteen-, or even thirty-two-team event. In turn, the recipients have learned to get better spam filters.

Yet despite such outward resentment over the sport's status quo, and with the BCS's original agreement with ABC about to expire, BCS officials announced in 2004 they were not only extending the arrangement for another four years, but that starting with the 2006 season, they would be adding a *fifth* BCS bowl game. Not a playoff game, mind you, just a chance for two more teams to play in prime time, presumably sometime between New Year's and Arbor Day. ABC responded to the news with a polite: "Thanks, but no thanks." Having already lost money on its original deal, the network proposed a new, "plus-one" BCS model in which the title game would involve the top two teams left standing *after* the bowl games. Though hardly a full-blown playoff, it would theoretically provide more clarity than the current setup by eliminating some of the contenders. When the idea was rejected, ABC chose to retain only the Rose Bowl, while FOX stepped in to claim the rest of the package, placing four of college football's most revered events on the same network as *Trading Spouses*.

---

*I don't know what it is, either.

By the end of 2004, college football's power brokers had been given the thumb by both their most loyal television partner (ABC) and their sport's most historic poll (AP), yet marched on unfazed to the tune of "four more years." If Microsoft did a survey and found that 75 percent of their consumers couldn't stand Windows, do you think they'd respond by putting out another edition? I doubt it. Which is why, on the surface, it must seem to the public as if the people who run college football are either extremely stubborn or lack the foggiest idea how to take a hint.

In reality, the politics involved in making any sort of formative change to college football's postseason are only slightly less complicated than bringing peace to the Middle East. In fact, college football's postseason quandary bears a striking resemblance to the political stalemates of Capitol Hill. You have your congressmen (the conference commissioners and athletic directors), your senators (university presidents and chancellors), your lobbyists (the bowl games, the smaller-conference schools), and your fundraisers (the television networks), each exercising their respective influence on the decision-making process while at the same time seeking to protect their own best interests. Meanwhile, there's no singular leader—like, say, the president—to steer the ship in any particular direction. The result: Nothing ever changes.

To better understand the dilemma, let's examine each of the aforementioned groups' respective agendas.

Conference Commissioners and Athletic Directors

If it were solely up to these guys, there would probably be, at the very least, a plus-one game by now. The commissioners and ADs, contrary to published reports, are not dumb. Their primary responsibility is to generate as much revenue as possible for their schools' athletic departments, most of which are entirely dependent on football and men's basketball to cover the expenses of all their swimmers, golfers, and fencers. While the new five-bowl model did garner a modest 5 percent hike in rights fees from FOX (reportedly $80 million per year, up from $76.5

million under the old ABC contract*), anything remotely resembling a playoff would have netted a mint. "An NFL-style football playoff would provide three to four times as many dollars to the Big Ten as the current system does," said Delany. "There is no doubt in my mind that we are leaving hundreds of millions of dollars on the table."

So why be altruistic? After all, the thirst for more moolah is why these guys created the BCS in the first place, wasn't it? It's also why they invented conference championship games (the SEC's event elicits an extra $1 million annually for each of its schools), regularly move games to other nights of the week at the behest of ABC and ESPN (which pays the ACC nearly $40 million a year to televise its contests), and recently convinced the NCAA to add a twelfth game to the regular season (allowing schools like Nebraska and Auburn to schedule an additional home game against McNeese State or Louisiana-Lafayette and pocket the extra $3 to $5 million in ticket sales that come with it).

Well, for one thing, the commissioners and ADs want to keep the spoils for themselves. "One big factor [behind the formation of the BCS] was that this would be a system controlled by the commissioners and the major conferences," a source involved in the original 1996 negotiations told *Sports Illustrated*. "There was noise back then about the NCAA getting involved in postseason football, and that was something nobody at the commissioner level wanted." It's no mystery why. Between TV rights fees and payouts by the bowls themselves, the four BCS games played in January 2006 generated $125.9 million in revenue, of which all but $7 million was pocketed by the six founding conferences (and Notre Dame). The rest was split among the other five Division I-A conferences ($5.2 million†) and eight I-AA conferences ($1.8 million). Any move to add games to the postseason, be it a plus-one or a multiround

---

*Those figures do not include the Rose Bowl, for which ABC has a separate contract worth a reported $300 million over eight years (2007–14). The deal includes two BCS titles games the years they're played in Pasadena.
†Starting with the 2006 season, the take for the five non-BCS conferences was raised to about $9 million, or 9 percent of net revenues. When one of those leagues' teams qualifies for a berth, as Boise State did in 2006, that share is doubled.

playoff, would have to be approved by the NCAA's entire Division I membership, of which the six BCS conferences are in the minority. It stands to reason that their peers would vote to let the NCAA take over control of any proposed playoff and, in turn, invoke a more egalitarian revenue distribution. "The foundation of college football is the institutions, the conferences and the bowls, and the sport is healthier than it's ever been," said SEC commissioner Mike Slive. "There's really no reason to look at it any differently." Not when your conference is raking in $17–$21 million a year by serving as its own BCS banker.

It should also be noted that the primary source of revenue for most athletic departments is not TV or bowl dollars but ticket sales for their home games—and the fact that schools are able to sell out their ninety-thousand-seat stadiums on a weekly basis is not something to be taken for granted. A primary reason most commissioners and ADs remain lukewarm about a playoff is their fear that it would devalue the twelve games leading up to it. College football's regular season is unique among all other sports in that every single week truly does matter. One loss is often all it takes to crush a team's national or conference title hopes, so a game between two top-ten teams in September carries as much weight as it would if they played in December. "In a sense, the BCS makes every weekend a playoff," said Slive, the BCS's coordinator in 2006–07. When rivals Ohio State and Michigan, both undefeated and ranked number 1 and 2 in the country respectively, met on November 18, 2006, the game served as a de facto championship play-in, creating intense national interest that resulted in the sport's highest regular-season TV rating in thirteen years.* Under a playoff, however, both teams would have already been assured of a berth. While the game would have still meant the world to fans of the two teams, to the rest of the country, they would have been playing for little more than seeding. "What we've got is a really exciting regular season that the BCS actually enhances by making so many games important, not only in the

---

*The game earned a 13.4 Nielsen rating (21.8 million total viewers), the sport's highest since another number 1 vs. 2 game, Florida State vs. Notre Dame, scored a 16.0 in 1993.

regions in which they were played, but nationally," said Slive. "Attendance is up, ratings are up, interest is up."

Beyond the championship race, there's also the fact that more than sixty teams—over half of Division I-A schools—remain in contention for a bowl berth right up through the final weekend, giving fans of even mediocre teams reason to stay interested. Even in a sixteen-team playoff, nearly 80 percent of Division I-A teams would be out of contention by the final weeks. ADs and commissioners rue the day when fans of an otherwise respectable 7–4 Arkansas team—which in the past would have been playing for a potential New Year's Day bowl berth—figure, "Why bother" attending the season finale, instead spending Saturday at Home Depot.

Finally, commissioners and athletic directors remain reticent to step on the toes of their friends at the bowl games. Bowls have been part of the fabric of the sport for more than a century, and any administrators old enough to remember life before the BCS—that is, every one of them—are devoted to preserving their place in the landscape. Of course, all the loyalty in the world didn't stop the founding BCS commissioners from walking all over the bowl tradition once already, so why would it stop them now? Because there's this pesky little matter of their bosses . . .

University Presidents and Chancellors

In theory, college athletic departments are merely one subsidiary of the larger university, their leaders ultimately reporting to the same head honcho as the dean of the business school or the head of the physics department. In reality, most major football programs long ago morphed into their own monstrous, nearly autonomous corporations. In the past, university presidents were too busy doing such menial things as raising money and hiring professors to bother poking their nose into the football team's business. It was the conference commissioners and athletic directors—not presidents—who played the biggest role in the original creation of the BCS.

But as the dollar amounts surrounding big-time college football grew to staggering proportions in the 1990s—and with them, an increasing number of embarrassing headlines about teams with 19 percent graduation rates and more players in police lineups than the starting lineup—calls for athletic reform at the presidential level began to sweep through the academic community. The movement's telltale moment came in 2002 when, for the first time in its history, the NCAA hired a university president, Indiana's Myles Brand, as its chief executive officer. Brand had become a household name two years earlier when he stood up to longtime Hoosiers basketball coach/bully Bob Knight, controversially firing the Hall of Famer for repeated bad behavior. Reformists viewed Brand as just the guy to usher in a new era of actually being able to say the term "student-athlete" with a straight face. Addressing reporters at his first NCAA basketball Final Four—an event for which the organization is netting *$6 billion* from CBS over an eleven-year period—Brand showed no reluctance whatsoever to put his foot down when necessary. "There was a request [to air the] Miller Lite catfight commercials [during the Final Four]," said Brand. "We exercised our option in the contract with CBS not to permit that."

It didn't take long for the newly energized presidents to offer their input on college football's postseason debate. When a committee of presidents and chancellors from the six founding BCS conferences convened in the summer of 2003 to begin exploring future postseason possibilities, they made it crystal-clear that one option was not on the table. "We have instructed the conference commissioners to not pursue . . . an NFL-style playoff system for postseason collegiate football," said Nebraska president Harvey Pearlman.

Pearlman's allusion to the NFL was no accident. University presidents have come to view the mere mention of the word "playoff" as a terrifying threat to college football's last remaining strand of innocence. To stage a playoff, they say, would be to turn the sport into a mirror of its professional counterpart and all the excess commercialization that comes with it—a somewhat feeble argument considering that their schools already participate in a gargantuan basketball tournament bathed in corporate influence (only water cups bearing a Dasani logo are permitted at courtside), as well as the Champs Sports Bowl, the Chick-fil-A Bowl, the Pioneer PureVision Las Vegas Bowl . . . need I go on? The presidents also contend that the season would become too long, intruding on players' academic calendars and interrupting either final exams in December or the beginning of a new semester in early January. Never mind that lower-division college teams already participate in playoff games during the time period in question, and that the March basketball tournament coincides with finals for schools on quarter systems. "There is no sentiment of any significance [among university presidents] for a national playoff, [with] academic reasons and the welfare of student-athletes being the primary reasons why that is opposed and opposed strongly," said Oregon president David Frohnmayer.

The presidents' continued adamancy against a Division I-A playoff is, in essence, a last stand. It's their most visible opportunity to show that the ideals of academics and amateurism remain a higher priority than financial motives. (And that Big Foot is real.) For that, there's at least one constituency that is eternally grateful . . .

The Bowl Games

Walk into the press box of any major college stadium during the heart of the season and you'll see what reporters affectionately refer to as "the blazers." They are the bowl scouts—staff members or volunteers from their respective games, donned in gaudy sport coats (orange for the Orange Bowl, yellow for the Fiesta Bowl) affixed with a seal of their logo. Their purpose, in principle, is to scout one or both teams as a possible participant for their upcoming contest, but in reality they mostly go for expense-account dinners and to watch a good game for free. The scouts' jobs were far more important in the old days, back when the bowl-selection process was a virtual free-for-all and back-room deals were brokered as early as October to send certain teams to certain bowls. Today, though, the pairings have been taken almost entirely out of the bowls' hands. The BCS selection process is spelled out on paper, leaving little room for flexibility, and nearly every other game has contractual partnerships with certain conferences that significantly limit their pool of potential teams. It's why Virginia Tech has played in the Gator Bowl seemingly every other year.

The blazers are, in essence, dinosaurs, and their industry in general operates under a cloud of fear that the games themselves will soon become the same. A Web site for the Football Bowl Association—a loosely organized coalition of the thirty-two current bowl games—breathlessly extols the virtues of the bowl system ("Bowl games are as much a part of the tradition of college football as any other aspect of the game," reads one passage) while not so subtly dissing playoff proponents ("A playoff system would be an unmitigated disaster," reads a 2003 quote from a Colorado columnist displayed prominently at the top of one page).

Mind you, few people if any want to see bowl games abolished—especially anyone who's ever participated in or attended one. Why would anyone want to voluntarily part with spending a week in a high-end resort being showered with gifts and attention? For the 2006 championship game hosted by the Fiesta Bowl, participating teams were housed in the Scottsdale Plaza and Fairmont Princess, treated to dinner at Drinkwater's City Hall Steakhouse, and feted with Torneau watches and XM satellite radios. Special events were held for visiting fans at numerous Tempe and Scottsdale bars and restaurants. Even my usually cranky colleagues in the media found themselves lacking for anything to complain about after spending a week at the opulent J.W. Marriott Camelback Inn.* "Everybody is treated like a king around here," Florida receiver Andre Caldwell told the *Arizona Republic*. "It's nice to relax and get pampered a bit."

Of the playoff concepts most commonly bandied about, the smaller-scale ones involve a short tournament played *after* the existing bowl games, while the more lavish ones suggest using the bowl games as playoff sites. For instance, the Rose or Fiesta Bowl might host a Final Four

---

*I spent the majority of the week drinking Fiji water, eating unlimited Tostitos, and bathing myself with scented Camelback soap. It would have been even better if I hadn't had to work.

game one year, the championship game the next. None of this, however, makes bowl honchos feel any better. For them, any sort of playoff is viewed as a death knell to their business, which is dependent on large numbers of people (for the major bowls, as many as forty thousand per school) traveling great distances to follow their team. Bowl types contend that if their games were to suddenly become just one step in a team's postseason path rather than an ultimate destination, fans might not be quite as eager to make the trip. Even if they did, they might not arrive as early in the week, thus reducing the financial impact for the local economy and rendering irrelevant such timeless traditions as the Orange Bowl Beach Bash and the Fiesta Bowl Block Party. In a playoff, the traditional, collegial atmosphere of bowl games, with the two teams' colors splitting stadium stands, would likely be replaced by a more buttoned-down, corporate crowd. "I've been to Super Bowls," said Fiesta Bowl CEO John Junker. "It's a big event, good for them, but they can keep it. I wouldn't trade the spirit in this stadium [for the Fiesta Bowl] for all the Super Bowls in the world." And that's assuming the bowls would actually remain a part of said playoff. "The big losers in a playoff are going to be the communities that host the bowl games," Rose Bowl CEO Mitch Dorger told *National Public Radio*. ". . . It's only going to take a couple of years of quarter-full stadiums before the conferences realize that they could do better by playing the games in the home stadium of the highest-ranked team, in the way that the NFL does. We think that that's the way that they would go to increase their revenues, and who's left out in the cold are the 935 volunteers for the Tournament of Roses and the city of Pasadena who've been supporting college football and universities and conferences for 102 years."

Joe Q. Fan, sitting in Pennsylvania miffed about the latest national championship controversy, isn't all that concerned about the welfare of those poor Tournament of Roses volunteers. Most school and conference officials, however, remain sympathetic to the bowls' unique circumstances—that is, unless they happen to represent the sport's "other half" . . .

Smaller-Conference Schools

In the summer of 2003, outspoken Tulane president Scott Cowen organized a coalition of forty-four schools from the so-called non-BCS conferences—leagues like the Mountain West and Conference USA, whose champions, unlike those of the Big Ten, SEC, and so on, do not receive automatic BCS bowl berths—to rally against the system's inherent unfairness. When the leaders of the six major conferences (and Notre Dame) originally set up the BCS, they hadn't given much thought to including their less prestigious colleagues because 1) that would mean having to share the money with them, and 2) it's not like there was any precedent that said they *should* be included. During the twenty years prior to the BCS's inception, all 160 teams that played in the Rose, Sugar, Orange, and Fiesta bowls were members of or went on to become members of the big six conferences (and Notre Dame).* Since World War II, all but one national champion (BYU in 1984) fit the same category. The Alabamas and Penn States of the world had been beating up on the Louisiana Techs and Toledos of the world for the better part of a century, so you'll have to excuse the BCS founders if they didn't spend a whole lot of time in those original meetings discussing their mostly harmless little stepbrothers.

As it turned out, a couple of fundamental changes took place that happened to coincide with—and partially resulted from—the BCS's creation. For one, the little guys started beating the big guys with more frequent regularity—including Louisiana Tech over Alabama in 1999 and Toledo over Penn State in 2000. While still hardly the norm, such upsets started giving credence to the notion that perhaps some of the elite smaller-conference teams could compete at a BCS level, such as when Fresno State of the WAC knocked off a Fiesta-bound Colorado team in 2001 or C-USA's Louisville upended eventual ACC champ and Sugar representative Florida State in 2002. Under the BCS's rules, though, the only way such smaller-conference schools could be assured

---

*Louisville, which played in the 1991 Fiesta Bowl, was a non-BCS school until 2005, when it joined the Big East.

a berth was by finishing in the top six of the BCS standings. It's not like the bowls themselves—whose lone concerns are selling tickets and producing TV ratings—were going to voluntarily pass up a Texas or Auburn in favor of a Boise State or Marshall. They'd sooner call the thing off. Only one such team, Alex Smith–led Utah in 2004, was able to climb that high during the first eight years of the BCS' existence, qualifying for that season's Fiesta Bowl.*

Beyond the on-field ramifications, the advent of the BCS also caused what its leaders would later refer to as "unintended consequences." The term "BCS" was only supposed to be a catchy name for the four major bowls. Just because they set the thing up to be as favorable as possible to their own teams while nearly doubling their revenues, never in a million years, swore the BCS commissioners, did they ever imagine the media and the public would start using the terms "BCS" and "non-BCS" as a de facto form of branding to distinguish between, say, a Michigan and a Western Michigan. The non-BCS schools did not take kindly to their newfound stigma, or to the fact that the BCS bowls were now paying out more than fourteen times as much as the lower-end bowls to which their teams found themselves relegated. "It is absolutely classic cartel behavior," State University of New York at Buffalo president William R. Greiner said of the BCS. "What we have is some people who think they are the 'haves,' and for reasons that escape me . . . do their damndest to beat on the have-nots." They don't *think* they're the haves, William—they *know* they're the haves.

In a teleconference with national reporters in July 2003, Cowen's group called the BCS a bunch of nasty names, then called for an all-inclusive Division I-A playoff, an utterly unrealistic goal considering the BCS-conference presidents' steadfast opposition to *any* sort of playoff. Cowen would, however, prove extremely successful in effecting change, especially upon convincing Congress to hold hearings that fall on

---

*The Utes' reward for their historic run was a forgettable matchup with 8–3 Big East champion Pittsburgh. It would become the only BCS game to date in which both teams' head coaches, Utah's Urban Meyer (Florida) and Pitt's Walt Harris (Stanford), had already accepted other jobs.

possible BCS antitrust violations. Uh-oh—potential lawsuits. Soon the BCS's Presidential Oversight Committee was holding a series of peace summits with Cowen's Coalition for Athletic Reform, with NCAA president Brand serving as a facilitator, and on February 29, 2004, the two sides announced a stunning agreement that caught even the BCS's own commissioners by surprise. From now on, they decreed, all 11 Division I-A conferences (and Notre Dame) would have a seat at the table when decisions were made; a fifth game would be added to the lineup starting in 2006; and while the Coalition conferences still wouldn't be afforded automatic entry to the BCS bowls, the rules would be loosened so that such a team need only finish in the top twelve instead of the top six.* In a teleconference from Miami's Fontainebleu Hilton Resort, site of the meeting where this historic agreement was brokered, Cowen proclaimed, "Today is a very good day for intercollegiate athletics and higher education. Our agreement is a positive and important step forward in developing an inclusive, fair system to govern postseason play in football." Gushed Brand: "This agreement that's been reached today is a significant victory for college sports and higher education. It will benefit the institutions of both groups, and most especially the student-athletes." A fifth bowl game—the greatest thing to happen to academia since the pencil sharpener.

One group not quite as thrilled by the news was the original BCS commissioners (and Notre Dame). "This [was] not a commissioner-driven decision," said Delany. "Scott Cowen did an exceptional job of selling his idea to national media members. Our presidents recognized that there was congressional concern, they recognized that no matter why we did what we did, it wasn't a winning argument why some were in, some were out. . . . What came out of the political pressure was this compromise." While the presidents had concerned themselves largely

---

*One of these teams can also receive a bid by finishing in the top sixteen and higher than the lowest-rated BCS-conference champion. For that, non-BCS teams are eternally grateful for the existence of the ACC.

with issues of fairness and collegiality, it was the commissioners who would be charged with actually implementing the presidents' inspired solution—which would mean attempting to sell the concept to a marketplace where fairness and collegiality rank a great bit farther down the priority list than, oh, Nielsen ratings . . .

Television Networks

On January 1, 2007, Boise State, a one-time junior college only a decade removed from I-AA competition, became the first non-BCS school to take advantage of the new, less stringent BCS requirements, finishing ninth in the standings and receiving a berth to that year's Fiesta Bowl. The WAC champion Broncos were listed as a touchdown underdog to Big 12 champion and college football aristocrat Oklahoma. Not only did the orange-and-blue-clad Broncos upset the Sooners, but they did so with one of the most thrilling finishes in bowl history, sending the game to overtime on a 50-yard, hook-and-lateral touchdown, then winning it with an old-fashioned Statue of Liberty play. To top it all off, Boise's star running back, Ian Johnson, got down on one knee and proposed to his cheerleader girlfriend, Chrissy Popadics, during a live postgame interview. "Lord almighty, I nearly fell out of my chair," legendary broadcaster Keith Jackson told the *Los Angeles Times* the next day. "What we saw was pure, raw emotion. What we saw, you can only see in college football."

Actually—not that many people saw it. Despite the obvious human-interest story and jaw-dropping finish, the Boise-Oklahoma Fiesta Bowl drew a disappointing 8.4 Nielsen rating, tying it for thirty-fifth out of the thirty-seven BCS games played to date. The two that finished lower? The Utah-Pittsburgh Fiesta Bowl 2 years earlier (7.4) and the Wake Forest-Louisville Orange Bowl played a night after Boise State-Oklahoma (7.0). It's no coincidence that all three games involved non-traditional powers.

It's numbers like these that ABC execs had feared when they declined to pony up for the BCS's new five-game, everyone's-invited format for 2006–2009.* Like any good business, the network was only interested in a concept that would bring "added value" to its product—that is, lure more eyeballs and advertising dollars. With ratings for the non-title games having declined in recent years, ABC felt the only way to accomplish this would be to create a "plus-one" game, which, at the very least, would increase interest for at least two of the four BCS bowls (the ones involving the number 1 and 2 teams) while putting the championship game itself on an even greater pedestal. While one of the most compelling aspects of CBS's NCAA tournament coverage is the presence of Cinderella teams—unheralded schools like George Mason or Coppin State that miraculously knock off one of the big boys in the early rounds—there's no evidence to suggest football fans are interested in a similar David-versus-Goliath element to their bowl games, particularly if there is no championship at stake. "Over the years, the marketplace has established that the major revenue streams go to the bigger schools and conferences because they generate larger audiences," said former CBS Sports president Neal Pilson. "That has nothing to do with the credibility of their education, nothing to do with the quality of their play, it has to do with the viewing preference of the American public."

As should be crystal-clear by now, college football's decision to stick with its current postseason format has very little to do with the viewing preference of the American public. It has everything to do with an institutional resistance to change, caused by the divergent interests of the sport's many decision-makers. In this most recent political go-round, it was the university presidents—particularly Cowen's coalition of smaller-conference schools—that got their way, somehow pushing through a new BCS model that did little to resolve the sport's national-championship dilemma while providing greater access to teams that the vast majority of fans don't care about enough to watch. Is there any doubt Cowen will one day be a senator? However, had FOX not been desperate to break into the college football market (the

---

*ABC did actually make an offer—for about $17 million per game, down from $25 million. That's when FOX stepped in.

network previously aired just one game all season, the Cotton Bowl) and offered just enough to make the BCS's five-bowl proposal financially viable, it's entirely conceivable that the BCS leaders would have had to go back to the drawing board, and that the commissioners, athletic directors, and television networks would have been able to adopt something more to their liking.

In fact, there's been a notable shift in the company line ever since Slive took over as BCS coordinator at the beginning of 2006. Whereas his predecessors* mostly evaded discussing anything radical, Slive has embraced the ongoing debate over the current format and has hinted on numerous occasions that he would endorse a plus-one game. "We need to continue over the next few years to look at the postseason to be sure it works the way we want it to work," said Slive. "I think the regular season has been enhanced [by the BCS]. The question is, where is the magic point where you maintain the quality of the regular season as it currently exists and at the same time maybe provide more opportunity for a deserving team?" Dissension is also being raised by a growing number of coaches, most of whom were content in the past to dish standard throwaway lines like, "The system is what it is." Auburn's Tommy Tuberville has been a relentless playoff proponent ever since his team got left out in 2004. "From a competitive standpoint, you can't make a good argument against it," Tuberville told *Sports Illustrated.* "Let's just go to a playoff and be done with it." Florida coach Urban Meyer was extremely vocal about the issue over the final few weeks of the 2006 season, when it appeared his team might be nudged out of the title game by a potential Ohio State–Michigan rematch, and did not let up even after his team was ultimately chosen over the Wolverines. "If you want a true national championship," said Meyer, "you have to let the teams go play it on

---

*The conference commissioners take turns serving two years as BCS coordinator. So far there have been five: the SEC's Kramer (1998–99), the ACC's John Swofford (2000–01), the Big East's Mike Tranghese (2002–03), the Big 12's Weiberg (2004–05), and the SEC's Slive (2006–07). "Being BCS coordinator is my two years in the penalty box," joked Slive.

the field." Even Michigan's Carr, one of the sport's most noted traditionalists, has changed his tune in recent years. "I never thought I would say this, [but] I think we should go to a playoff," he said in 2005. "I think we should play the top sixteen teams, and do it on the field, because I think that's only fair to the guys that play the game." Let me guess—Carr then turned on his iPod Nano and started text-messaging on his Blackberry?

The coaches can stand on their soapboxes all they want, but they do not have the final say on the matter. And the people who do are only slightly closer to installing a sixteen-team playoff than they are to launching giraffes into space. However, many observers believe the BCS's move to a stand-alone championship game, not to mention its unusually late date (the first such game was played on January 8, 2007, four days later than the previous year's), is a not-so-subtle precursor toward eventually converting the game into a "plus-one" when the current contract expires in 2010. The BCS bowls themselves may even prefer it to the current model because it might make nonchampionship games more meaningful. In 2006, for instance, number 1 Ohio State, number 2 Florida, and number 3 Michigan could have all gone into the bowls with their national-title hopes still intact. "We'd be encouraged by [a plus-one]," said the Fiesta Bowl's Junker. "We believe there is merit and value to a plus-one after the bowls." "It's no secret that every one of the [TV] folks we talked with would prefer to see us move in the direction of some sort of a plus-one type of approach," said the Big 12's Weiberg. "That was a very uniform message throughout our television negotiations."

In a December 31, 2006, article, the *New York Times* polled all eleven commissioners (and Notre Dame) as well as several athletic directors and presidents from those conferences. Nine of the eleven commissioners were open to the possibility of a plus-one, as were the five athletic directors. "There is more open-mindedness at this point than there was a few years ago," ACC commissioner John Swofford told the *Times*. "We have some presidents and athletic directors that are very sold on the Plus One model as the next step." Just as they were a decade ago, however, commissioners and presidents from the Big Ten and Pac-10 remain adamantly opposed to any such change. "I oppose a Plus One," Pac-10 commissioner Tom Hansen told the *Times*. "All you do is weaken the bowl games to set it up." "The system we have right now is a good system," said Penn State president Graham Spanier. "The overwhelming majority of the presidents in the Big Ten are against any type of expansion." Once again, the future of college football's postseason will be directly tied to its impact on the Rose Bowl, which was able to host its preferred Big Ten–Pac-10 matchup just twice in the six seasons from 2001 to 2006. While one scenario for a plus-one involves the bowls returning to their traditional conference tie-ins—which the Rose Bowl would obviously love—more realistically, the numbers 1 through 4 teams would have to be seeded, effectively ending conference tie-ins altogether. "The Rose Bowl is the most important external relationship we have," Delany told the Associated Press. "It's more important than the BCS." Suffice to say, the other BCS bowls aren't big fans of the Rose Bowl.

Within the rest of the presidential ranks, the traditionally united stand against a playoff is starting to show some cracks. In March 2007, SEC presidents for the first time formally added a playoff discussion to the agenda of their regularly scheduled meetings. "A playoff is inevitable," Florida president Bernie Machen told Bloomberg News in 2006. "The public strongly favors a playoff, but university presidents are in denial about that. They just don't see it. Whatever the format, I believe we need to get ahead of it and create the system rather than responding to the external pressures." Florida State president T.K. Wetherall has joined Machen in supporting a playoff. Like many, Machen points to Boise State's Fiesta Bowl victory—which, combined with Ohio State's BCS title-game loss a week later, left the Broncos as the nation's only undefeated team that season but with no way of playing for the national title—as an indictment against the status quo. "The Boise State game makes it clear that there is no longer a clear delineation between BCS and non-BCS schools," Machen told the *Palm Beach Post*. "It's going to make the case that this small collection of six conferences has no right to control how college football settles who's the champion." Machen is unlikely to receive many Christmas cards next year from his colleagues within those six conferences.* In fact, there are plenty of presidents who are diametrically opposed to his viewpoint. "A number of [presidents] in the Big Ten and Pac-10 would rather go back to the old bowl system than go to a playoff," said Oregon's Frohnmayer. No word whether they would also cheerfully return to the days of horse and buggy or outdoor plumbing.

The fact is, the precedent has now been set for a true national championship in college football, and there will be no turning back. In fact, the large majority of fans would happily spit in the face of tradition altogether if it meant finally resolving the sport's repeated, frustrating end-of-season controversies. But like the bowls themselves, controversy has been a part of the sport since nearly its inception, and it won't be going away anytime soon, even if a plus-one comes to pass. "You're never going to eliminate controversy," a by-then-retired Kramer told the *Florida Times-Union* in 2004. "Fans of the number 3 team this year may be unhappy, but if you have an eight-team playoff, fans of the number 9 team will be unhappy. If you have a sixteen-team playoff, number 17 is going to be unhappy."

Rightly or wrongly, college football will turn to a playoff one day. As Machen said, it's inevitable. The presidents will not be able to defy the wishes of the general public forever, nor will the commissioners be able to resist the potentially absurd financial benefits.† However, barring a dramatic change of heart by either group—or a particularly harsh kick in the rear from the television networks—that day is at least a decade away. In the meantime, fans would best be advised to save their voices. There's going to be a lot more yelling to come.

---

*Machen has seen the other side of it firsthand, however: he was Utah's president in 2004 when the Utes went undefeated but had no chance to play for the national title.
†No one has ever managed to pin down with any certainty exactly how much more lucrative a playoff would be than the current system. Television experts have estimated anywhere from a 60 percent spike in rights fees to about triple the current amount. As it stands now, the BCS's annual TV revenue (about $120 million) pales in comparison to that of the NCAA tournament ($545 million).

2

Pulling Rank

The polls are a caste system, and there are people out there who really believe their school is better simply because their football team is No. 1. Too many people whose lives aren't full overly invest.

—Dr. Miguel Franco, University of Notre Dame sports psychologist, to the South Bend Tribune, *1998*

I did it at 2 A.M. in the morning. Maybe I had a brain fart. Based on what you're telling me [about Arizona State], I probably made a mistake.

—AP voter Jimmy Watson explaining a puzzling inclusion on his ballot to the Seattle Post-Intelligencer, *2001*

S *eptember 5, 2006, 2:37 A.M., Room 2620, Biscayne Bay Marriott: Before leaving for the Florida State–Miami game earlier tonight, I ranked twenty-three of the twenty-five teams on my AP ballot, leaving space to move up the winner and move down the loser of Monday night's contest. However, after watching the teams' utterly inept offensive performance, I'm not sure either team should be ranked any higher than, say, Prairie View. Florida State, the winner, rushed for a total of 1 yard. Miami, the loser, rushed for 2. The game went right down to the last minute, yet I couldn't have been any further from the edge of my seat. I take a quick look at my preseason ballot, drop FSU two spots, from twelfth to fourteenth, and Miami six spots, from seventeenth to twenty-third, then send the thing in so I can try to get a few hours' sleep before heading to the airport. The next day, it will be pointed out to me that as a result of dropping the 'Noles two spots for beating a ranked team on the road, Iowa moved up two spots, from thirteenth to eleventh, for beating I-AA Montana on its own field. Whoops.*

We are a society of people obsessed with rankings, and personally, I blame Casey Kasem. So many generations of pimply-faced American teenagers grew up listening to the host of *America's Top 40* tell us where our favorite Madonna or Bee Gees song was on the charts that week (in addition to those painful long-distance dedications) that now we crave rankings for nearly every aspect of our lives. *U.S. News & World Report's* Top 25 law schools. *Sports Illustrated's* Top 20 Hottest Female Athletes. *E!'s* Top 10 Celebrity Breakups of All Time. Of course, those rankings are mostly for amusement. The issue of ranking college football teams is a decidedly more serious matter—at least to fans of those teams being ranked.

Here's how it usually works. On Saturday, they play the games. Late Saturday night or early Sunday morning,* most likely while you're sleeping, a panel of sportswriters and coaches evaluates the results of those games and compiles their rankings of the twenty-five best teams in the country for that given week. Then, on Sunday afternoons, fans of those teams scurry to their computers to find out the latest results—and to fire off a nasty e-mail to whoever might listen (in this case me) detailing the grave injustice that has occurred as a result of their 7–2 team coming in sixteenth while a 6–2 team that their team beat by a field goal six weeks earlier is four spots higher. The e-mail will inevitably include some off-shoot of the following phrase: "What were the voters thinking?"

Since 2005, I have been one of those voters, submitting a Top 25 ballot to the Associated Press at the completion of each Saturday's games. (This ballot also constitutes my weekly Power Rankings for SI.com, which I've been publishing since the 2002 season.) Utilizing firsthand knowledge, I can assure you that the process of comparing two or more teams with identical records that don't necessarily play the same opponents and whose most recent performance may or may not have been affected by injuries, venue, weather, kickoff time, a bad call by an official, or all of the above is only slightly less subjective than ranking those Celebrity Breakups. While every voter I know in the media takes his responsibility very seriously,† the reality is that none of them, nor I, have any true way of knowing the exact order of the best teams in the country unless they were to all somehow play each other. In fact, for all the sport's other technological advancements, the only thing that's changed about voter polls in seventy years is that today you can e-mail your ballot to the AP rather than call it in. And yet these archaic, largely arbitrary rankings still manage to create an indisputable craze among anyone with any attachment to the sport.

According to longtime *Sports Illustrated* writer and college football historian Dan Jenkins's 1973 book *Saturday's America*, the first person

---

*AP ballots are due by noon EST on Sunday, *USA Today* coaches' poll ballots by 10:00 A.M.

†The same cannot necessarily be said of coaches. But more on that in a bit.

to attempt this insane endeavor was a University of Illinois economics professor named Frank G. Dickinson, who ranked every team in the country using his own, seemingly arbitrary mathematical formula. After years of doing this for his own private enjoyment, Dickinson went public with his ratings beginning in 1926.* A whole slew of copycats soon followed, but Dickinson's was regarded as the authoritative poll of that era.† Most of these polls, however, were not widely distributed, appearing in such annals as *Spalding's Football Guide* and *Illustrated Football Annual*, and their sole purpose was to determine the mythical number 1 team at the end of the season.

The man responsible for bringing college football rankings to the masses—on a weekly basis, no less—was Associated Press sports editor Alan J. Gould. In the mid-1930s, when college football still towered over the relatively infant National Football League in terms of popularity, newspapers were scouring for anything they could find to quench the football appetites of their readers. So midway through the 1935 season, Gould began authoring his own college football rankings and sending them to the AP's subscriber papers. "It was a case of thinking up ideas to develop interest and controversy between football Saturdays," Gould reflected fifty years later. "Papers wanted material to fill space between games. This was just another exercise in hoopla." Oh, he got his hoopla all right. According to a 1990 *Dallas Morning News* feature, when Gould made the innocent mistake of ranking three undefeated teams—Minnesota, Princeton, and SMU—number 1 at the end

---

*In historical records, Dickinson's first poll is considered to be 1924. According to Jenkins, when Notre Dame coach Knute Rockne heard about the poll, he invited Dickinson to lunch in South Bend and suggested he predate the poll two years so that his 1924 "Four Horsemen" team could be proclaimed national champion. "That was actually how polls began, and how Notre Dame won its first official national title," wrote Jenkins. "At lunch."

†The NCAA officially recognizes thirty-seven different "national championship selectors" dating to 1869, but with the exception of those crowned by sportswriter Caspar Whitney from 1905 to 1907, all champions prior to Dickinson's were selected retroactively by the respective organizations.

of the season, Gophers fans hung him in effigy. Perhaps if said Minnesotans knew there would come a day seventy years later when they'd feel fortunate to be ranked at all, they would have built a statue of Gould instead.

The first official AP poll began the following season when Gould washed his hands of it, turning the rankings into a poll of AP-member sports editors. From 1938 to 1959, the poll was open to any AP-affiliated media member interested enough to call in a ballot, causing the electorate to soar as high as two hundred-plus. Eventually, the number would be pared down to about fifty* specially selected writers and broadcasters dispersed regionally throughout the country. In 1950, the nation's other major wire service, UPI, entered the football rankings business as well, but instead of writers, it enlisted a panel of thirty-five (now sixty-three) coaches. Other rankings systems would come and go, including those of the Football Writers Association, the National Football Foundation, and the Helms Athletic Association, but over time, the AP and UPI[†] came to be recognized as the sport's two authoritative polls—mostly because they ran in all the papers.

Today, newspapers don't have to worry about filling space between games. And thanks to ESPN, one needn't ever fret about a shortage of hype. And yet, Gould's creation remains as central to college football as the footballs and the helmets. "All I had mind," said Gould, who passed away in 1993 following an award-winning career as the AP's executive editor, "[was] something to keep the pot boiling."

Mission accomplished.

October 15, 2006, Jordan-Hare Stadium press box, Auburn, Alabama: I've just filed my column about Auburn's 27–17 victory over Florida. Now, I'm trying to construct my AP ballot (because there's no point

---

*This number would later rise back up to as high as seventy-four in the 1990s before falling back down to its current total of sixty-five.

[†] *USA Today* took over administration of the coaches' poll from UPI in 1991. CNN co-sponsored the poll until 1997, ESPN until 2004.

joining the traffic on College Avenue before I have to) and realizing that the SEC teams have created one colossal mess. Florida, Auburn, Tennessee, and Arkansas all now have one loss. Logic says the Tigers, who I had thirteenth last week, should move ahead of the Gators, who I had second. Let's say Auburn seventh, Florida eighth. But what about number 12 Arkansas, which came to this same stadium last week and whooped Auburn 27–10? Common sense says they stay ahead of the Tigers, but that would mean moving them up six spots for beating Southeast Missouri State. And shouldn't the Gators stay above number 7 Tennessee, who they beat on the road earlier in the season? Besides, despite what the final score said, Florida was the better team here tonight. They held Auburn without an offensive touchdown and lost in large part due to a questionable fumble call while driving for the go-ahead score in the final minutes. And their sole loss came on the road at night in a hostile venue, while the other three SEC teams lost at home. Therefore, I only drop Florida two spots. Auburn moves up five spots for the win. Tennessee (which had a bye) and Arkansas stay where they were. Apparently my fellow pollsters disagree. They wind up dropping the Gators seven spots, all the way down to number 9. We'll see who looks smarter at the end of the season.

So who votes in these polls anyway, you ask? And what exactly qualifies them to evaluate football teams? The first question I can answer. The second one is open to debate.

The AP poll consists of sixty-five voters, sixty-one of which are "districted" state-by-state much like Congress or the Electoral College. States with one to three Division I schools get one vote, states with four to six such schools get two, and so on. In 2006, Texas and California had the most voters with four apiece; Florida, North Carolina, and Ohio had three; everyone else had two or one. There were also four national voters, of which your humble author was one.* While AP's

---

*The others: ESPN's Chris Fowler, ABC's Craig James, and College Sports television's Brian Curtis. ESPN's Kirk Herbstreit, a Columbus, Ohio, resident, was also a voter, but his vote counted toward Ohio's total.

national office in New York mandates how may votes each state gets, it is up to the respective regional AP bureaus to choose the actual voters. According to my own, unofficial research, thirty-nine of the sixty-one state-by-state voters were newspaper beat writers who cover a specific team; eight were general-assignment college writers covering multiple teams or conferences; six were general columnists who cover all sports; five were local TV or radio personalities; two were newspaper sports editors; and one, Mike Radano, was the Philadelphia Phillies' beat writer for the *Courier-Post* in Camden, New Jersey.*

I know many of the aforementioned beat writers personally, and many of the others I read regularly. They are all extremely dedicated to their jobs, highly knowledgeable about the sport they cover, and sensitive to the importance their vote carries with so many people. "It's a privilege and a responsibility to be closely affiliated with college football in that small way, and it's something I take very seriously," said *Austin-American Statesman* columnist Kirk Bohls, an AP voter since 1989. The ultimate irony, however, is that most see far fewer games on a given Saturday than the average fan does sitting at home.

Take it from me. Covering a college football game—which most voters in the poll do nearly every Saturday—is an all-day affair. Let's say the game kicks off at 3:30 P.M. EST. To beat traffic and get to the press box in time to get settled, I probably leave my hotel around noon. Consequently, I am in the car listening to the radio, or walking from the parking lot, during the first half of the noon games. Once I arrive, usually there are televisions in the press box airing at least one major national game. I try to keep an eye on them, but realistically my attention is mainly focused on getting ready for the game at hand—studying game notes, chatting up the teams' sports information

---

*As you can imagine, I was a bit puzzled when I came across this one. When I asked someone at AP about it, I was told Radano—of whom they'd been previously made aware—had covered college football in the past and had managed to retain his vote through "a glitch in the system." He was expected to be replaced in 2007. Sorry to out you, Mike.

directors.* However, thanks to ESPN GamePlan, it's now possible to see games on my computer, so I definitely watch the ones that go down to the wire. Once the game I'm covering starts, I try to keep tabs on some other games on my computer, but by the second half such multitasking becomes more difficult, and because you need to go down to the field with about five minutes remaining to do interviews, it's a given that I won't see the endings of the other games live. I usually return to the press box about an hour later and frantically write a column. By the time I get back to the hotel (or, more often, to a sports bar), I'm able to catch about the last quarter and a half of the prime-time games.

All of which leaves myself and my fellow voters extremely dependent on ESPN's Saturday night wrap-up shows and/or *SportsCenter*. "Without fail, I try to catch ESPN's final highlights show," said 2006 AP voter Tim Griffin of the *San Antonio-Express News*. "If I can catch it before I go to sleep on Saturday night, so much the better." The other problem is, most of us have flights to catch before the ballots are due. "I try to catch as many games as possible, but, of course, covering a game takes a large chunk out of my Saturday," said another voter, Mitch Vingle of the *Charleston (West Virginia) Gazette*. "More than once I've stayed up until Hawaii or a late West Coast team completed its game in order to vote—with a four A.M. wakeup call set up to catch a plane." Indeed, finding out what happened in the games ranks right at the top of the list of tasks a voter should probably undertake before casting his ballot. In 2006, the AP booted one of its voters, Jim Kleinpeter of the *New Orleans Times-Picayune*, after he admitted to mistakenly dropping Oklahoma nine spots because he'd failed to check the final score of the Sooners' game against Texas Tech. Oklahoma had rallied to win 34–24. "I was in the press box after the LSU game that night and I remember . . . asking somebody, Did Oklahoma get beat? and somebody said 'Yes.'" Kleinpeter told the *Tulsa World*. "When I woke up the next morning, I rushed through my stuff and when I

---

*Actually, I mostly eat the free food and talk to other writers. But that's neither here nor there.

looked in the paper, I didn't see the score. It was still in my head that they lost."

Fortunately, the national scope of my beat allows me to get to different parts of the country and see most of the top teams in person at some point.* If, however, you're a beat writer covering, say, Michigan State, chances are the only teams you'll see in person all season are the Spartans' Big Ten opponents and annual nonconference foe Notre Dame. "I have often said that a regular college football fan has access to way more games on a weekend than a beat writer who is often on the road and is tied to one game," AP voter Dave Rahme of the *Syracuse Post-Standard* told the *Daily Oklahoman*. "I saw much more college football before getting on the beat than I do now."

If there's one set of voters that sees even less games than AP writers, it's the coaches. In theory, the idea of *USA Today* sponsoring a coaches' poll makes sense. After all, who knows more about football than the coaches? The problem is, while coaches do spend a large chunk of their week watching football, 99 percent of what they watch is tape of their upcoming opponent or the game their own team just played. Ask a coach in mid-November about a team in his own conference and he'll likely be able to give you an off-the-cuff scouting report about nearly every player at every position on the field. Ask the same coach about a team in another conference and he'll likely resort to: "Well . . . we have a lot of respect for that program. They have a great coach, great players. I haven't seen them play much . . ." Indeed, if you think Tennessee coach and coaches' poll voter Phillip Fulmer has a couple of spare hours on a Saturday to catch some of the UCLA–Oregon game, you're mistaken. From the moment he wakes up until the moment his team's game kicks off, he's with his team, either in meetings or in the locker room, or going over final preparations with his coaches. After the game, he has media obligations, visiting recruits to entertain, and perhaps a postgame celebration with family back at his house. Chances are,

---

*In 2006, I covered games involving seven of the top ten teams—and ten of the top fifteen—in the final AP poll.

when he fills out his ballot at the end of the night, he's doing it based on nothing more than final scores.

That is, assuming he actually fills it out himself.

The age-old dirty secret about the coaches' poll is that often the coaches themselves aren't the ones ranking the teams. Due to the afore-mentioned time constraints, many enlist their sports information director or other support staff with the dirty work. "I'd give a lot of thought to who was No. 1 and No. 2. Then I'd just pass it on and say, 'Vote for who you think,'" former Arkansas coach Frank Broyles told the *Dallas Morning News*. "I probably did that 90 percent of the time. And I'd say 90 percent of the coaches did the same thing." Few other coaches have been as candid as Broyles, but occasionally, examples of their hands-off approach to voting have slipped out. After watching undefeated Michigan rout his previously undefeated team in November 1997, Penn State coach Joe Paterno was surprised to learn that Florida State, not the Wolverines, was the new number 1 team on his ballot. "I have somebody who helps me with the voting, and we didn't vote for Michigan No. 1," Paterno unwisely admitted. "That bothered me." Not as much as it bothered fans across the country to find out one of the nation's most revered coaches doesn't cast his own ballot. Then, less than a year later, at the Big Ten's preseason media event, Paterno was asked who he voted as his preseason number 1 team. "Geez," he replied. "I'd have to check with the staff." At that same event, Purdue coach Joe Tiller disclosed that his son, a University of Wyoming junior at the time, had filled out his preseason ballot. "He buys all the [prognostication] magazines," Tiller said. "He has fun with it." And in 2006, Ohio State coach Jim Tressel caused a mini-uproar during the week leading up to his top-ranked team's game against number 2 Texas by mistakenly proclaiming, "I've got [the Longhorns] ranked No. 1 on our ballot." This came as a surprise to the folks at *USA Today*, who let it be known that no, Tressel had the Buckeyes number 1 on his ballot and Texas number 3. The discrepancy was quickly blamed on the staff member, associate director of football operations Stan Jefferson, responsible for calling in Tressel's vote, who apparently took it upon himself to change the order of Tressel's preseason ballot without informing the coach. Jefferson called it "an honest mistake."

So we've established that most AP voters are too busy covering games to keep tabs on the others and most coaches'-poll voters are too busy coaching in the games to fill out their own ballots. But they at least take a fair and unbiased approach to their duties, right? Yes . . . and no. College football's inherently paranoid fan base has been crying for years about any number of perceived regional biases in the AP poll. After all, it stands to reason that, say, a USC beat writer, who spends nearly every waking hour of the fall around the Trojans' program and has seen them play far more often than any other team, would tend to vote the Trojans higher than his fellow writers, right? Not necessarily. While I can't vouch for how it was in the old days, since I've been following the poll, I've rarely found homerism to be a problem. Unlike the coaches' poll, individual AP ballots are made public every week, so voters know they're going to be scrutinized. And as hard as this may seem for the average fan to believe, 99 percent of reputable beat writers do not root for the team they cover. I've always found it amusing that fans assume reporters would be so attached to the team they cover as to eschew the most basic tenant of their professional code, which is to be objective. If you're that paranoid, you might as well also assume that your doctor is passing out copies of your personal medical records to his buddies. I'm not saying there aren't exceptions out there—on the contrary, I encounter a few such yokels in nearly every press box I visit—but you'd be hard-pressed to find these types represented in the poll.

If anything, many writers tend to overcompensate and vote the team they cover *lower* than does the general electorate. In 1997, when Michigan and Nebraska both finished undefeated, *Omaha World-Herald* writer Lee Barfknecht—the state of Nebraska's lone AP voter—took no shortage of flak locally after casting his final number 1 vote for the Wolverines. Michigan wound up finishing number 1 in that poll, but Nebraska finished number 1 in the coaches. "I haven't the foggiest idea why the coaches did what they did, but I thought there was no doubt [about Michigan]," Barfknecht told the *South Bend Tribune*. In 2004, *Huntsville (Alabama) Times* writer Paul Gattis resisted considerable pressure to vote Auburn ahead of fellow undefeated teams USC and Oklahoma in his final poll, keeping the Tigers at number 3. "The fact that Auburn and I share the same state is meaningless," Gattis wrote in his paper. "That's part of a reporter's objectivity. There's no pulling for the home team, no pulling for the team in the home conference." The AP monitors ballots and, in instances of blatant homerism, often takes action. In 1991, when Miami and Washington both finished undefeated and wound up splitting the national title, one West Coast voter tried to rank the Hurricanes fourth—no other voter had them lower than second—in a transparent effort to help the Huskies finish on top. He lost his voting privileges the next season.

There is one poll, however, where biases and agendas not only go uncorrected but are almost par for the course. You guessed it—the coaches' poll. As you might guess with a poll where the electors are also the sport's participants, many coaches incorporate personal agendas onto their ballots. "It is a popularity contest," former Texas A&M coach R. C. Slocum, who voted in the poll for more than a decade, told the *Austin-American Statesman.* "There's a couple of [coaches] who are good guys, you might put their teams in there, while a guy who's a halfway jerk, you don't put in there. It's just human nature." For decades, voting coaches have been afforded the protection of anonymity, their weekly ballots kept under wraps by the American Football Coaches Association so as not to create storylines (such as a coach voting his opponent that week unusually low). As a result, a few coaches were able to cast some pretty objectionable ballots without scrutiny. In 1995, after undefeated Florida completed its regular season 12–0 but lost to Nebraska 62–24 in the Fiesta Bowl, two apparently vindictive rivals dropped Steve Spurrier's team all the way to number 11 and number 13 on their final ballots. As a result, the Gators finished number 3 in the final poll—one spot behind a Tennessee team it had beaten 62–37 during the season. It was assumed at the time that one of the offending coaches happened to be the head man in Knoxville.

Following years of public pressure, the AFCA finally agreed in 2005 to publicly release the coaches' final regular-season ballots—and we quickly found out why they've been trying so hard to keep them a secret. The level of provincialism was downright mind-boggling. On average, coaches voted their own teams 1.7 spots higher than did the general electorate, and ranked other teams from their conference about one spot higher than did coaches from the other conferences. Miami, ninth in the general poll, came in fourth on 'Canes coach Larry Coker's ballot. Spurrier ranked his South Carolina team twenty-first; the Gamecocks didn't make the overall poll. And Arkansas coach Houston Nutt flat-out forgot to put number 11 West Virginia on his ballot. That year's biggest BCS controversy revolved around which two teams out of Notre Dame, Ohio State, and Oregon would secure the Fiesta Bowl's two at-large berths. Ducks coach Mike Bellotti voted his team fourth and the Irish ninth; Ohio State's Jim Tressel put his team fourth and Bellotti's team ninth. A year later, fifteen of the eighteen coaches who voted for their own team ranked them higher than the general electorate, most notably Rutgers's Greg Schiano (tenth vs. seventeenth), West Virginia's Rich Rodriguez (seventh vs. twelfth), and Tennessee's Fulmer (thirteenth vs. eighteenth). Amazingly, this giant conflict of interest accounts for one-third of the standings used to determine the national championship and other BCS bowl matchups —not to mention that countless coaches have financial incentives tied to their team's finish in the poll as part of their contracts. It's like having a serial bank robber go to trial only to find out half the jury is comprised of all the people he's accused of robbing.

The AP poll, meanwhile, has been dealing with its own conflict-of-interest crisis for the better part of seventy years. As noted earlier, the poll was created largely for entertainment purposes. During the early part of the twentieth century, the notion of a national champion in college football was taken about as seriously as that of a spaceship landing on the moon. "Nobody even cared," wrote *SI*'s Jenkins. "You told a friend that your school was number 1 in those days and all he said was, 'Listen, that's great. But excuse me. I've got to go invent the airplane.'" As the poll grew in popularity, however, the chase for number 1 quickly became a matter of utmost importance, and soon there was no escaping the reality that writers were helping to determine a very important aspect of the sport they were covering. This, coupled with the fact that bowl invitations worth millions were also becoming unofficially tied to a team's ranking, would seem to run contradictory to the journalist's creed of wanting to report the news, not make it. "In no other sport do media types have say or sway," wrote *Daily Oklahoman* columnist Jenni Carlson. "Not basketball, not baseball, not softball, not anything." As recently as 1997, the AP seemed to be fine with its unusual role in the proceedings. "There is a lot of money tied to it, true," said longtime AP sports editor Terry Taylor. "But I don't think the poll created this."

But then the BCS came along, creating for the first time an official national championship game and formalizing the selection process for the other major bowls. BCS organizers incorporated the AP poll into their standings (which also included various computer ratings detailed in the previous chapter), apparently without the AP's consent, though no one bothered to mention this during the first 6 years of its existence. In 2004, however, the whole conflict-of-interest issue came roaring to a head, as voters found themselves at the center of two controversies. Three major-conference teams, USC, Oklahoma, and Auburn, all finished the regular season undefeated. When it became apparent over the final weeks that the Tigers were going to be the team left out, their fans found the e-mail addresses for AP voters and began campaigning them en masse. "I don't take the responsibility lightly, but it's a struggle," said *Fort Worth Star Telegram* voter Jimmy Burch. "There's more riding on your vote this year than ever." Gattis, the aforementioned Huntsville, Alabama, writer who kept Auburn at number 3, was not only deluged with hate mail, but, in a classic case of small-town politics, the paper's own editor, Melinda Gorham, authored an apologetic letter to its readers. "I wouldn't necessarily have voted the way he did," she said.

Meanwhile, with Cal and Texas both 10–1 and engaged in a near-deadlock for an at-large berth to the Rose Bowl, Longhorns coach Mack Brown issued a public plea to the voters after his team's last game. "You need to help this team out," he said. A week later, when the Bears declined to go in for one last score against Southern Miss, finishing with a modest 26–16 victory, nine voters—including three in Texas—

moved Texas ahead of Cal on their final ballot. *Mobile (Alabama) Register* writer Neal McCready, who said he'd received more than a thousand e-mails from Longhorns fans, bumped them from ninth to fifth. It was enough to move Texas up to fourth in the final BCS standings, guaranteeing them a spot in the $14 million Rose Bowl and relegating the Bears to the $2.5 million Holiday Bowl—and to cause a whole bunch of sports editors to pull their writers from the poll. "This isn't the poll we all grew up with," said *Palm Beach Post* sports editor Tim Burke. "Reporters should not have a say in who gets a $14 million payday." Faced with a possible mass mutiny, the AP sent a letter ordering the BCS to stop using its poll in the standings. "The AP has never sanctioned use of our poll by the BCS or anyone else," Darrell Christian, AP's director of sports data, told the *Washington Post*. "Obviously, we weren't unaware the BCS was using the poll in its formula. . . . It had finally gotten to the point that it was causing too many problems for the AP and its members."

So if you're the BCS, and you need to find yourself a new set of voters to replace the writers, and the coaches are already taken, who do you tap? How about *former* coaches (and former players and administrators) who now have all the spare time in the world? That's the idea the BCS came up with when, in 2005, it asked the Harris polling service to devise a new Top 25 poll to be incorporated into the BCS standings. Each conference was asked to nominate potential voters, from which Harris randomly selected 114 to participate. Of those, only 23 would be media members. The list of voters, made public that summer, read like a who's who of college football has-beens, from ancient coaches (Bill Yeoman, Foge Fazio) to long-retired commissioners (Fred Jacoby, Harvey Schiller) and athletic directors (Homer Rice, Bump Elliott). "There are several people on the panel who have long since departed their active roles in football," former Illinois, Texas, and Arizona coach John Mackovic, himself a Harris invitee, wrote in the *Palm Springs (California) Desert Sun*. "To tell you the truth, I did not know a couple of them were still alive." The inclusion of several former players better known for their NFL exploits (Terry Bradshaw, Boomer Esiason, Steve Largent) certainly raised some eyebrows, as did the inclusion of one still-active NFL player (at the time), Brentson Buckner, a former Clemson standout,* as well as one former basketball coach, UAB's Gene Bartow. As writers around the country scanned the list of voters, one name, Jason Rash, drew a blank. It would soon be revealed that Rash's only connection to the sport was as the son-in-law of Troy State coach Larry Blakeney, who nominated him via the Sun Belt Conference. "I did it because I knew he'd be credible and accountable," Blakeney told CBSSportsline.com. Rash, the president of an Atlanta masonry company and self-described "avid football fan," resigned from the poll a day after he was named, which is a shame. It's not like you would have had to worry about him ranking Troy State too high.

The poll has served its purpose, however. With such a large number of voters, any off-the-wall ballots have been largely minimized and, in its first two seasons, the Harris Poll basically mirrored the AP and coaches' polls. "I think the Harris Poll was put together with one hundred fourteen different pollsters consistent with acceptable polling principles," said SEC commissioner and BCS coordinator Mike Slive.

What? There are principles involved in these things? Who knew?

November 18, 2006, 11:12 P.M., Ruby Tuesday's, Columbus, Ohio: A couple of my fellow writers and I, having just covered the Ohio State–Michigan "Game of the Century," have gathered for a late-night dinner. Laptop open, I'm putting the finishing touches on my AP ballot, but one issue has me stumped: Who should be number 2? For weeks, I have resisted in print the notion that should number 1 OSU and number 2 Michigan stage a thriller, the loser should not drop in the polls. The idea of a national-championship rematch seems ridiculous. And yet, with images from the two teams' 42–39 classic still fresh in my mind, I can't bring myself to move another team above the 11–1 Wolverines. Arkansas, the team I had third last week, has won ten straight games, yet I'm no

---

*Buckner took his new responsibility extremely seriously, posting his ballot each week on his official Web site complete with an explanation. In 2006 he even named his own All-American teams to go with it.

*longer comfortable putting them ahead of 9–1 USC, a team that beat
the Razorbacks 50–14 the first week of the season. The Trojans appear to
be the next best candidate, but they're only three weeks removed from a
bad loss at Oregon State. And Florida, itself 10–1, hasn't looked good in
about a month. I poll the table, and everyone is in agreement that under
the circumstances, you've got to keep Michigan number 2, so I do. It's a
decision I'll regret two weeks later when Florida wins the SEC title.*

Because there is no playoff in major college football, the voter polls have
become the sport's ultimate arbiter. As a result, it's also the only known
sport where the teams are essentially seeded before they ever play a
game. Preseason polls, long a subject for lively debate and conversation,
have become even more controversial with the advent of the BCS, seeing as they effectively give the highest-ranked teams a leg up on everyone else in the chase for the national title. It's hard, though not
impossible, for a team that starts the year ranked twentieth to finish
number 1, even if it goes undefeated. The number 4 preseason team,
however, can lose a game and know it still has plenty of time to climb
back up. Starting number 1 in the preseason is like having pole position at the Daytona 500 or the inside post in the Kentucky Derby.
Fourteen times since 1936, the team that started the season number 1
in the polls also finished there. Lately, the pollsters have served as pretty
good prognosticators, too: for five straight years, from 2002 to 2006,
the AP and coaches' preseason number 1 reached the BCS championship game. And either or both the preseason number 1 or 2 teams
have reached the title game every year since the BCS's 1998 inception.
Three of those teams (Florida State in 1998 and 2000 and Oklahoma
in 2003) did so despite suffering a loss.

Every year, coaches and fans alike gripe about the existence of preseason polls, which, as any voter will tell you, are an exercise in educated
guesswork. "If you're going to have this system, then [polls] should start
around the first of October," said Auburn coach Tommy Tuberville,
whose undefeated 2004 team failed to reach the title game in large part
because it started the season ranked eighteenth. "People will have a little bit of an idea on how [teams] are doing rather than guessing." He's

probably right, but reality dictates that preseason polls aren't going anywhere. Why? Because there's an insatiable public demand for them. Even before the AP and coaches issue their official preseason edicts in August, one can walk into a bookstore as early as May and see racks and racks of preseason magazines (*Athlon, Sporting News, Street & Smith*) with their own Top 25 lists.* And thanks to the Internet, the poll conversation now begins almost as soon as the last season ends. SI.com published my first Top 25 for the 2007 season on January 16, a full seven months before teams report for fall camp—and not surprisingly, it got hit like mad. The organizers of the new Harris Poll tried a noble experiment in delaying the release of their first poll until the last week of September. Of course, when the poll did finally come out, it looked almost exactly the same as that week's AP and coaches' polls. Even if the AP and coaches did delay their polls (which will never happen), it's naïve to think the voters would sit down with a blank piece of paper and list twenty-five teams from scratch. Inevitably, they would use an Internet poll or other unofficial ranking as their starting point. Let's face it—most pollsters don't have the time to be original.

So as long as there are going to be preseason polls, one might as well gain an understanding of how they work. I've been studying and conducting these things myself for the better part of a decade and in doing so have noticed four common criteria most voters emphasize:

1. *Number of returning starters:* You hear this statistic a lot in the months leading up to the season. Because it's nearly impossible to gain an intimate knowledge of twenty-five different teams' entire eighty- or ninety-player rosters, we focus primarily on the twenty-two starters. A team that was pretty good the year before and returns sixteen or more is generally considered to be loaded. Ten to fifteen returning starters is about average and a sign of a fairly experienced team. Single digits is considered a rebuilding year. While this statistic is a decent starting point in determining

---

*Which the AP and coaches' voters then use as a reference in filling out their ballots.

the strength of a team's roster, it hardly tells the entire story. For one thing, while only eleven guys can play on a side at once, most teams rotate in far more than that during the course of the game. Second, just because a team returns fifteen starters doesn't necessarily mean they're all good. What if the seven who graduated happened to be the seven best players on the team?

In the 2006 preseason, I fell for the returning starters trap with LSU. I saw a team that had finished 11–2 the year before but lost eleven starters, including two all-conference defensive tackles and three all-conference offensive linemen. I assumed there would be a drop-off and ranked the Tigers outside the top 10. What I didn't truly appreciate was the amount of accomplished veterans still in the fold (QB JaMarcus Russell, WR Dwayne Bowe, and S LaRon Landry, among others) and had no way of knowing that one of the new starting defensive tackles, Glenn Dorsey, would wind up blowing away his predecessors and becoming a consensus All-American. A few hundred Bayou Bengals fans reminded me of my mistake when the Tigers again went 11–2 and finished the season third in the country.

2. *The presence of a star quarterback and/or running back:* We've all heard the old adage "defense wins championships," a theory national champion Florida proved true yet again in 2006, but that doesn't stop us from continuing to be entranced by the more glamorous offensive positions. Without fail, a team that returns veteran star power on offense will be rated higher than a comparable team whose strength lies on defense. Part of that is because it's easier to predict whether a team will field a powerful offense (generally, if they did the year before and they return most of the players, they will again) than it is for defense (where breakdowns and missed tackles can happen to anyone). Teams with a star quarterback or fifteen-hundred-yard rusher tend to get more hype than a team with anonymous skill players but a loaded defense—and voters aren't immune to the hype.

In 2006, I and a whole bunch of other voters fell for this with

Notre Dame. In a year when nearly all the other logical contenders had lost their marquee names (Defending champion Texas had just lost QB Vince Young, runner-up USC had lost Heisman winners Matt Leinart and Reggie Bush), the Irish, 9–3 a year earlier, were a sexy pick what with the return of star QB Brady Quinn, running back Darius Walker, and receivers Jeff Samardzija and Rhema McKnight. In ranking the Irish as high as number 2 in the preseason polls, the voters conveniently overlooked the fact their defense had just allowed 617 yards to Ohio State in their last game. The assumption was that the defense, with nine returning starters, would improve. Well . . . it did not. And not only that, the offense, after losing a couple of key linemen, regressed from its 2005 level. Notre Dame finished with a similar record (10–3) but got blown out in its three losses and finished the season significantly lower than second in the polls (seventeenth in AP, nineteenth in coaches').

However, voters had used basically the same criteria in choosing that season's preseason number 1 team, Ohio State, which returned a boatload of offensive stars (QB Troy Smith, RB Antonio Pittman, WR Ted Ginn Jr.) but just two starters on defense, and the Buckeyes lived up to their billing by going undefeated during the regular season. This goes to show that offensive firepower can indeed take a team a long way—but you'd better make sure they've got some players on defense, too. And while quarterback is without question the most important position on the field, the often overlooked offensive line is a close second in my book.

3. *A big bowl win:* College football is a sport of "what have you done for me lately," and the preseason polls are no exception. Whether a team won or lost its last game the previous season can cause about a six-point swing in the team's rank to start the next season. I have a real problem with this one. As mentioned elsewhere in this book, non-BCS bowl games (and even some nonchampionship BCS games) are often in no way reflective of a team's entire season leading up to it. The teams are coming off a long

layoff, some of them are more motivated for the bowl than others, and coaches often use the games to experiment with personnel and play-calling in ways they would never consider during the regular season. Therefore, bowl wins and losses—particularly big upsets—often create false expectations for the following season.

Textbook example: Auburn in 2003. After upsetting Penn State in the Capital One Bowl to finish 9–4, the Tigers suddenly became the darlings of the following preseason, rocketing from fourteenth at the end of the previous season to sixth in the preseason AP poll. The *Sporting News* took it one step further, dubbing Auburn its preseason number 1 team. Voters were so enamored by the returning tailback tandem of Carnell Williams and Ronnie Brown that they overlooked the Tigers' brutal schedule and highly questionable passing game. They lost their season opener 23–0 to USC, finished 8–5, and nearly got their coach fired.* Other recent, memorable bowl poll flops: 2004 Clemson (started fifteenth following a Peach Bowl upset of 10–2 Tennessee, finished 6–5), 2005 Tennessee (started third following a Cotton Bowl trouncing of Texas A&M, finished 5–6), and 2005 Iowa (started eleventh following a dramatic Capital One Bowl win over LSU, finished 7–5). To me, a team that performed well over the final month of the regular season is better poised for a breakthrough than a team that had a ho-hum regular season but turned it on in the bowl.

4. *Schedule:* In a sport where the schools and conferences make their own schedules, you can't evaluate a team's prospects for the upcoming season without evaluating the favorability of its schedule. How many home games? Does its nonconference schedule include Michigan and Louisiana State or Western Michigan and Louisiana-Lafayette? If it plays in a twelve-team conference,

---

*As it turned out, the voters were a year early in hailing Auburn, which went 13–0 the following season with Williams and Brown as seniors, but, because of the disappointing 2003 season, started 2004 ranked just eighteenth.

which opponents does it miss? The schedule can go a long way toward determining whether a perfectly talented team winds up 9–3 or 6–6. It only makes sense that voters would factor in the schedule when making their preseason prognostications. Doing so, however, raises a thorny question: Is the preseason poll supposed to be a starting-off point or a prediction of how it will look at the end?

In my experience, most voters take the latter approach. "If we're doing our jobs correctly," wrote Austin's Bohls, "those ballots five months apart should closely resemble each other within reason." While I don't necessarily disagree, I do wonder whether that's really fair to the teams. In 2006, several voters placed West Virginia at or near number 1 in their preseason ballots, not necessarily because they thought the Mountaineers were the best team in the country, but because of what appeared to be a ridiculously favorable schedule. In doing so, however, they gave West Virginia a built-in advantage on top of what was already perceived to be a huge advantage by giving them less ground to make up in the polls. Meanwhile, another team might start lower than it would have because of a perceived difficult schedule, but if both teams finish with the same record, shouldn't the team that mastered the harder schedule finish ahead of the team with the easier schedule? If anything, the team with the harder schedule should start higher because it has the bigger handicap. But that would make too much sense for something as arbitrary as a preseason college football poll.

Once upon a time, "arbitrary" was a good word to describe the end-of-season poll as well. Back in the old days, they'd let the season play out, and if come the end of the year* there was more than one team tied with the best record, the voters chose the number 1 team based on . . . nobody's really sure. Tradition? Regionalism? School colors? "In the

---

*Prior to 1965, the final AP poll was released at the end of the regular season. The UPI poll did not select its first post-bowl national champion until 1974.

Southwest we all stay pretty depressed until we're still unbeaten and Notre Dame and everybody in the Big Ten has been knocked off," then-Texas coach Darrell Royal said in *Saturday's America*. His paranoia was well within reason. For all the criticism directed these days at the BCS, bizarre national championship races date all the way back to the first official season of the AP poll in 1936, when Northwestern and Minnesota both finished 7–1, the Wildcats beat the Gophers head-to-head during the season . . . and Minnesota was crowned number 1. In 1966, number 1 Notre Dame famously played for the tie against number 2 Michigan State, choosing to run out the clock in the final minutes of a 10–10 game. The 10–0–1 Irish retained the final number 1 ranking over both the 10–0–1 Spartans and 11–0 Alabama. In 1978, AP voters selected the 11–1 Crimson Tide as their champion after they knocked off number 1 Penn State in the Sugar Bowl; UPI went with 12–1 USC, seeing as the Trojans had beaten 'Bama 24–14 during the season. And in 1983, 11–1 Miami, which lost its first game of the season 28–3 to 9–2–1 Florida, shot from fifth to first in the final poll after stunning top-ranked Nebraska in the Orange Bowl, much to the dismay of number 2 Auburn, whose only blemish had been a 20–7 loss to 11–1 Texas.

While the aforementioned decisions were all debatable, they were accepted by the public because of the general acknowledgment that the polls were a matter of opinion—specifically, the so-called experts' opinion as to which was the best team. But somewhere along the way, the debate began to gradually shift from the largely nebulous issue of "which team is best" to the more dicey issue of "which team is most deserving." A key moment in this transformation was the 1984 season. BYU, a high-scoring outfit from the lesser-regarded Western Athletic Conference, swept the number 1 spot in the final polls in large part because the Cougars were the only team to finish undefeated. They'd done so, however, in large part by playing a weak slate of opponents whose combined record was an atrocious 60–86. In its Holiday Bowl coronation, BYU beat a 6–5 Michigan team 24–17. This hardly seemed fair to fans of 11–1 Washington, which had beaten Big 8 champion Oklahoma 28–17 in the Orange Bowl. "Washington deserves to be No. 1," Sooners coach Barry Switzer said after the game. "They are 11–1, have the next-best record and I guarantee you they are a better team than Brigham Young." Sportswriters were not as sympathetic to the Sooners' plight. "Brigham Young is the national champion. It's official," wrote *Los Angeles Times* columnist Mike Littwin. "Even though BYU's schedule might not challenge Burbank High's. Even though winning the Western Athletic Conference title is not unlike winning the Utah surfing championship."

This idea that strength-of-schedule should matter had caught on by 1990, when AP voters tabbed a Colorado team that had gone 11–1–1 (and won a game against Missouri thanks to receiving an errant fifth down in the final seconds) over an unbeaten Georgia Tech team (11–0–1) because the Yellow Jackets' ACC schedule was deemed inferior to Big 8 champion Colorado's. The coaches voted Georgia Tech number 1. Meanwhile, plenty of teams from conferences like the WAC have gone undefeated since BYU did, including Utah in 2004 and Boise State in 2006, yet none have come close to finishing number 1. "The thing that bothers me about the whole deal is that nobody has ever clarified what you're voting for," then-Nebraska coach Tom Osborne said in 1985. "Are you voting for the best record? Are you voting for the best team? There seems to be a lot of confusion on that issue and I think that the writers and the coaches should get together and lay out some guidelines." Umm . . . yeah. That's never happened.

In fact, Hall of Famer Osborne was directly involved in one of the most heated number 1 controversies in the modern era when in 1997 both his Nebraska team and Michigan finished undefeated. The Wolverines had supplanted the Huskers atop both polls in November after Nebraska needed a controversial kicked-ball touchdown catch to survive Missouri in overtime while Michigan had stomped heavyweights Penn State and Ohio State. But following the bowl games, in which the Wolverines beat number 8 Washington State 21–16 in the Rose Bowl and the Huskers routed number 3 Tennessee 42–17, at least twenty-three coaches moved Nebraska ahead of Michigan on their final ballots, giving the Huskers a share of the national title. Most believed the coaches were giving their friend Osborne, who had previously announced his retirement, a going-away present. "As I watched Nebraska play last night and saw their team out there, I felt like I had to vote for Nebraska and hopefully they could get a tie in this thing," Colorado State coach Sonny Lubick told the *Omaha World Herald*. ". . . It would have been a crime for either team to go 12–0 or 13–0 and not be [national champs]." The coaches' poll: where everyone goes home a winner.

With the arrival of the BCS the following season, the decision regarding which team should finish atop the polls was essentially taken out of the voters' hands, as now the top two contenders were guaranteed to play each other in a bowl game. Only once since the BCS's 1998 debut, in 2003, has there been split champions, and even that case was not a voter-rendered decision. USC, the number 1 team in both polls at the end of the regular season, finished number 3 in the BCS standings, sending the Trojans to the Rose Bowl to face Michigan and BCS-number 1 Oklahoma to the Sugar Bowl to face BCS-number 2 LSU. By mandate of the coaches' association, LSU, the winner of the BCS game, was automatically crowned the coaches' national champion. (AP voters stuck with USC.) To this day, if any writer dares to even acknowledge USC's claim to that season's championship, he will receive a batch of angry e-mails from LSU fans reminding him that "LSU won the only championship that was agreed to by all participants before the season . . . blah, blah, blah."

In response to the mess, the BCS altered its formula the following season to place much greater emphasis on the two human polls, thus lessening the possibility of a future split. In instituting the change, however, poll voters now found themselves with more influence than ever before in determining the participants in the national championship game, one reason the AP dropped out a year later. During the first six years of the BCS, there had been no discernible change in voter tendencies. When two of three remaining undefeated teams, Kansas State and UCLA, lost the final weekend of the 1998 season, voters did what they'd always done: move up the next team, 11–1 Florida State, which itself led 10–1 Ohio State primarily because it had lost less recently. And when controversy ensued over the second title-game participant a couple of years later, the blame was placed not on the pollsters, who had tapped majority favorites Miami (2000) and Oregon (2001), respectively, but the BCS computers, which helped send Florida State to the game instead of the Hurricanes, and Nebraska instead of the Ducks. But then came 2004 and the Auburn and Texas/Cal controversies. While the Tigers fell victim to a decades-old poll tradition that you don't drop a number 1 or number 2 team (in this case USC and Oklahoma) that hasn't lost, the eleventh-hour poll swing that sent Texas to the Rose Bowl was the first explicit example of voters behaving in a manner cognizant of the impact their vote would have on the BCS.

If that moment was not enough to indicate a tangible shift in the role of pollsters, the end of the 2006 season iced it. Heading into the final weekend of the season, the BCS standings were: number 1 Ohio State (12–0), number 2 USC (10–1), number 3 Michigan (11–1), number 4 Florida (11–1). The Buckeyes had defeated the Wolverines 42–39 in both teams' season finale two weeks earlier to fill one spot in the national championship game, and the Trojans were widely expected to defeat 6–5 rival UCLA to clinch the other spot. The Gators, despite playing for the SEC championship that weekend against Arkansas, had barely entered the discussion despite much public lobbying by their coach, Urban Meyer. But then the Bruins stunned the Trojans 13–9 in a game that ended around halftime of the Florida–Arkansas SEC title game. As the Gators pulled away in the second half of a 38–28 victory, CBS game analyst Gary Danielson urged voters to tab Florida over Michigan for the number 2 spot. Meyer did much the same in his postgame comments. "Another team had their shot [at Ohio State]," he said, in a reference to the Wolverines. ". . . If you're going to tell me that we can go 12–1 against the toughest schedule in the country and don't deserve a shot, I have a problem with that."

Whether the voters succumbed to the lobbying or acted on their own, we'll never know. But when the final ballots were cast, an estimated 40 of 113 Harris Poll voters and 25 of 65 coaches moved the Gators ahead of idle Michigan, according to BCS expert Jerry Palm, enough to lift Florida from number 4 to number 2 in the final BCS standings. "It's safe to say we would have never seen that much movement if this was November third and not December third simply based on the results of last weekend," wrote Palm. "However, the voters weren't simply picking this week's number two team, they were choosing who would play for a national championship." Never before had voters behaved in this way—and the ensuing controversy was heated. Jilted Michigan coach Lloyd Carr blasted Meyer for his lobbying tactics, calling his comments "inappropriate," and pointed out, correctly, that had USC won, voters likely would have kept the Wolverines ahead of the Gators. Ohio State coach Tressel, faced with voting on his potential title-game opponent, created his own mini-controversy by abstaining from voting in the final poll, a move Carr referred to as "real slick" and ever-outspoken Texas Tech coach Mike Leach called "a bunch of sanctimonious bunk." And South Carolina coach Spurrier, a former Heisman-winning quarterback and record-setting coach at Florida, exposed for the umpteenth time the transparent agendas afoot in the coaches poll, saying he voted the Gators over Michigan because, "Heck, I'm a Gator."

Even though my AP ballot bore no influence on the BCS matchup, I, too, bumped Florida to number 2. It was the right thing to do. Earlier in this chapter, I used the word "arbitrary" to describe the polls, and for the most part, it's true. When you're trying to decide between three 5–2 teams for the number 15 ranking in the middle of October, you don't have much to go by besides your own personal eyeball test. But by the end of the season, teams have built up a fairly comprehensive body of work by which to judge them. By the end of the 2006 regular season, the Gators had won their conference championship and beaten three ranked opponents and eight bowl teams; Michigan had finished second in its conference while beating two ranked foes and six bowl teams. At the time, I couldn't have told you with any certainty which was the better team—the Gators would bear that out pretty convincingly come bowl season—but there wasn't much question which team was more deserving. Apparently, other voters felt the same way.

So, while on the one hand the idea of voter polls in college football may seem completely outdated and archaic, not to mention ripe with conflicts of interest and other pitfalls, at least there's been one positive advancement: voters who actually put some thought into their ballots. No longer does the next team automatically move up when the one ahead of it loses. No longer are matters of common sense like head-to-head matchups or strength of schedule thrown out the window. Voters will never get the order of teams exactly right—if they could, they'd be smart to move to Vegas and start a new, more lucrative career—but they're coming closer today than ever before.

Which, of course, is not to say that you're going to agree with them.

January 8, 2007, 9:25 P.M., University of Phoenix Stadium press box, Glendale, Arizona: The fourth quarter of the national championship game is playing out below me, with Florida's victory over Ohio State well in hand. I'd like to be concentrating on my column that's due later tonight or figuring out the quickest route to the field to conduct interviews, but my final AP ballot is due as soon as the game ends. Now I must decide how far Ohio State should fall and where 13–0 Boise State, now the lone remaining undefeated team, should finish. I quickly decide that the Buckeyes, by virtue of their perfect regular season, deserve to remain above everyone but Florida. LSU, USC, and Boise will round out the top five. I quickly review the rest of my ballot, which I prepared before the game, before hitting the "Send" button. A smile crosses my face as I see Penn State at number 25. All season long, Nittany Lions fans have been pestering me about their poll absence, despite the fact they hadn't beaten anyone of merit, but after upsetting Tennessee in the Outback Bowl, I slip them into the final poll. I figure they'll be pleased.

My final ballot gets posted on SI.com shortly after the game. Upon finishing my column a couple of hours later, I check my e-mail. The first message reads: "Got an idea for you . . . FIND A TALL BUILDING AND JUMP OFF IT!!! Ranking Tennessee ahead of Penn State after Penn State thumped them in the Outback Bowl!!! Are you insane?? How do you still have a job?" Ah, the rewards of being a pollster.

3

He Won the Heisman?

Few relics that we know of have created more
melodrama in college football than the Heisman
Memorial Trophy, an award that is supposed
to go to the outstanding player in the United
States every year, and sometimes does.

—*former* Sports Illustrated *writer Dan Jenkins, 1973*

I can't go back on the field and change anybody's
perception. I got a trophy at home. They can
say whatever they want.

—*former Heisman Trophy winner Gino Torretta, 2004*

L adies and gentlemen, a moment of your time, please. I am here to educate you about a heretofore overlooked crisis of rapidly increasing concern to our fine nation. Put aside, for a moment, your consternation over the price of gas or access to health care. Forget, at least temporarily, about lack of funding for schools or the wads of fatty French fries your kids are eating. As an American citizen, your biggest cause for distress right now should be this: our country has become incapable of picking the right Heisman Trophy winner.

Exhibit A: Eric Crouch. In 2001, the Heisman electorate decided to hand out their esteemed award to a Nebraska quarterback who threw more interceptions (10) than touchdowns (7) and wound up losing his last two games of the season by scores of 62–36 and 37–14. Crouch, it should be noted, was primarily an option quarterback who ran around a lot, but his most memorable moment was his lone pass reception of the season, a 63-yard touchdown on a trick play against Oklahoma. Crouch, drafted in the third round by the St. Louis Rams, was out of the NFL almost before they had time to stitch the name onto the back of his jersey and by now is likely selling insurance door-to-door in Omaha. Nonetheless, he has a nifty portrait of himself hanging in New York City and a lifetime invitation to one hell of an annual banquet (which he attends every year because—well, what else does he have to do in early December?).

Exhibit B: Gino Torretta. It's never a good sign if you're a Heisman Trophy winner from the 1990s, yet almost no fan in the country could pick you out of a police lineup. To his credit, Torretta was Miami's starting quarterback for twenty-six consecutive victories, though his team won games more on the strength of its defense than the nation's nineteenth-rated passer. This, however, did not prevent Torretta from running away with the balloting in 1992, finishing more than three hundred points ahead of a San Diego State running back by the name of Marshall Faulk. Incidentally, Torretta, a low draft pick who wound up playing in just one NFL game, *does* sell insurance, or something like it, for Prudential Services, and is more easily recognizable than you might think. During each year's Heisman ceremony, when the camera pans to the past winners in attendance, he's the guy who looks like someone's lost wedding date.

Exhibit C: Reggie Bush.* This one's not an indictment against Bush, who, as anyone with a TV can tell you, is a once-in-a-lifetime athlete who will wind up redefining the tailback position. For the Heisman electorate (of which I was a member by this point), 2005 seemed about as big a no-brainer as they come. Nearly every week of the season, we'd watched, both live and on countless replays, as Bush juked, spun around, sprinted by, and, at one point, hurdled over opposing defenders. We were bombarded with constant comparisons to Bears legend Gale Sayers and the never-ending usage of the phrase "most dangerous player in the country," and basically, we fell for him like lovestruck schoolboys. Unfortunately, we never once stopped to consider that there may have been an even more dangerous player that year, Texas quarterback Vince Young, who could not only run really fast but throw a pretty nice deep ball. He finished a distant second to Bush in the voting. So what happened? The Longhorns upset the Trojans in the national championship game, with the unstoppable Young serving as his own one-man wrecking crew. Bush wasn't even his team's most effective rusher. Whoops.

Exhibit D: Troy Smith. Ohio State's dynamic quarterback was the most deserving candidate in 2006, regardless of what his future may hold. It wasn't exactly the finest hour for the Heisman winner, however, when, just a month after posting one of the most lopsided victories in

---

*In 2006, Yahoo! Sports reported that Bush and his family had received hundreds of thousands of dollars in benefits from a prospective agent while still a member of the Trojans, which, if proven true, would have meant he was ineligible under NCAA rules. This led to speculation as to whether Heisman officials would revoke his trophy. No decision had been issued at the time this book went to press.

the history of the trophy, Smith ended up on the wrong side of another blowout, Florida's 41–14 national-title upset of Smith's Buckeyes. Your Heisman-winning numbers: 4–of–14 for 35 yards, five sacks, and two turnovers. Smith wound up the last pick in the fifth round of the following spring's NFL Draft.

Do you see what's going on here, people? The aforementioned men have all been awarded membership to one of our nation's most exclusive fraternities, one to which only seventy-one players in the storied history of college football have been deemed special enough to join, while other, more luminous football players have been . . . well, stiff-armed. Dick Butkus? Not a Heisman Trophy winner. Ron Dayne? Heisman Trophy winner. No room for you at the table, Peyton Manning. Feel free to have another drink from the open bar, Chris Weinke. Jim Brown? Nyet. Rashaan Salaam? Oui. And who needs a John Elway at your party when you have a Jason White?

If you're still not grasping the enormity of the situation by now, then, by golly, you just don't understand the significance of the Heisman Trophy. There must be something special about that 50-pound piece of hardware that causes us to follow its annual contest with nearly the same intensity as the actual national-championship race. Even before kickoff of the first game, nearly every newspaper and Web site in the country chimes in each week with its list of the top candidates. And in the climactic period leading up to the presentation, various organizations go into all-out Gallup mode, surveying voters in a desperate attempt to project the winner, à la a presidential election. Literally, the Heisman is a bronzed, 14-inch statue sculpted in the likeness of a ball carrier sidestepping and stiff-arming an invisible defender on his way to untold glories. Figuratively, it's the most coveted individual honor in American sports—or at least it was until they started handing them out to any old schmo with a high passer rating.

The prize has been awarded every year since 1935, when members of the Downtown Athletic Club, a high-end, members-only sporting and fitness facility in lower Manhattan, took it upon themselves to hand out an award to the nation's "most outstanding college football player." John W. Heisman, the legendary former Georgia Tech coach and inventor of the center snap, had recently retired and moved to New York, where he became the club's first athletic director. It's unclear what exactly his official duties entailed (was Heisman the guy you went to if you wanted to reserve a bowling lane or request a new locker?), but he did become the primary figurehead behind the new award, identifying candidates and organizing the voting system. The members commissioned sculptor Frank Eliscu, a twenty-three-year-old graduate of the Pratt Institute, to create the new trophy, which he modeled after Ed Smith, the star halfback of that venerable college football juggernaut, NYU. For the first year, the accolade was named the Downtown Athletic Club Trophy, and University of Chicago passer/runner/kicker Jay Berwanger was the landslide winner, beating out Army's Monk Meyer, Notre Dame's William Shakespeare (yes, Shakespeare was a real player, not a Seymore Butts-style write-in hoax) and Princeton's Pepper Constable.* Today, the announcement of the winner is a grand spectacle, broadcast live on national television following months of breathless speculation and debate over his identity. Berwanger, however, simply received a letter at his fraternity house informing him of the award and inviting him to New York for a dinner in his honor. "I didn't know what it was," Berwanger recalled to the *Orlando Sentinel* in 1999, three years before his death at age eighty-eight. "The thing that excited me most was, it would be my first plane ride."

The following year, Heisman died of pneumonia, and the award was renamed in his memory. In both 1936 and 1937, the Heisman went to players from Yale, end Larry Kelley and back Clint Frank. One might have been tempted right then to start the first of what would eventually be countless cries of East Coast bias, if not for the fact that in 1938, the voters smartly tabbed gunslinging TCU quarterback Davey O'Brien, thus legitimizing the Heisman as a truly national award. Within a few years, imitators like the Maxwell and Walter Camp awards started sprouting up around the country, but the keepers of the Heisman had already solidified its place as the highest honor in all the land.

---

*Why were players' names so much cooler back then?

At this point, you might be wondering, how exactly did a bunch of cigar-chomping New York socialites come to hold such influence in the national college football scene? I have no earthly idea. Maybe it was the immaculateness of the trophy itself that captured the imagination of the American public. Perhaps it was the glitz and glamour of the trophy's home, New York City, not to mention its proximity to the nation's most influential football writers, that turned the otherwise drab Downtown Athletic Club* into something of a sporting Mecca. Or maybe the award itself was simply an idea whose time had come, and the members of the Downtown Athletic Club just happened to be the ones to make it happen. Whatever the case may be, in the years and decades following its inception, the Heisman became to college football what the Oscars are to movies and the Emmys are to television: one of the nation's most revered individual achievements, with the added bonus of no Joan Rivers.

Year after year, the biggest gridiron heroes of their era would etch their names into Heisman immortality. There was Michigan's Tom Harmon, "Old '98," the two-way bandit who ran for three touchdowns, passed for two others, intercepted three passes, and averaged 50 yards punting in a 40–0 rout of archrival Ohio State in 1940. Then there was Army's Doc Blanchard, "Mr. Inside," and his teammate Glenn Davis, "Mr. Outside," winning the award in consecutive seasons, 1945 and 1946. And who could forget SMU running back Doak Walker, who would one day have his own award named after him, in 1948. "Early on, like in the forties with Glenn Davis, Doc Blanchard, [Notre Dame QB] Johnny Lujack, Doak Walker, [Notre Dame end] Leon Hart—God, it really was a 'Who's Who' of college football," said Bernie Kish, former executive director of the College Football Hall of Fame.

Notice that Kish mentioned two Notre Dame players. That's no small coincidence. From the award's earliest days, the Heisman electorate—primarily newspapermen from around the country—began exhibiting

---

*My main memory of the place from my lone visit there in 1995 was that it smelled like a mixture of chlorine and aftershave.

some of the unofficial criteria that remain in effect to this day. With the exception of Hart, who was primarily a lineman, every winner for more than sixty years was a passing, rushing, or receiving star on the offensive side of the ball (though in the one-platoon era prior to 1941, and again from 1953 to 1965, many played defense as well). Nearly every winner during the first fifty years was a senior, and none were younger than a junior. And while many different schools, from Princeton to Wisconsin to Oregon State, produced Heisman winners, none did so more prolifically than Notre Dame, which spawned six from 1943 to 1964 alone. Some of them even deserved it.

Not every Heisman winner of that era would go on to gain reverential status. Certainly Pete Dawkins (Army, 1958), Joe Bellino (Navy, 1960), Terry Baker (Oregon State, 1962), and John Huarte (Notre Dame, 1964) do not often come up when discussing college football's all-time greats. And in retrospect, there were some pretty glaring oversights. Jim Brown, the legendary Syracuse running back who set a new standard for the modern tailback, finished just fifth in the voting in 1956. Purdue's Bob Griese, considered one of the top quarterbacks of his generation, came in just eighth in 1965. And Alabama's Joe Namath, whose fame would grow exponentially once he moved up to the spotlight of New York City but was nevertheless the unquestioned leader of Bear Bryant's 1964 national title team, failed to even crack the top 10. For the most part, however, the Who's Who feel to the Heisman continues to stick out as you read down the list of winners through the 1950s (Texas A&M's John David Crow, LSU's Billy Cannon), 1960s (Navy's Roger Staubach, USC's O.J. Simpson), 1970s (Nebraska's Johnny Rodgers, Ohio State's Archie Griffin, the award's only two-time winner; Pittsburgh's Tony Dorsett; Texas's Earl Campbell), and 1980s (Georgia's Herschel Walker, Auburn's Bo Jackson, Boston College's Doug Flutie, and Oklahoma State's Barry Sanders).

So when, exactly, did the Heisman jump the shark? When did the image of the Heisman Trophy winner as mythical superhuman begin to suffer its first cracks? When did the once-holy halfback start to look more like a slightly droopy guy in a funny helmet? "To me, when it started dropping off was in the late '80s," said Kish. "Maybe then it started becoming more of a beauty contest." I have my own theory, and it can be summed up in two words: Andre Ware. In 1989, the Heisman electorate made what seems in hindsight to be one of the strangest choices in their history. Ware, a junior quarterback for the University of Houston, spent much of that season shattering NCAA passing records, throwing for a staggering 4,699 yards and 46 touchdowns. That he did it while running Cougars coach Jack Pardee's wild, pass-happy run-'n'-shoot offense, one that in ensuing years would elicit similar numbers from nearly every quarterback who played in it, did not at the time serve as a mitigating factor. Nor did the fact that Ware put up much of his numbers against such stalwart opposition as UNLV, Temple, Baylor, SMU (whom the Cougars actually beat 95–21), and the rest of the probation-ravaged Southwest Conference. Heck, the voters did not even seem to mind that most of them never actually saw Ware play, seeing as Houston, one of several SWC teams paying its NCAA penance for various sins committed throughout the 1980s, was banned from appearing on television that season. In what was deemed a particularly weak but crowded field of contenders (though a noteworthy Florida running back by the name of Emmitt Smith finished seventh), Ware became enshrined into the Heisman fraternity amidst a notable shroud of cynicism. "Ware is a good college quarterback, maybe a great one," *Newsday's* Tim Layden, now with *Sports Illustrated,* wrote at the time. ". . . But what of the competition? And what of the system that allowed Ware to attempt 52 passes a game? The SWC is woefully weak, and Houston lost to the only two decent teams in the conference: Texas A&M and Arkansas."

Layden and the others who shared his skepticism would prove to be prophetic. Ware, who skipped his senior season to enter the NFL draft and was selected seventh by the Detroit Lions, never came close to duplicating his college success at the next level. He started just six games in four NFL seasons and served primarily as a backup in the CFL. One of the greatest players in college football history? More like one of the greatest players in the history of the run-'n'-shoot. And yet his name is permanently attached to one of the proudest legacies in all of sports, forever immortalized alongside the Harmons and Lujacks, the Doaks and the O.J.s. Don't think about it for too long—you might start to cry.

For whatever reason, Ware's enshrinement marked the beginning of an era where the so-called Heisman bust would become more and more the norm. Of the fifteen players to win the award from 1989 to 2003, only four—Ohio State running back Eddie George (1995), Michigan cornerback Charles Woodson (1997), Texas running back Ricky Williams* (1998) and USC quarterback Carson Palmer (2002)—would go on to have any significant success after winning the trophy. Some, like Weinke and Crouch, flopped as soon as their final bowl game. Others, like BYU quarterback Ty Detmer and Michigan receiver Desmond Howard, spent more than a decade in the NFL (Howard even earned a Super Bowl MVP award with the Packers for his 99-yard kick return in the 1997 game) but never lived up to their college acclaim. And one, Florida State quarterback and two-sport star Charlie Ward, never even attempted to play professional football, opting instead for an NBA career as a point guard for the New York Knicks. "Everyone has different goals," Crouch told *USA Today* in 2003. "Just because you win the Heisman, doesn't mean you're supposed to have a long NFL career."

Indeed, most college purists balk whenever one dares bring the NFL into a Heisman discussion. "The award is presented for what the young man does in his college career," Rudy Riska, the Downtown Athletic Club's longtime executive director, told the *Dallas Morning News* in 1996. "We would be very upset if the voters suddenly started voting on pro potential." You won't hear any argument from me there. The problem, however, is that perception is reality. Back when the college game was still our nation's primary obsession, it didn't particularly matter for posterity's sake whether 1944 winner Les Horvath went on to become a more prominent doctor than pro football player, or that 1951 winner

---

*Many would consider Williams a Heisman bust as well, seeing as he pot-smoked himself out of the NFL for two seasons, but he was pretty darn good when he did play.

Dick Kazmaier forsook the pro-sports industry for the sporting goods industry. Back then, legends could be built entirely around one's brief but distinguished college career. But like it or not, the NFL has since become the dominant brand of football in our nation's conscience. A spectacular college career only gets a player so far in the eyes of the public. Ultimately, he is judged by whether he lives up to his potential at the next level. Thus, each Torretta or Salaam-caliber flop can't help but reflect poorly on the Heisman, stripping away another layer of its luster and eliciting yet another round of questioning over how the player won in the first place. "It's gotten to the point where you look at the draft, not the Heisman, to see who the best player is," former Oklahoma and Dallas Cowboys coach Barry Switzer told the *Morning News*.

To get a glimpse at just how drastically the award's credibility has fallen, one need look no further than the virulent backlash endured by 2003 winner Jason White. After missing almost all of the previous two seasons to knee injuries, the Oklahoma quarterback set the college football world on fire upon his return, throwing for 3,446 yards, 40 touchdowns, and just 6 interceptions during the Sooners' 12–0 start. He was the farthest thing from flashy, but he got the job done, and, in a close two-man race, he beat out Pittsburgh receiver Larry Fitzgerald for the trophy. However, when it came time for his two biggest tests of the season, the Big 12 title game against Kansas State and the Sugar Bowl national-title game against LSU, White—who, undisclosed to the public at the time, was nursing fairly severe knee and hand injuries—fell flat on his face, going just 13-of-37 for 102 yards and 2 interceptions in the Sugar Bowl. "Is the Heisman Trophy subject to a recall vote?" *San Diego Union-Tribune* columnist Tim Sullivan wrote after the game. "It's safe to say that the Sooners' first 12 games managed to mask some inherent weaknesses," I wrote on SI.com, having endorsed White's Heisman worthiness just a month earlier. ". . . No, he was not the best player in college football this season."

White, having been granted a sixth year of eligibility due to his injuries, came back for another go-round in 2004 and produced yet another spectacular regular season and 12–0 start. But this time around, the Heisman voters weren't buying it. White finished a distant third in the balloting behind USC quarterback Matt Leinart and one of his own teammates, Oklahoma running back Adrian Peterson, and by the time of the ceremony seemed visibly fatigued and perturbed by the criticism. "Are you kidding?" he said when asked by a reporter about his chances of repeating. "I guess you didn't read the papers after our final two games last year. They pretty much threw me out the window after the season." In his last college game, an Orange Bowl matchup with USC for another shot at the national title, White was once again humbled, throwing three interceptions in a 55–19 loss. Adding insult to injury, not a single NFL team selected him in the following spring's draft, thus sealing his legacy as a Heisman bust—and once again calling into question our intelligence as voters.

What can be done to curtail this ever-growing tide of Heisman embarrassments? College football and the NFL are different games, and there will always be a certain type of player who excels at one and not the other. That said, the two levels have never mirrored each other more closely than they do today, what with coaches frequently jumping between the two and importing pro schemes to the college game. You wouldn't think it would be that hard to identify a single player each year whose abilities are so clearly transcendent as to ensure his stature as a worthy heir to the Heisman legacy. Like Riska said, by no means should voters start basing their choices on pro potential. But obviously, something's got to change, and it would behoove all of us to stop and take stock of the archaic process by which our Heisman Trophy winners are selected.

Part of the Heisman's allure, of course, is its ambiguity. The Downtown Athletic Club didn't exactly go out of its way to lend guidance to the voters upon establishing the trophy, leaving them with only the vaguest of instructions to select "the most outstanding college football player in the country." Not another word about the criteria. It would be akin to plopping a naïve bachelor in the heart of South Beach and telling him to pick the "perfect girl." Would that mean the girl with the most unbelievable body? The most beautiful smile? The best conversationalist? Help a brother out! It's the same way with the Heisman. Does "most outstanding player" mean the one who makes the most dazzling plays? Puts up the biggest stats? Is the most valuable to his team? Wins the most games? Nobody knows.

As documented earlier, certain voting patterns emerged and certain precedents were established during the earliest years of the trophy's existence, creating what came to be known as the Heisman prototype. There's nothing unseemly about that. What's unacceptable, however, is the fact that despite all the radical changes to the sport over the past sixty years—from the expansion of playbooks to the growing size of the players to the specialization of their skills—the Heisman prototype has remained virtually unchanged. In fact, in some areas the parameters are even more limited today than they were then. "How can anyone continue to pretend that in the age of football specialization the Heisman Trophy represents, even in theory, the outstanding college football player in the country?" *Slate* magazine's Allen Barra wrote in 2003. Don't kid yourself, Allen. Most of us stopped pretending the moment Torretta stepped to the podium.

No one I know has devoted more time and energy to analyzing and dissecting Heisman voters' tendencies than Chris Huston, a former USC sports information assistant who publishes the popular blog HeismanPundit.com. One of the sections of the site, which tracks the Heisman race 365 days a year, is Huston's ten "Heismandments"— hard-and-fast rules for winning the trophy. Rather than going through all ten, I asked him to summarize what he feels are the most important criteria a potential winner must exhibit. "You've got to be a junior or senior, and you've got to be a quarterback, running back, or all-purpose threat," said Huston. "And it really helps to be part of a program that has a lot of cachet. If you play for a Notre Dame or USC or Oklahoma or Nebraska . . . the voters take you more seriously. There are about nine schools that have that built-in advantage. If you're not all those things, it makes it almost impossible. You have to have a superhuman season, like Barry Sanders [who ran for an NCAA-record 2,628 yards in 1988] or Andre Ware did."

Take a moment to process what Huston is saying. There are 120 teams in Division I-A, yet only about 9 are deemed capable of producing the most outstanding player in the country.* It takes, at a minimum, twenty-two different players to win a football game, but only three of them—the quarterback, running back, or receiver/return man—are considered noteworthy enough to merit consideration for the trophy. And while at least 60 percent of most teams' rosters are comprised of freshmen (either true or redshirt) or sophomores, unofficially, the award is only open to the other 40 percent, the juniors and seniors. By my count, that would mean that no more than twenty-seven players in the entire country have a realistic chance at the trophy in any given season. On the surface, that seems preposterous, yet the evidence is overwhelming. No freshman or sophomore has won the award during its entire seventy-two-year history. The only true defensive winner, Woodson, was also a return man, which qualifies him under the "all-purpose" requirement. And of the past twelve Heisman winners, eleven have come from the so-called cachet programs—USC, Oklahoma, Nebraska, Florida, State, Texas, Michigan, Florida and Ohio State. The lone exception was Wisconsin's Dayne, who, like Sanders and Ware, did something truly exceptional, breaking the NCAA career rushing record of 6,279 yards. Lately, the voters have been limiting the pool even further by tying the Heisman into the sport's national-title race. (Not surprisingly, the trend coincides with the dawn of the BCS era.) Since 1996, eight of the eleven winners' teams played in a national-championship game. In other words, the chances of a freshman defensive tackle from a 6–5 Bowling Green team winning the Heisman are about as remote as that of a pimply, flat-chested fifty-five-year-old woman winning Playmate of the Year.

It should be noted that several players have come close to breaking the mold in recent years. Ohio State's Orlando Pace, an overpowering offensive lineman, finished fourth in the voting in 1996. A freshman, Oklahoma's Adrian Peterson (2004), and a sophomore, Pittsburgh's Fitzgerald (2003), both finished as high as second in the balloting, and

---

*Of the five schools that have produced Heisman winners in the 2000s (Florida State, Nebraska, USC, Oklahoma, and Ohio State), four rank among the NCAA's top eight all-time in winning percentage.

another freshman, Virginia Tech's Michael Vick, placed third in 1999. And players from such nontraditional locales as Marshall (Randy Moss in 1997, Chad Pennington in 1999), TCU (LaDanian Tomlinson in 2000), Fresno State (David Carr in 2001) and Utah (Alex Smith in 2004) have all placed in the top five. None, however, have managed to ascend to the ultimate level, and one can't help but wonder what Herculean feats of strength it will take for someone to do so. If, for example, Peterson's 1,925-yard season in 2004 was only good enough for second, what will it take for some future phenom to become the first freshman winner? Score 100 touchdowns? If Arizona State defensive end Terrell Suggs's NCAA-record 24 sacks in 2002 didn't even get him a spot in the top 10, what has to happen for a solely defensive player to actually win the thing? A sack or interception on every other play? "There's still a huge barrier between second and first," said Huston. "The Heisman gods will entertain all kinds of third- and second-place candidates. But first always has to be a certain way."

Which brings us to another pressing question: Who exactly are the Heisman gods? Who are the 923 individuals entrusted with choosing which college football player to immortalize each December? The Heisman voting process is structured so that every living former Heisman winner, of which there were fifty-two in 2005, gets a vote. There is also one fan vote, tabulated through an online poll. The remaining 870 ballots—divided evenly among six geographic regions— are reserved for members of the media. There are six designated "sectional representatives" for each region, who in turn appoints a "state representative" for each state in his region, who in turn maintains the voter list in his/her state. Still with me? Basically, it works much the same way as the Electoral College, where each state is allotted a certain number of votes based on its size (Oregon, for example, has 10; California has 55).

It's no secret that sportswriters and broadcasters are constantly changing jobs and beat assignments—a person covering college football one season could be covering hockey or world politics the next. Therefore, one might figure it a priority of the Downtown Athletic Club to make sure the people facilitating the process are out on the front lines, privy to the latest developments within the industry. Not exactly. While the Heisman's complete voter registry is protected like a state secret, the six sectional representatives are listed right on its official Web site. They are Dave Campbell, retired sports editor of the *Waco (Texas) Tribune-Herald*; Jimmie McDowell, a longtime Mississippi sports columnist who began covering college football in the late 1940s; Bob Hammel, retired sports editor of the *Bloomington (Indiana) Herald Times*; Pat Haden, former star quarterback for USC and the Los Angeles Rams who now broadcasts Notre Dame games for NBC; Beano Cook, the longtime ESPN analyst whom the network still props up in front of the camera when it needs a good sound bite about Joe Paterno; and my personal favorite, Don Criqui, longtime network NFL play-by-play guy and, until recently, weekend co-host of the tabloid news show *Inside Edition*.* No one would dispute that each gentleman has had a long and distinguished career in his chosen profession; how that qualifies them to oversee Heisman voting is beyond me. Most state representatives are fairly diligent about checking and updating their voter rolls every year, but some inevitably slip through the cracks. I hear a few stories every year like that of a Midwest writer who'd switched from covering college football to covering hockey yet unexpectedly received a ballot.

Now, you may be asking yourself, why so many voters? Are there really 870 people who cover college football closely enough to merit a Heisman vote? Are there even 87? Well, let's do the math for a second. Figure that each of the 120 Division I-A teams has an average of four full-time beat writers (some of the big-name programs have far more, and some of the Sun Belt and WAC teams are lucky to have one). That's 480. There are about 25 so-called national writers who, like myself, don't cover one team specifically. Let's put the new total at a cool 500. Who, then, are the other 370? Well, they're either 1) general

---

*Criqui did return to the college football world in 2006, becoming the play-by-play voice for Notre Dame's national radio games. Which means that between him, Haden, and noted Domer Beano Cook, the Heisman is almost literally run by Notre Dame.

columnists, like a Bob Ryan or Jay Mariotti, who spend the majority of their time covering the NFL and Major League Baseball and whose lone appearance in a college press box all season is usually for the national title game (or if Notre Dame's playing a really big game); 2) TV and radio personalities from across the country who, with the exception of a Chris Fowler or John Saunders, are about as impartial as Rush Limbaugh; or 3) long-retired college football writers who manage to hold on to their votes in perpetuity, so long as they keep turning in the ballots. In 2006, Dave Rhame, a college beat writer for the *Syracuse Post-Standard* and AP poll voter, complained in print that he had not been made a Heisman voter despite repeated calls over the years to the Heisman brass but that a retired reporter from his paper continues to receive a ballot. "There are way too many voters, and 800 of 'em are idiots," Dan Jenkins told the *Fort Worth Star Telegram*. "There are too many voters who don't have a passion for the game."*

Even the ones who do have a passion for the game—and I know plenty of them—aren't necessarily in the best position to evaluate the candidates. As mentioned in the "Pulling Rank" chapter, it's difficult for most writers covering a game on Saturdays to see anything but highlights of the others. That makes it awfully difficult to track the various candidates across the country. Of the top two candidates in 2005, I saw Reggie Bush and Vince Young each play five times, either in person (three of Bush's games, two of Young's) or on television. That's about 40 percent of their seasons. And that I was able to see them that much was due largely to the freedom of my beat, which allows me to travel to games like Ohio State–Texas or Notre Dame–USC. I would imagine that the more typical Heisman voter, who spends every Saturday covering the same team, saw both players far less. Think about that for a second. If this were the Oscars, it would be like voting for Best Picture having seen only one or two of the nominated films.

---

*The Web site StiffArmTrophy.com has compiled a list of 470 known Heisman voters. As an active beat writer who tries to read as many articles from around the country as possible every day, most regular college football writers' bylines are familiar to me. I'd never heard of about a third of the people on that list.

Considering these circumstances, it's almost inevitable that many voters' decisions are based on influences besides their own judgment. Much has been made through the years about Heisman hype, the long-time tradition of schools' publicity departments inundating voters with postcards, magnets, and other promotional items in support of their candidates. Some of the more creative gestures, like BYU sending out cardboard ties for Ty Detmer in 1990 or Memphis's DeAngelo Williams mini-stock cars in 2005, can't help but catch your attention. Your garden-variety Joe Hamilton CD-ROMs or Antwaan Randle-El mouse pads, on the other hand, wind up becoming gifts for your co-worker's nephew.

Maybe such efforts were necessary in an earlier era, when highlights and statistics of players from across the country weren't so easily accessible. (In the late 1960s, Notre Dame publicity director Roger Valdiserri took things so seriously as to change the pronounciation of quarterback Joe Theismann's name from "thee-sman" to "th-eisman.")

Today, however, it's hard to believe any reasonable voter could be manipulated into voting for someone based on a bobble-head doll. In fact, most major programs rarely orchestrate formal Heisman campaigns anymore, other than perhaps e-mailing voters in the final weeks of the season to lobby for their candidates. Such public-awareness campaigns are more useful to players from lower-profile programs that might otherwise be left out of the Heisman discussion entirely. The most effective stunt by far in recent years was Oregon's audacious decision to spend $250,000 to plaster a ten-story billboard of quarterback Joey Harrington across from Madison Square Garden in 2001.* While the billboard itself probably did little more than confuse a lot of Japanese tourists, there's no doubt in my mind that the massive coverage it generated around the country directly contributed to Harrington becoming a Heisman finalist that season alongside higher-profile candidates like Crouch, Florida's Rex Grossman, and Miami's Ken Dorsey.

---

*In a hilarious response the next year, Washington State spent $2,500 to plaster a twenty-five-foot poster of quarterback Jason Gesser on a grain elevator in rural Dusty, Washington.

But when it comes to influencing voters, however, no billboard or mouse pad can come close to the power of television. By the end of the season, you can usually make a solid argument for any number of different candidates based on their eye-popping stats, but time and again, the player who hoists the trophy is the one who put up big performances in major, nationally televised games. Such was the case for all three of USC's recent winners, Palmer, Leinart, and Bush, all of whom saved some of their best performances of the season for their final, nationally televised regular-season games (Palmer and Leinart against Notre Dame, Bush against UCLA). Ditto Ohio State's Smith, who threw for nearly 600 combined yards and six touchdowns in huge number-1 versus number-2 games against Texas and Michigan; Crouch, whose infamous touchdown catch came in his biggest game of the year against Oklahoma; Texas's Williams, who broke Tony Dorsett's all-time rushing record with a 60-yard touchdown in the 'Horns' nationally televised day-after-Thanksgiving game against rival Texas A&M; and Michigan's Woodson, whose punt return for touchdown and end zone interception sealed the Wolverines' season-ending showdown with Ohio State.

Woodson's controversial and historic Heisman victory over Tennessee quarterback Manning probably did more than any other to illustrate the power of television in the modern Heisman race. On the same day as Woodson's epic Ohio State performance, Manning passed for a staggering 523 yards in a victory over Kentucky. Woodson's game, however, was broadcast nationally on ABC and viewed in 7.64 million homes, while Manning's was shown on ESPN2 and drew just 212,000 households. Bring up this subject to nearly any Vols fan, however—most of whom are still as bitter about the result today as they were the day it was announced—and you will hear a more sinister explanation.

"ESPN . . . stole the Heisman Trophy from [Manning]," a Vols fan by the name of Wrangler95 posted on CollegeFootballNews.com's fan forum 5 years after the fact. "No one had even heard of Charles Woodson until four or five weeks before the voting was to take place. ESPN saw that Peyton Manning would win the trophy [and] they would talk about Charles Woodson every chance they got." These are not the rantings of some lone, deranged fanatic. To this day, most of the Orange Nation believes that ESPN and its corporate partner, ABC, influenced the voting with its relentless hyping of Woodson at the expense of Manning during the final weeks of the regular season. Over and over and over again, its commentators extolled the cornerback's game-changing abilities and showed endless replays of his interceptions and touchdowns. Some theorize it was because ABC holds the rights to Big Ten games, while the SEC is aired by CBS. Maybe ESPN, which airs the Heisman presentation, was seizing an opportunity to broadcast a historic moment. Others believe it was just another case of good old-fashioned bigotry against the South by the Northern media establishment. In an interview with the *Tennessean* two years later, ESPN commentator Chris Fowler strongly denied any validity to the conspiracy theories. "We were just doing our job and reporting that it was a two-player race when everybody else was giving it to Manning," he said. "We were not trying to stir it up or campaign for anybody. Woodson had solid support around the country, and it had nothing to do with ESPN." Fowler didn't help his standing in the Volunteer state when, after fielding one too many vulgar phone calls and e-mails about the controversy, he went on national radio and described the reaction as "a trailer park frenzy." He later apologized.

Personally, I didn't see any big injustice about Woodson winning the Heisman that year. It was actually a rare instance of the voters abandoning their conventional thinking—Manning, a prototypical golden-boy quarterback, was the preseason favorite and went out and threw for a whole lot of yards, therefore he should automatically win the trophy—and rewarding a player who was the biggest difference-maker in the entire country that season, lifting Michigan to the national title on the strength of his performances in the Wolverines' biggest games (including the ensuing Rose Bowl victory over Washington State). What made it bizarre was that the voters had never exhibited any such tendencies in their logic in any of the previous decades nor the entire decade since. Therefore, it's reasonable to assume that in literally any other year, a quarterback with both a pedigree and a performance (3,819 yards, 36 touchdowns) like Manning's would have won the award.

Clearly, something different entered the equation that year, and the ESPN hype machine may have been it. Whether Fowler and his colleagues want to admit it, ESPN's hugely popular *GameDay* shows, both at the beginning and end of each Saturday, hold tremendous influence in shaping public opinion about college football, and nowhere is that more evident than with the Heisman. This can be as subtle as which highlights the producers and editors elect to show from each candidate, and it can be as overt as a prominent personality's on-air comments in support of a particular player. Two recent and apparent examples of this phenomenon were the second-place finishes of Iowa quarterback Brad Banks in 2002 and Pittsburgh receiver Fitzgerald in 2003. If you go by the traditional Heisman criteria, Banks was almost a total anomaly. He was a first-year starter with absolutely no name recognition coming into the season playing for a nontraditional power, and he put up impressive but hardly amazing statistics (2,573 yards, nearly 1,500 less than that year's winner, Palmer, but with 26 touchdowns and just 5 interceptions). However, week after week as the season progressed, ESPN analyst Trev Alberts,[*] among others, beat the drum for Banks's candidacy. By the time the ballots were tallied, Banks had defied the odds and finished ahead of a 2,000-yard Penn State rusher (Larry Johnson) and a national-champion Miami quarterback (Ken Dorsey). Similarly, the next year, just when it seemed like much of the media was ready to concede its vote to Jason White, Alberts's on-air sidekick and proud Pitt alum Mark May relentlessly pushed Fitzgerald, who statistically was having one of the best receiving seasons in modern history (92 catches, 1,672 yards, 22 touchdowns). Receivers have traditionally fared poorly in the Heisman race, unless they also return kicks. That Fitzgerald managed to finish a close second despite being not only a receiver, but a *sophomore* on an 8–5 team was a testimony to the power of all those touchdown-grabbing highlights and the Mark May gushing that accompanied them.

The ESPN factor, while troubling to some extent, may not be such

---

[*]Though he was an All-American at Nebraska, Alberts is a native of Cedar Falls, Iowa. Just throwing it out there.

a bad thing in the long run. In each of the aforementioned cases, the network shed light on the type of candidate who in the past might have been largely ignored, and, in turn, perhaps helped to expand Heisman voters' traditionally limited perspectives. For years, fans and pundits have been crying for changes to the Heisman voting process—reduce the number of voters, postpone the presentation until after the bowl games, lay out more specific criteria—that would significantly alter certain aspects of the Heisman lore at a time when its keepers are already fighting tooth and nail to preserve its tradition. (Sadly, the Downtown Athletic Club went bankrupt in 1998 and its lower Manhattan building was irreparably damaged in the September 11 attacks. Since then the ceremony has been held at several different locations, most recently the newfangled Nokia Theatre Times Square.) Heisman organizers have in fact taken several progressive steps in recent years, like initiating online voting and actively weeding out ambivalent voters, resulting in higher response rates—96.6 percent of the registered electors voted in 2005, up from an embarrassing 63.3 percent 4 years earlier.

If anything, the responsibility of ensuring the Heisman's continued significance and legitimacy in the twenty-first century—and avoiding increasingly common sentiments like that of *Houston Chronicle* columnist Fran Blinebury, who observed that the Heisman race has become "silly and irrelevant in recent years"—rests solely on the shoulders of we, the voters. Only we have the power to decide once and for all to shuck the commonly held, outdated criteria and truly seek out the "nation's most outstanding player." In my first year as an elector in 2004, I was proud to cast my first-ever first-place vote for a freshman, Peterson, and was encouraged to see that 153 of my colleagues did the same. In 2006, my third-place vote went to Boise State running back Ian Johnson, a player from the relatively obscure Western Athletic Conference who was arguably the best running back in the country that season. (Alas, he finished eighth.) But this isn't just about throwing out the underclass and small-school biases. The Heisman should be open to all players, regardless of position, TV appearances, preseason standing, or other factors. Had such modernized criteria been invoked over the past few years, I believe you would have seen several different names enshrined in the Heisman fraternity, among them:

- Michael Vick, Virginia Tech quarterback (1999): The prevailing feeling at the time was that in a relatively weak field of contenders, Dayne's Heisman was something of a career appreciation award, seeing as he broke the same all-time rushing record as the previous year's winner, Williams. The most spectacular player in the country that season, however, was unquestionably Vick, the lightning-fast quarterback who led a previously middling Hokies team to the national title game, where he proceeded to put on one of the most spectacular individual performances in bowl history. Vick was automatically discounted by most, however, because he was a freshman with zero name recognition coming into the season, and it was considered an accomplishment at the time that he even finished third. He doesn't seem to have that name-recognition problem anymore.*

- Roy Williams, Oklahoma safety (2001): Williams, who finished seventh in the voting that season, was the most dominant defensive player college football had seen in years. Equally adept as a pass rusher and in coverage, he made 101 tackles, had 11 tackles for loss, intercepted 5 passes, broke up 22 others, and made 3 fumble recoveries. And in what was unquestionably the play of the season, with the Sooners clinging to a 7–3 lead over archrival Texas late in the game, Williams hurdled over a Longhorn blocker to hit quarterback Chris Simms just as he was releasing the ball, which linebacker Teddy Lehman then intercepted and returned for a game-sealing touchdown. Do you think maybe, just maybe, Williams, who has gone on to play in four Pro Bowls for the Dallas Cowboys, would have been just a little more distinguished of a Heisman representative than Crouch?

- Ben Roethlisberger, Miami of Ohio quarterback (2003): Compared with that year's winner, White, Roethlisberger, a junior,

---

*He does have some other, well-documented problems.

threw for more yards (4,486), had a higher completion percentage (69.1 percent), had the same number of interceptions (10) and threw only three less touchdowns (37). He never had a chance, however, because he played for a Mid-American Conference team that, despite going 13–1, rarely made an appearance on television. Two years later, Roethlisberger became the youngest player in history to lead his team, the Pittsburgh Steelers, to a Super Bowl victory; White presumably watched the game on TV with the rest of us.

Obviously, it's a lot easier to reach such conclusions with the benefit of hindsight. When the actual voting takes place, at the apex of a three-month-long debate, amidst a season not yet even completed, it's easy to get lost in the noise and swayed by the highlights. I'll admit to being guilty of that myself, making a decision based not so much on my own judgment but instead on the several thousands of voices that inevitably permeate my brain on the subject throughout the course of the season, reminding me over and over and over again that "Reggie Bush is the most dangerous player in the country" or "Troy Smith is simply a flawless quarterback," to the point where such messages seem less like bravado than fact.

Needless to say, it's not an easy job, this Heisman voting thing. There's an awful lot of pressure associated with that single vote. Seriously. How would you like to go to sleep every night for the rest of your life knowing you were partially responsible for tarnishing the Heisman legacy by picking the wrong guy? Heck, I'd go so far as to say it's an even more important decision than voting for president. At least if you screw that up, you can correct your mistake four years later. Gino Torretta, on the other hand, will stay with us 'til the end of time.

4

FireMyCoach.com

We won't let this program gravitate to mediocrity.

*—Nebraska AD Steve Pederson, in announcing head coach
Frank Solich's dismissal following a 9–3 season, 2003*

―――――――

We Got Him!

*—Headline on FireGlenMason.com following the
Minnesota coach's firing, December 31, 2006*

Midway through the 2006 season, I received a press release from the UCLA blog Bruins Nation that read like something you'd expect to see about a president or other elected official: "AN ASTOUNDING 8 out of 10 UCLA football fans disapprove of the way UCLA head football coach Karl Dorrell is doing his job, according to an online opinion poll released this week." Said one of the 250 fans who was surveyed, "I can deal with a loss here and there, but when you don't even try to win the game then it's just spitting in the face of loyal fans. I simply cannot believe that any fan who has actually watched the football team play a game in the last-year-and-a-half could still want Dorrell as the head coach." During that year and a half, the Bruins had compiled a 14–4 record, finishing the 2005 season 10–2, and ranked sixteenth in the country following a 50–38 Sun Bowl victory over Northwestern. What was Dorrell's Bruin Nation "approval rating" at the end of that season? "An all-time high of 50 percent."

College football coaches are held to a higher performance standard, and operate with less job security, than virtually any other profession in our society. They aren't paid millions of dollars annually to merely win more often than they lose, lead teams to bowl games, graduate players, and run a clean program; no, there must be regular national and conference championships, annual top-five recruiting classes, and lopsided victories over hated rivals. It's the equivalent of expecting a teacher to not only educate her students, but help them all to achieve perfect SAT scores—and to fire her if too many of them don't. Think of it another way: the president of the United States can lead the country into an ill-fated military campaign or have an affair with an intern and keep his job until the end of his term; a college football coach can lose to Auburn on Saturday and be out of a job by Monday.

What else would you expect in a profession where the constituents one serves are not investors, shareholders, voters, or any other form of rational human being, but rather, college football fans? True, a team's fans don't technically hold any control over a coach's job status; in most cases, he reports to a university's athletic director and president. In actuality, however, fans hold the ultimate power over such decisions due to the most coveted of assets: their checkbooks. Without the substantial revenue generated by booster donations, seat licenses, season-ticket renewals, and merchandise purchases, the athletic director has no budget to support all of the other sports that Title IX requires— leaving a whole bunch of softball players without uniforms and gymnasts without balance beams. And the president, for reasons that could never be rationally explained to a foreign scholar, will have a much easier time raising money for that new library if the football team is winning. Therefore, it is in the best interests of both parties to keep the fans happy with their football program—and that, as you'll soon see, is no easy task.

Based on years of highly scientific research (reading my e-mails) and sound, quantitative methods (counting the number of teams that play football), I've developed a theory: At any given time only about 25 percent of college football fans are completely happy with their team's current coach. Sounds inordinately low, right? Surely in a sport that brings so much enjoyment to so many people, 75 percent of them aren't walking around in a disgruntled funk, bitching about the coach's play-calling? You'd be surprised. The fact is, all fans desire the same thing— championships. But in any given year, only one team in the country (sometimes two) can claim a national title, and only one team in each of the eleven Division I-A conferences can claim league superiority. I'm not saying all the fans of the other hundred-plus teams are ticked off— just most of them.

Heading into the 2007 season, for example, one could say with reasonable certainty that fans of the following major-conference teams were content and confident with the leadership of their program, either because its coach has delivered a recent championship or has significantly raised the school's profile: Florida (Urban Meyer), Ohio State (Jim Tressel), Texas (Mack Brown), USC (Pete Carroll),

Oklahoma (Bob Stoops), Notre Dame (Charlie Weis), Auburn (Tommy Tuberville), Georgia (Mark Richt), West Virginia (Rich Rodriguez), Rutgers (Greg Schiano), Virginia Tech (Frank Beamer), Wake Forest (Jim Grobe), Cal (Jeff Tedford), Wisconsin (Bret Bielema), and South Carolina (Steve Spurrier). There are sixty-six teams in the six BCS conferences if you include Notre Dame; the above list comprises 15 of them, or 23 percent.* And keep in mind, Brown and Tuberville would have not have made the list just a couple of years earlier, back when significant contingents of their fan bases were ready to run them out of town. "Mack Brown . . . just needs to be put out to pasture,'" a twenty-eight-year-old Texas alum named Peter told the *Denver Post* in 2003, just a year before Brown's team began a run of twenty straight wins and a national championship.

To get a sense of just how fickle the college coaching world can be, one need only look at some of the names who were *not* on that list: the nation's two all-time-winningest coaches (Florida State's Bobby Bowden and Penn State's Joe Paterno) and two others who have won national titles (Michigan's Lloyd Carr and Tennessee's Phillip Fulmer). Meanwhile, the coach who entered 2006 with the highest winning percentage, Miami's Larry Coker, wound up getting fired following a 6–6 regular season. Coker, who just 4 years earlier had won twenty-four straight games and played for consecutive national championships, finished his six-year tenure with a record of 60–15 (.800).† Not that Hurricanes fans didn't see the move coming: Earlier in the season, several of them had paid to fly a banner over the Orange Bowl before a game that read FIRE COKER NOW.

It seems poison tongues and pink slips have been a part of the coaching profession practically since its inception. More than a hundred years before the first "Mack Brown can't beat Oklahoma" column,

---

*Louisville's Bobby Petrino was on this list before bolting for the Atlanta Falcons, as was Iowa's Kirk Ferentz before going 6–7 in 2006.
†The figure is a bit deceiving, seeing as Miami's record got worse each year under Coker, from 12–0 in 2001 to 12–1 in 2002 to 11–2 to 9–3, 9–3, and, finally, 7–6.

Texas's first-ever coach, R. D. Wentworth, who began the 1894 season with a 6–0 record, saw his popularity take a sharp downward turn after getting crushed by Missouri 28–0 in the season finale. According to Texas's media guide, "Wentworth's judgment in the final game was questioned by Texas fans," who, without the luxury of talk radio or chat rooms, presumably used carrier pigeons to send word of their displeasure. Wentworth did not return for a second season, eventually moving to New York and entering the marine insurance industry. Fate would not be much kinder to a couple of his successors, either—Bill Juneau (1917–19) was fired after just three seasons despite a decent 19–7 record, as was E. J. Stewart (1923–26), who went 24–9–3. Future generations of fans would find new and innovative ways to voice their criticism, like posting a FOR SALE sign in the coach's front yard after a particularly embarrassing loss. In 1988, then-Alabama coach Bill Curry was the recipient of a brick tossed through his office window following a Homecoming loss to Ole Miss. Just imagine if it had been Vanderbilt.

Without question, however, the voice of the fan has never been more influential in the firing and hiring of coaches than it is in the twenty-first century—and for that, the embattled subjects can thank Al Gore. The Internet, the same technological advancement that allows us to bid on secondhand junk, steal term papers, and download lesbian porn, has provided an unprecedented window into the prevailing mood of a certain team's fans.

On a random April afternoon in 2006, three months removed from the disappointment of a 7–5 season and Alamo Bowl loss to Nebraska and nearly five months away from the start of a new season, visitors to the "Stadium and Main" message board on Michigan's Scout.com fan site were engaged in a heated discussion about twelfth-year coach Lloyd Carr's competency. A user going by the name of PietaSterx wrote:

> Lloyd Carr is not a good football coach. You can say all you want, quote all the numbers that you want, but all you have to do is watch him coach a game and it's apparent. Conservative, Predictable, Unaggressive, and zero killer instinct.

Any coach will win Big 10s and go to Rose Bowls at Michigan. Lloyd hasn't sniffed a NC [national championship] for 10 years. We should at least be on the radar every 3 years for a NC. Lloyd is not a good game-time coach, in fact he's poor.

Posts like these can be found on similar message boards—there's one for nearly every team on both Scout.com and Rivals.com—twenty-four hours a day, nearly every day of the year, wherever a significant segment of the fan base is disgruntled and, we can only presume, bored. While these forums remain the most popular online outlet for fan frustration, another form of cybercritic has joined the realm in recent years: bloggers. Anyone with an Internet connection and an excessive amount of free time can become a pundit these days, and, unlike a mainstream sports columnist, these writers aren't bound by the conventional rules regarding partisanship (on the contrary, it's almost a requirement), slander, or the use of obscenities. Staying with the Carr example, the maize-and-blue-bleeding author of a popular blog entitled "Straight Bangin'" posted this diatribe less than an hour after the Wolverines' 2005 loss to Minnesota:

Lloyd Carr is ruining this program. Period.

Michigan . . . is led by a gutless relic whose game plans are always inspired by fear, complacency, and stubbornness. Listen, Lloyd: YOU DO NOT WIN GAMES BY KICKING FIELD GOALS, SO STOP PLAYING LIKE YOU CAN. AND STOP BLOWING DOUBLE-DIGIT LEADS!!!!!!!!!!!!!!!!

Would you have ever guessed from the above comments that Carr has won 76 percent of his games and led the Wolverines to four Rose Bowls and a national title?

For all the various coaching critiques that have plastered the Internet in recent years, however, one stands squarely above the rest in the effect it had on both the coach in question and the profession as a whole. In January 2002, Steve Spurrier, the uniquely cocky and innovative coach who turned traditionally mediocre Florida into one of the preeminent powers of the 1990s, stunned Gator Nation when he resigned to become the head coach of the Washington Redskins. In the frantic days following Spurrier's announcement, Florida athletic director Jeremy Foley attempted unsuccessfully to woo two of the sport's most prominent figures, Oklahoma coach Bob Stoops (formerly Spurrier's defensive coordinator) and two-time Super Bowl champion Mike Shanahan of the Denver Broncos, as replacements. When both turned him down, Foley turned to a far more surprising choice: New Orleans Saints assistant Ron Zook, known by the seven people who had heard of him as an intense workaholic and masterful recruiter. While the arrival of a new coach is normally a time of eager anticipation and excitement, Zook's hiring sharply divided the Gator faithful, many of whom considered the career assistant—whom Spurrier had once demoted—unfit for the job. One such cynic, a 1996 Florida grad by the name of Mike Walsh, decided to publish his skepticism online. Just a day after Zook's hiring, Walsh (who didn't reveal his identity until years later), a New York–based salesman, launched a Web site that would change college football forever: FireRonZook.com.

Throughout the three tumultuous seasons that followed, as the Zooker led the Gators to their worst records (8–5 in 2002 and 2003, 7–4 in 2004) since the late 1980s, Walsh's Web site became synonymous with the downtrodden state of Florida football. Visitors to the site were treated to weekly rants from its then-anonymous publishers, a countdown to the expiration date of Zook's contract, a message board for fellow anti-Zook ranters, and an online store that sold Fire RonZook.com T-shirts, coffee mugs and—not making this up—thongs. Its ubiquitous name garnered more than five hundred mentions in the nation's newspapers and magazines, as well as frequent acknowledgment on ESPN's airwaves. More notably, it spawned an army of copycats from similarly disgruntled fans across the country, among them, FireMackBrown.com, FireLouHoltz.com, and JoePaMustgo .com. In a preemptive strike, Ohio State fan Chris Stassen, a software engineer in Newark, Ohio, purchased the domain name FireJim Tressel.com for the mere purpose of shielding the Buckeyes coach from such a creation. Stassen's simple HTML page contained a headline that read: "Fire Jim Tressel? Are you NUTS?" Below it was one line of text: "This domain is parked to keep it out of the hands of folks who shouldn't be trusted with kitchen utensils, let alone web sites." This automatically qualified Stassen as the most rational college football fan in the country.

When the ax finally fell on the embattled Zook following a humiliating loss to SEC bottom-feeder Mississippi State in the seventh game of the 2004 season, there was no denying the role Zook's namesake Web site had played in influencing popular opinion and, in turn, Foley's decision to cut his losses. "I always thought it was unfair to Ron," acknowledged the athletic director. "As the noise built, it became divisive. It became apparent it wasn't going to work." In an interview with *The State* newspaper in Columbia, South Carolina, a few weeks after Zook's firing, Walsh reflected on the impact of his creation. "[FireRonZook.com] became more than we ever expected," said the publisher. "Fans saw you can have a voice without [spending] thousands of dollars. . . . I didn't get Zook fired, he did it to himself. But I think we applied pressure." Responding to the obvious criticism that a Web site devoted entirely to attacking an individual's job credentials and demanding he be sent to the unemployment line might seem a tad, oh, I don't know, mean?, Walsh replied, "With the money coaches make, if you paid me Zook's salary, you could criticize [me] all you wanted."

Money has a great deal to do with the backlash aimed at many coaches. Over the past decade, their salaries have skyrocketed astronomically. As recently as 1999, there were only five coaches making more than $1 million annually. As of November 2006, that number had risen to at least forty-two, according to *USA Today*.* USC's Pete Carroll, Notre Dame's Charlie Weis, and Oklahoma's Bob Stoops each made at least $3 million per season, with ten others (Spurrier, now at South Carolina; Texas's Brown; Tennessee's Fulmer, Auburn's Tuberville;

USA Today could not obtain official contract information for 12 Division I-A coaches, so it's likely this number was even higher. The average compensation package among the 107 *USA Today* did obtain was $950,000.

Florida's Meyer; Virginia Tech's Beamer; Georgia's Richt; Ohio State's Tressel; Iowa's Ferentz; and Louisville's Bobby Petrino) in the $2 million club. In January 2007, Alabama raised the bar even higher, making former LSU and Miami Dolphins coach Nick Saban the first $4 million man. "As one school pays more, it starts a domino effect that impacts everybody," Texas athletic director DeLoss Dodds told the *Fort Worth Star Telegram*. At the current rate, coaches' salaries will exceed the Gross National Product by 2013.

The spiraling salaries have caused no shortage of outrage in the academic community, where most professors make only a fraction of that amount and are routinely dealing with budget cuts and overcrowded classrooms.* But for the men and women charged with balancing the athletic budget, there's no understating the value of having the right guy in charge of the football program—like a Stoops (who took over a long-dormant Oklahoma program and won a national title in just his second season) or Carroll (who won national titles in his third and fourth seasons and played for another in his fifth)—considering that football revenues at a powerhouse program can exceed $40 million. "The value is obvious," Oklahoma athletic director Joe Castiglione told the *New York Times*. "From a business standpoint, we can justify every penny that we pay Bob and his staff."

As a result, schools often bend over backwards to keep their coach happy, offering raises and contract extensions on a near-annual basis. After all, you never know when a bunch of deep-pocketed boosters from another campus or a filthy-rich NFL owner will come after your guy. Such was the case with Saban just 2 years before he became Alabama's coach. After leading LSU to the 2003 national championship, the school's first since 1958, Saban, a notoriously frenetic multitasker who has the amazing ability to devise masterful game plans and assemble top-ranked recruiting classes all the while negotiating with his next employer, was able to cash in on a fortuitous clause that had been added to his contract just a year earlier, one that required LSU

---

*Saban's salary is nearly seven times that of his university's president, Robert E. Witt.

to automatically make him the highest-paid coach in the country if he won a national title. The school happily complied, offering a new seven-year deal that immediately bumped his salary from $1.6 million to $2.3 million with an escalation to $3.4 million by 2010. Even those seemingly staggering sums, however, couldn't stand up to the reported five-year, $22.5 million deal the Miami Dolphins dangled in front of him less than a year later.* Meanwhile, in the summer of 2006, Louisville AD Tom Jurich offered his coach at the time, Petrino, a ten-year, $25 million contract extension—a staggering amount for a program that only two years earlier had been competing in the lower-level Conference USA. In doing so, it was hoped that Petrino, who had turned the Cardinals into a national power almost overnight, would stop entertaining offers from other suitors, something he had done literally every season since his 2003 arrival.† "For me and my family, Louisville is my home," Petrino said after signing the extension. "I also wanted to make sure that everyone understood—and I know I've said it—that this is where my family wants to be and where I want to be." Six months later, after leading the Cardinals to their first-ever Orange Bowl, Atlanta was where he wanted to be after the NFL's Falcons offered him a five-year, $24 million deal.

Speaking at a Ball State University summit in December 2004, NCAA president Myles Brand expressed his dismay with the spiraling trend. "It's a very dangerous path, all for the wrong reasons," said Brand. "Winning does not produce more revenues, it really doesn't. The data doesn't support that. Don't get me wrong. I don't think you should engage in the games unless you want to win. But you could be so overwhelmed by that, that you could make bad decisions."

---

*Saban coached the Dolphins to a two-year record of 15–17, angrily insisted to reporters that, "I'm not going to be the Alabama coach"—then became the Alabama coach two weeks later. It's believed he's attempting to become the first football coach to work in all fifty states before he retires.

†In 2003, Petrino secretly interviewed with Auburn. In 2004, he interviewed with Notre Dame and was a finalist at LSU, and in 2005 he turned down a lucrative offer from the Oakland Raiders.

By bad decisions, Brand wasn't referring to those of Oklahoma or USC,* but rather the other 90 percent or so of schools whose coaches aren't likely to have such wild and dramatic success as Stoops or Carroll. Because the marketplace demands it, these teams' coaches are likely to be blessed with fairly cushy salaries themselves, but that's not necessarily a good thing. The more a school invests in its coach, the more it expects in return, making it tougher to justify retaining a coach who isn't meeting anything but the loftiest of expectations. In most cases, the school's investment isn't limited to payroll, either. As the amount of money at stake has grown over the past decade, through both the BCS and increased television and marketing opportunities, an arms race has broken out among schools to see which can provide the most extensive training facilities, design the most garish offices, and build the most elaborate stadium renovations. Many major-conference schools have pumped tens of millions of dollars into their football programs in recent years, making it all the more imperative to have the right leadership in place, lest those locker-room plasma screens get wasted on a 7–4 team.

It's no coincidence that coaches these days seem to be working on shorter and shorter leashes. Once upon a time, there was an unwritten rule that, barring extenuating circumstances (committing major NCAA infractions, getting caught with a hooker), a coach would be given at least four or five years—the amount of time it takes to stock the roster entirely with "his" recruits—to be properly evaluated. As was seen with Zook, however, the twenty-first-century window for many coaches has been reduced to three seasons or less. The rapid success of coaches like Stoops, Carroll, Tressel, and Meyer, all of whom won national titles in just their second or third years at their schools, have upped the already demanding standard by which fans and athletic directors across the country now judge their coaches. "The reason coaches are getting fired is because they've changed the market," said Brand. "Just like the pro coaches, college coaches are so subject to winning and losing that they

---

*Nor, presumably, the hundreds made every year by his own organization.

can lose their job in three years before the contract is over—just like professional coaches."

While Brand is on the money (pun intended) in pinpointing the economic factors behind the sport's increasing coaching churn, one would be unwise to overlook two important human elements that often play a role in such decisions: pride and ego. At its core, college football is all about bragging rights. For Michigan fans, few things in life are more important than maintaining superiority over Ohio State. For a Miami fan, watching the Hurricanes lose to a Clemson or North Carolina is no less insulting than someone making fun of his mother. There's no point trying to temper such lofty expectations with something as unsatisfying as reason, because that would be asking an intrinsically emotion-driven being, the fan, to think with his head, not his heart. You'd have a better chance convincing him that *Star Wars* was a documentary.

There is one group of people who are, theoretically, paid to conduct rational assessments of coaches: athletic directors. But even though these walking suits aren't calling the plays or lacing up the chin strips, they often engage in their own form of competition. In the old days, many athletic directors were themselves former football coaches (only a handful remain, like Arkansas' Frank Broyles and Alabama's Mal Moore) who stayed at the school forever and tended to take care of their own. These days, however, most ADs are savvy, upwardly mobile professionals who, as in any field, are striving for achievement and recognition among their peers. What better way to brand one self a visionary than being the man or woman who hires the next Tressel or Carroll?

With those factors in mind, let's take a look at four recent coaching changes that best illustrate the largely unmerciful climate in which college coaches are now evaluated.

Nebraska, 2003

For more than forty years, the Nebraska Cornhuskers were synonymous with dominance. Generation after generation of hard-working, farm-bred teenagers from across the state headed off to Lincoln each fall to play for legendary coaches Bob Devaney (1962–1972) and Tom Osborne (1973–1997), whose old-fashioned brand of power running and option offense helped the Cornhuskers annually steamroll their overmatched Big 8 opponents and regularly compete for national titles. For a long time, oddsmakers automatically labeled them at least a 17-point favorite just for donning those intimidating "N" helmets. The very end of Osborne's tenure happened to coincide with their most spectacular run to date—three undefeated, national-championship seasons (1994, 1995, and 1997) in the span of four years.

Upon retiring in 1997, Osborne ran for Congress in Nebraska, where he became the first candidate in political history to receive more than 100 percent of the votes. And just as Devaney had once passed the Huskers' coaching torch to his trusted offensive coordinator Osborne, the Hall of Famer handed over the reins to *his* longtime coordinator, Frank Solich, a mild-mannered, lifelong Nebraskan with squinty eyes and the personality of a librarian. At the start of Solich's tenure, Nebraska looked very much like it always had, going 12–1 in 1999 and 10–2 in 2000, and winning their first eleven games en route to the national championship game in 2001. However, after closing that season with a pair of uncharacteristic blowout losses to Colorado (62–36) and Miami (37–14), then posting an abysmal 7–7 record in 2002, whispers began to arise about Solich's job security. Columnists began raising the question of whether Nebraska's old-fashioned offense could still match up with the game's more modern, complex defenses—just as they had in 1992, 1987, 1982 . . .

The Huskers appeared to be back on the right track in 2003 when they finished the regular season with a 9–3 record. But by then the school had hired a new athletic director, Steve Pederson, a forty-five-year-old Nebraska alum who had earned acclaim for overseeing the resurrection of Pittsburgh's long-struggling football and basketball programs. An oft-described egomaniac with ambitions of modernizing his alma mater much the same way he had Pitt, Pederson pulled the plug on Solich—despite his holding one of the highest active winning percentages (.753) in the country—following that year's regular-season finale, citing the lopsided nature of two of that season's three losses. "I was concerned after the Texas game, and in the Kansas State game, when I saw a seeming disparity. I certainly think that we are not recruiting the way we were a number of years ago," said Pederson. ". . . I refuse to let the program gravitate into mediocrity. We won't surrender the Big 12 to Oklahoma and Texas."

A year later, Nebraska surrendered the conference to not only the Sooners and Longhorns but to Texas Tech, Texas A&M, Oklahoma State, Iowa State, and Colorado, posting their first losing season in forty-three years. The state's famously loyal, football-crazed faithful, already peeved at Pederson for his callous treatment of the home-grown Solich, were now being asked to embrace a complete outsider, deposed Oakland Raiders coach Bill Callahan, who had the audacity not only to change nearly every aspect of Nebraska's football culture—installing a pro-style West Coast offense, shifting the program's recruiting emphasis from its own state to the rest of the country, and de-emphasizing its longtime tradition of embracing walk-ons—but to let the school's NCAA-record streak of bowl appearances end on his watch. He couldn't have made himself any less popular if he'd walked out to the 50-yard line of Memorial Stadium and dropped trou on the Nebraska logo. In 2006, his third season, Callahan led the Huskers to their first division title in seven years, but his team still lost five games,* a far cry from the Nebraska of old.

In fairness, Callahan walked into something of a no-win situation, one not unlike that of Zook's at Florida. This one, however, wasn't born out of a legendary coach's departure, but rather the ego of an overzealous athletic director.

Notre Dame, 2004

In 2002, his first season in the most pressure-filled job in sports, Tyrone Willingham, the first African American head coach in school

---

*Following Nebraska's 21–7 loss to Oklahoma in the Big 12 title game, Callahan apologized to Huskers fans for his coaching performance in the game—a great way to inspire confidence from the faithful.

history, took the college football world by storm when the Irish jumped out to an 8–0 start and top 5 ranking. Notre Dame, which had posted losing records in two of the previous three seasons, wound up winning ten games for the first time in nearly a decade while upsetting the likes of Michigan and Florida State. A book entitled *Return to Glory* chronicled the historic season. The Notre Dame–Willingham marriage, however, would last about as long as one of Pamela Anderson's.

Even during that seemingly triumphant first season, the Irish often appeared to be more lucky than good, winning in spite of their own offensive ineptitude. Their flaws would finally be exposed in the final two games, a 44–13 whitewashing by USC and a 28–6 Gator Bowl loss to N.C. State. Heading into the 2003 season, Willingham's stoic, almost robotic persona was already starting to grate many in typically rah-rah South Bend, where pep rallies are as much a part of campus life as priests and pizza. When a core group of key seniors from the 2002 team graduated, Willingham was forced to throw several members of his first full recruiting class into the fire as freshmen. Their inexperience was evident as the 2003 team limped to a 5–7 record, including painfully lopsided losses to Michigan (38–0), USC (45–14), Florida State (37–0), and Syracuse (38–12).

Though he'd been on the job for just two seasons at that point, barely enough time to make significant recruiting inroads, numerous Notre Dame loyalists decided they'd already seen enough. In January, the university's board of trustees received an angry letter signed by 412 alumni from across the country denouncing "the pronounced and persistent deterioration of the Notre Dame football program." While insisting the letter was "not a call to fire Tyrone Willingham," the authors quickly added, "Although we continue to support [Willingham] and hope he succeeds, his performance, marked by unprecedented and humiliating defeats, deficiencies within his coaching staff, and his inconsistent record as a head coach, indicates that he may not. Absent significant progress in 2004, a coaching change will become necessary." No pressure there.

Following an up-and-down third season in which the Irish beat top 10 foes Michigan and Tennessee but also lost to BYU and Boston

College, the 6–5 Irish received an invite to play in the 2004 Insight Bowl. However, just two days after a third consecutive lopsided loss to USC to end the regular season, the school's trustees held an emergency meeting and decided to grant the letter-writing alumni—and disgruntled Notre Dame fans everywhere—their wish. With a 21–15 record, Willingham was relieved of the final two years of his contract, completing the shortest tenure of any Irish coach since 1933. In disclosing the rationale behind the decision—one in which he had little input—athletic director Kevin White offered up a stomach-turning explanation that could easily apply to nearly every other coaching change in the country. "From Sunday through Friday, our football program exceeded expectations in every way," said White, referring either to the players' academic progress or some *really* impressive practices. "But on Saturday, we've struggled."

Notre Dame being Notre Dame, Willingham's firing provoked impassioned reactions from fans and writers across the country, most of them blasting the school for abandoning its supposedly noble ideals. Even the school's own outgoing president, Reverend Edward Malloy, was aghast. Speaking at a sports business summit the week after Willingham's firing, Malloy, whose successor, John I. Jenkins, had called the emergency board meeting, said, "In my eighteen years, there have only been two days that I've been embarrassed to be president of Notre Dame: Tuesday and Wednesday of last week."

So if neither the president nor the athletic director were behind the move, who, exactly, precipitated Willingham's firing? In this case, chalk it up to the alums. Notre Dame, with its nationwide constituency, has no shortage of impassioned and influential alumni. The alums made their feelings about Willingham well known, and clearly the trustees moved to appease them. So far, things seem to be working out about as well as the alumni could have hoped. New coach Charlie Weis managed to bring more excitement and optimism to South Bend in his first season alone than ever existed under Willingham or predecessor Bob Davie, nearly upsetting top-ranked USC at home and reaching the Fiesta Bowl. He followed that up with a Sugar Bowl bid in his second season. So the cruel lesson to be taken from the Willingham experiment may be this: crucifying a coach before he's even gotten a fair chance to prove himself can in fact pay off.

Ole Miss, 2004

When you think of Ole Miss football, one thing immediately jumps to mind: The Grove. If tailgating were a sport, Ole Miss would be number 1 in the standings every year. Hordes of Southern belles in sundresses and frat boys in khakis and ties descend on a gorgeous, tree-lined patch of campus to gorge on all varieties of home-cooked delicacies* under an endless sea of red-and-blue tents. It's a scene so beatific it makes you temporarily forget that many of these people's ancestors owned slaves.

When it comes to the actual football, however, Ole Miss is largely a historical afterthought. Try as they might, the Rebels just can't seem to crack the upper echelon of the ever-competitive Southeastern Conference, having gone without a league championship since 1963. For much of the 1970s, 1980s, and 1990s, the Rebels continually seesawed between two levels: decent and mediocre. Upon taking over the Ole Miss reins in 1998, former Tennessee offensive coordinator David Cutcliffe brought a level of consistency to the program rarely seen in the modern era. No, the Rebels didn't suddenly morph into Auburn or Tennessee, but they did post winning records in each of Cutcliffe's first five seasons, culminating in a particularly successful 2003 campaign in which the Rebels, led by future number 1 draft pick Eli Manning, posted their first ten-win season since 1971 and played in a New Year's Day bowl, the Cotton Bowl, for the first time in thirteen years.

Less than a year later, Cutcliffe was out of a job. Following the graduation of Manning and eleven other senior starters, Ole Miss stumbled to a 4–7 finish in 2004, including a particularly embarrassing loss at Wyoming. Cutcliffe, who was never fully embraced by the locals even when the Rebels were winning, became popular fodder for Internet

---

*There may be some adult beverages involved as well.

posters, including those behind the requisite FireDavidCutcliffe.com. Surely athletic director Pete Boone, paid to be more cognizant of the big picture, would tune them out, right? Wrong. After the last game had been played that season, Boone spent two full days meeting with Cutcliffe, at one point calling in university president Robert Khayat. According to reports, Boone, a former bank president, demanded the coach fire several of his assistants; Cutcliffe refused, and in turn it was he who got the pink slip, despite posting a higher winning percentage (.603) during his tenure than any Ole Miss coach since 1973. "He preferred the status quo, keeping things how they are," said Boone. "I didn't hear a plan to make [things] better."

While news of Ole Miss firing its football coach doesn't exactly receive the same kind of ink as Notre Dame, it did create a minor uproar among Cutcliffe's colleagues, including his former boss, Tennessee coach Phillip Fulmer. Speaking at that year's Cotton Bowl, Fulmer said, "Having a good friend at Ole Miss go through what he went through after one of the best eras at Ole Miss in recent history and getting fired, I think we're headed in the wrong direction." The authors of FireDavidCutcliffe.com, however, had a slightly different reaction: "We're glad this journey has come to an end! Now we can get on to hiring someone with a little more fire in his gut . . . someone with a little more desire to win . . . someone who knows how to recruit . . . someone who isn't scared to go for it on fourth and 2!"

Based on that description, Ole Miss fans got exactly what they wanted. New coach Ed Orgeron is a fiery Cajun who served as recruiting coordinator at USC when the Trojans assembled a series of star-studded classes that formed the core of their 2003 and 2004 national title teams. During his short time in Oxford, Orgeron has already raised the Rebels' recruiting profile significantly. He also, however, lost two assistants to alcohol-related arrests before even coaching his first game (Orgeron himself had been fired from Miami in 1995 under similar circumstances), ran off his offensive coordinator following a 3–8 debut season, and was accused of trying to poach players from Tulane's Hurricane Katrina–stricken program. For his part, Cutcliffe returned to

Tennessee in 2006, where he immediately resuscitated the Vols' struggling offense and helped them improve from 5–6 to 9–4.

Maybe Orgeron, who improved slightly to 4–8 his second season, will go on to become the guy who leads Ole Miss to the fabled land of BCS bowl bids and national titles. Based on the program's history, however, I'd have to say it's highly unlikely. In an SI.com Mailbag in 2003, I coined the term "Auburn/Clemson Syndrome" to describe the phenomenon by which fans of historically second-tier programs delude themselves into thinking that one isolated period of greatness—like Clemson's 1981 national title season—is more representative of their team's rightful place in the sport's hierarchy than its other one hundred or so years of football. These fans are chronically unhappy with whoever the current coach is because invariably he's not living up to their idealized standard. Since that time, however, Auburn has posted an undefeated season, and its loyalists now revere Tuberville, the same coach whom the school president once tried to secretly replace. Therefore, in light of what happened to Cutcliffe, I hereby rename the phenomena "Ole Miss/Clemson Syndrome."

Minnesota, 2006

In the nineteen seasons prior to Glen Mason's hiring at Minnesota in 1997, the Gophers compiled an embarrassing 80–117–3 (.400) record spanning four different coaches. Their last appearance in a bowl game had come eleven years earlier. None of this was particularly surprising, considering that it's not exactly easy to entice elite recruits to come to one of the coldest cities in America to play in a faceless domed stadium and routinely get their butts kicked by Ohio State and Michigan. Mason, therefore, could be considered something of a miracle worker. Starting in 1999, he took the Gophers to seven bowl games in an 8-year span while accumulating the highest winning percentage (.529) of any Minnesota coach since 1944. His teams, however, never could get above the middle of the pack in the Big Ten, and after a while, the novelty of playing in annual Sun and Music City bowls began to wear off for Gophers fans. Their patience was further tested by Mason's uncanny penchant for losing games in the most heartbreaking fashion known to man, from a last-second Hail Mary by Northwestern in 2000 to a 21-point fourth-quarter comeback by Michigan in 2003 to a last-second blocked punt against Wisconsin in 2005.* By 2006, as the Gophers struggled through a 6–6 regular season, "Fire Mason" chants had become commonplace during home games at the Metrodome, and not one but two different Web sites—FireGlenMason.com and Fire-Mason.com—were created. Who knew anyone cared enough about Minnesota football to go to such lengths?

For most of the season, it was assumed AD Joel Maturi would ignore the wishes of those critics. For one thing, it had been generally understood by most informed followers that after losing star running back Laurence Maroney and a veteran offensive line, 2006 would be a rebuilding year for the Gophers. Furthermore, Maturi had just rewarded Mason with a lucrative five-year, $8.25 million contract extension less than a year earlier. But then Mason committed what was apparently a cardinal sin. Facing Texas Tech in what would have otherwise been a forgettable Insight Bowl, Minnesota allowed the Red Raiders to stage the biggest comeback in bowl history, blowing a 38–7 third-quarter lead to lose 44–41 in overtime. Two days later, Maturi fired Mason. In explaining his decision at a press conference, Maturi said, "If we had not lost [the Insight Bowl] the way we had lost, we probably wouldn't be here today."

Excuse me? Did he really just say he based an enormous decision that will shape the future course of the program on a blown lead in a meaningless third-tier bowl game? Was he serious? Yes and no. More realistically, the bowl collapse served as the final boiling point for what had already been a rapidly increasing number of disgruntled Gophers fans, many of whom lit up Maturi's voice mail and in-box immediately fol-

---

*This is just the abridged version. There was also a second blown lead against Michigan, a last-second bowl loss to Virginia, a controversial pass-interference call against Penn State . . . honestly, I've never seen a team so cursed.

lowing the game. Faced with a crisis in confidence among his fan base, Maturi felt he had no choice but to pull the plug, even at a cost of $3.5 million to buy out Mason's contract. Chalk it up to yet another reality of college football's current climate: past or overall achievements in a coach's tenure don't carry nearly as much weight as his performance *at that very moment.* At the time of Mason's arrival, Minnesota fans would have been thrilled just to go to an Insight Bowl; by the time of his ouster, losing in one had become cause for mass outrage. For Mason's replacement, Maturi tapped largely unknown NFL assistant Tim Brewster. Perhaps he will be the guy to take the Gophers to the long-awaited next level; all too often, however, fans of programs like Minnesota fall victim to the "be careful what you wish for" syndrome. History says Minnesota has a much better chance of falling back to the realms of 4–8 every year than they do of reaching the BCS anytime soon.

Unfortunately, few supporters of any program, no matter the tradition, are willing to accept this reality. Remember our friends at Bruins Nation? Shortly after their Dorrell disapproval survey in 2006, the coach played right into the hands of his critics by losing three straight games, including blowing a late lead at Notre Dame. UCLA closed the regular season, however, by winning three straight games, including an epic, season-ending upset of second-ranked archrival USC that seemed to reenergize the fan base. Bruins Nation quickly tempered that. "Despite the euphoria of December 2, 2006 [the day of the USC game], Dorrell is nowhere close to off the hook," wrote the authors. ". . . If Dorrell doesn't at least win the Pac-10 in [2007], we need to hold him accountable. Going to the Holiday Bowl may be cause for hero worshipping at other programs in the Pac-10, but this is freaking UCLA." Freaking UCLA has won the Pac-10 exactly twice in the past twenty years. It was, however, a regular Rose Bowl participant in the 1950s and 1960s—back when USC and UCLA were the only two programs of any significance in what was then the Pac-8—and that is the standard to which all Bruins coaches now and forever will be held.

As long as coaches are making seven-figure salaries and entire athletic budgets remain dependent on selling out one-hundred-thousand-seat stadiums, the pressure not only to win, but win big, will continue to hover over coaches like the Goodyear blimp—which, for the right price, may soon be renting out its siding for FireMyCoach.com-type messages. The fact is, coaches who don't bring instant gratification to their perpetually hungry fan bases will be fired. And in an effort to stay one step ahead of the mob, the ones who do win early will always be a threat to jump to the next stop. After all, who wants to be the guy who passes up a cushy new gig only to be out of a job three years later when the wins taper off?

Just ask former Western Michigan coach Gary Darnell. After leading the Broncos to consecutive MAC division titles in 1999 and 2000, Darnell was courted by the likes of Oklahoma State and Missouri but passed in hopes of landing a more desirable opportunity that never came. Four years later, after the program slipped all the way to 1–10, Darnell, not surprisingly, found himself unemployed—and apparently a bit deranged. "I think I want to be a duck," Darnell told the *New York Times.* "A duck goes in the water when he wants and goes on land when he wants. He goes south for the winter and north in the summer. He eats good. He only eats fish and vegetables. I might be a duck for a while. How about that?"

The sad by-product of this trend is that once the game's two patriarchal deans, Penn State's Joe Paterno (forty-two seasons) and Florida State's Bobby Bowden (thirty-two), finally retire, it will just about mark an end to the sport's fabled history of coaches whose faces were synonymous with their schools—Alabama's Bryant, Oklahoma's Bud Wilkinson, Ohio State's Woody Hayes, Georgia's Vince Dooley, et al. Going forward, fans should expect most programs to undergo regime changes every three to six years, not exactly an ideal recipe for success and stability. In fact, nearly half of the nation's Division I-A schools—56 out of 120—have changed coaches just since the end of the 2004 season. While not much can be done to discourage sought-after coaches from jumping from job to job—last we checked, the coaching profession operated under the same free-market forces as the rest of the American workforce—one can only hope that universities and their constituents exercise at least some degree of pragmatism in the treatment of their coaches.

Without question, however, the one positive to emerge from this trend has been the newfound weight of the voice of the people. In a sport where the fans often find themselves ignored, if not patronized, by the powers-that-be—they've only been asking for a playoff for the past twenty years now, and they sure do appreciate being bumped out of their 40-yard-line seats to make way for more luxury boxes—there's no denying their increased influence in many schools' coaching decisions. Today's fans may be unrealistic, overly demanding, and, in some cases, downright delusional, but one thing they are not is ignored. "Fans don't make [coaching] decisions, but fans can create a climate that's not healthy to success," said Florida's Foley. "There's no question, with the different forms of communication today, the noise can get turned up very loudly."

So perhaps the college football world owes a debt of gratitude to Mike Walsh, the visionary Florida fan who, in following a whim and launching FireRonZook.com, unknowingly empowered a new generation of fans. Not that he'll be getting any thank-you cards from coaches anytime soon.

5

What's the Deal with Notre Dame?

Notre Dame football is special.
It has a national constituency.

—*NBC Sports president Ken Schanzer, 2003*

———

The time has come for the people at Notre Dame to
stop acting as if they, and their school, are special.
They aren't.

—*Boston Globe, 2004*

In the spring of 2006, I published a column on SI.com offering a fairly straightforward explanation of the new BCS rules set to go into effect that season. One of the items, however—the one about Notre Dame receiving an at-large berth if it finished in the top 8 of the BCS standings—managed to cause quite a bit of confusion, if not outrage, among readers like Rick from Richmond Hill, Georgia, who wrote:

> I'm not sure if I missed out on some attempt at humor on your part, but whose idea was it to put Notre Dame on such a lofty pedestal as to guarantee them an at-large berth for finishing in the top eight? Why not Alabama, why not Penn State, why not Wake Forest for that matter? It seems ludicrous to single out one school with special favors, regardless of how many times the movie *Rudy* has been shown on television.

Murray from Athens, Georgia, chimed in:

> This new BCS system is totally biased. Why should Notre Dame get treated so special, receiving a BCS bid if they're in the top eight? So they're Catholic, well I am too. Quit this crap and join the Big Ten!

Then there was this transatlantic e-mail from a guy named David that pretty much said it all:

> Hello, I'm a college football fan from Belgium. What I don't understand is why Notre Dame is so privileged? Is there any background story that I should know about?

Oh, David. Where to begin?

In a sport of 120 teams, it's easy to see why someone from another country—not to mention plenty of people in *this* country—might be confused as to why one team seems to play by an entirely different set of rules than the other 119. Why, for instance, when nearly every other team in the country is a member of a conference, do the Fighting Irish remain an independent? Why, when the other teams have to fight one another for broadcast time on networks like ABC, ESPN, and CBS, does Notre Dame have its own exclusive contract with NBC? Why do the Irish get to latch onto the Big East's bowl partnerships when they don't even play in the conference? Why, as the above e-mailers wondered, does Notre Dame have its own special provision in the BCS qualifying rules? And why oh why does seemingly every Brady Quinn touchdown pass, Darius Walker stiff-arm, or Jeff Samardizja fly pattern merit coverage by every major newspaper from New York to Los Angeles when the school is located in South Bend, Indiana?

Year after year, the obsession of the college football establishment with anything and everything Irish drives fans of the nation's other glamour teams absolutely bonkers. During the height of the 2005 season, when the Irish were rapidly rising up the national polls due to a late-season winning streak, I was able to fill nearly an entire Mailbag column solely with submissions from Ohio State fans incredulous about their two-loss team being ranked lower than the two-loss Irish. When 9–2 Notre Dame wound up receiving an invitation to the Fiesta Bowl that December over higher-ranked, 10–1 Oregon, the cries of injustice could be heard from Eugene to Eau Claire. "Notre Dame supposedly locked up a BCS game Saturday night with its 38–31 victory over Stanford," wrote *Contra Costa (California) Times* columnist Eric Gilmore. "Pardon me for a minute while I throw up."

The mere fact that a writer in Northern California would devote precious column space to a team from South Bend illustrates precisely why Notre Dame has its own bowl rules and TV network. Whether you love them (as a significantly large number of people do) or hate them (as an even larger number do), chances are you have some sort of discernible feelings toward the Fighting Irish. So when Notre Dame finds itself playing in a big game, it's no coincidence that more fans than usual tune in, even if it's to root against them. "Growing up a [New York] Yankees fan, I always found no matter where you went, people had an opinion on the Yankees. They either liked them or disliked them," said current Irish coach Charlie Weis. "I think that's very similar to what we have to deal with." For me, the realization that Notre Dame truly is America's team came while returning from a game I'd covered one Sunday during the 2004 season. Sitting in the back of a cab from La Guardia, I was engaged in a cell-phone conversation with my editor about possible topics for that night's column when the driver—clearly not from this country—asked me what I was talking about. When I replied, "College football," a big smile broke out on his face as he asked me, in heavily accented English, "Notre Dame—doing good, no?"

But don't take it from my cabdriver buddy. There are plenty of other metrics to demonstrate that the Golden Domers have more than just Jesus on their side. Let's see: There's the eleven consensus national championships, tied with Alabama and USC for the most of any Division I-A team. There are the seven Heisman winners, tied with USC and Ohio State for the most all-time. There are the two hit Hollywood films, *Knute Rockne All-American* (1940) and *Rudy* (1993), both of which centered on Notre Dame football and sent generations of moviegoers grabbing for the Kleenex. There are the 173 consecutive games the Irish have played on national television and the thirty-eight straight seasons broadcast on national radio.* The school's official athletics Web site is the most trafficked of the two hundred fifty operated by CSTV.com and set a company record for monthly page views with 7.8 million in September 2006, the *New York Times* reported. Finally, according to the Harris Interactive polling service, Notre Dame has been ranked the most popular team in the country every year since the company started asking the public to identify their favorite college football team in 1997.

---

*Notre Dame has a contract with the syndicated Westwood One Radio Network to broadcast every play of every Irish game to its various affiliates.

Even the respondents who voted for someone else can probably sing most of the lyrics to "Victory March." (Admit it, you know 'em: "Cheer, cheer for old Notre Dame, wake up the echoes . . .")

At this point, you're probably wondering, how did this happen? How exactly did one college football team manage to supersede all others in the departments of mystique and adulation? How, in a sport overflowing with Tigers and Buckeyes, Sooners and Bruins, did a team named after a European ethnic group achieve such a permanent place in the American sports culture? Strangely, it began with the work of a Norwegian immigrant. And ironically, the story of college football's greatest juggernaut is actually steeped in underdog roots.

In the early twentieth century, college football was still largely dominated by teams from the Northeast, mainly Ivy League stalwarts like Harvard and Yale and service academies Army and Navy. Michigan had established itself as the lone power in the Midwest, and Stanford was beginning to gain notoriety out West. However, seeing as universities were still largely the domain of elite rich folk, and seeing as Notre Dame was a small, private Catholic school in a remote Midwest town, there was little reason for most of mainstream America to pay its football team a lick of attention. Even so, one Notre Dame player had achieved at least some level of notoriety. In 1913, Knute Kenneth Rockne, a 5-foot-8, 160-pound starting end, teamed with his roommate, quarterback Gus Dorais, to unleash the sport's first true passing attack, stunning highly respected Army 35–13 thanks to their unprecedented reliance on the forward pass. Rockne, a senior, was named to the prestigious Walter Camp All-America third team. After graduating that spring, Rockne became an assistant to Fighting Irish head coach Jesse Harper and in 1918, at the age of thirty, took over as head coach for the retiring Harper.

Exercising the same innovative spirit that once caused him to practice pass routes on the Lake Michigan beach with Dorais, Rockne set out to bring gridiron glory to his alma mater. As the little Catholic school began beating up on college football's elite—the Irish would post a staggering 105–12–5 record in thirteen seasons under Rockne— Notre Dame became a source of pride for the nation's large but heavily persecuted Catholic population, many of them immigrants like Rockne, and most of them clustered in large metropolitan areas. Helping spawn this new legion of "subway alumni"—Notre Dame fans from across the country who had never attended the school and would likely never step foot on its campus—was Rockne's barnstorming nature. At a time when intersectional matchups were still extremely rare, Rockne would stick his team on a train and travel all the way to Los Angeles to face USC, with fans coming out to greet the convoy at stops along the way. A defining moment came in 1925 when the Irish went to the Rose Bowl and beat powerhouse Stanford.* Meanwhile, Notre Dame's annual showdowns with Army became such a spectacle that they were eventually moved from West Point to larger venues like New York's Polo Grounds and Yankee Stadium.

But the appeal of the Notre Dame teams of that day transcended mere wins and losses. This was the 1920s, the so-called Golden Age of Sport, when athletic heroes like Babe Ruth, Red Grange, and Jack Dempsey took on larger-than-life personas thanks to breathless newspaper accounts of their sporting exploits. Rockne made a concerted effort to befriend prominent sportswriters like the *New York Herald-Tribune's* Grantland Rice, whose epic account of the Irish's 1924 game against Army began:

> Outlined against a blue-gray October sky, the Four Horsemen rode again. In dramatic lore they are known as Famine, Pestilence, Destruction and Death. These are only aliases. Their real names are Stuhldreher, Miller, Crowley and Layden. They formed the crest of the South Bend cyclone before which another fighting Army football team was swept over the precipice at the Polo Grounds yesterday afternoon as 55,000 spectators peered down on the bewildering panorama spread on the green plain below.

---

*After watching Rockne's players miss nearly a month of classes to play in the game, Notre Dame administrators placed a ban on the Irish participating in bowl games that remained in effect for forty-five years.

The story spawned the most famous nickname in college football history, and it served to further propagate the increasingly heroic image of Notre Dame's gridiron warriors. (Not to mention that it beat the pants off *USA Today*'s lead, which read, "Notre Dame stomped Army yesterday. See full story, Page C9.") While the players changed from year to year, Rockne served as the face of Notre Dame, becoming one of the biggest sporting figures of his generation. First and foremost, Rockne was known as a master motivator whose fiery pregame and halftime speeches—"Fight, fight, fight! Win, win, win!"—quickly became the stuff of legend. Most famous of all is the account of his address to the troops at halftime of the 1928 Army game. The Irish weren't particularly good that season, while Army was undefeated. In hopes of springing an upset, Rockne chose that occasion to relay to his team an emotional request that the late George Gipp—a former Irish great who died of pneumonia shortly after his playing career ended in 1920—had supposedly made from his hospital bed: "Sometime, Rock, when the team is up against it, when things are wrong and the breaks are beating the boys, tell them to go in there with all they've got and win just one for the Gipper." Notre Dame rallied to knock off the Cadets 12–6.

The story, which would later be dramatized in the 1940 movie *Knute Rockne All-American*—with future president Ronald Reagan playing the part of the Gipper—was a certifiable tearjerker, and illustrates why Rockne became so beloved by working-class America. There's only one problem: It most likely never happened. Numerous historians over the years have pointed out inconsistencies in the story, that it's unlikely Rockne was even in a position to visit Gipp* during his dying days, nevertheless receive such an astounding request. The speech was likely a product of Rockne's imagination. This revelation shouldn't be viewed as entirely surprising, seeing as Rockne, a master showman, was by no means adverse to a little deception and chicanery. According to an ESPN Classic *SportsCentury*

---

*Another aspect of the famous story that often gets conveniently overlooked was the fact that Gipp was a hard-drinking, gambling-addicted renegade.

biography, Rockne often devised misleading stories about the Irish's opponents to inspire his squad. One time, he falsely claimed his six-year-old son was hospitalized and urged his players to pull out a win for him. "They were all lies, blatant lies," Jim Crowley, one of the Four Horsemen, would later recall. "The Jesuits call it mental reservation, but he had it in abundance."

Rockne was also a master at manipulating the press to his advantage. During the week leading up to Notre Dame's 1930 showdown with USC, the coach managed to convince the nation that his team, despite having won eighteen straight games, stood no chance against the 8–1 Trojans due to injuries to his top two fullbacks. "I'm afraid we're going to take a beating from Southern California next Saturday in Los Angeles," Rockne said on a radio show. "I am willing to wager we will not be defeated by four touchdowns, as some Los Angeles newspapermen have predicted, but if we can hold the Trojans to a two-touchdown difference we'll go home feeling pretty good." The L.A. newspapers ate it up. What Rockne didn't tell the press was that he had secretly pressed Paul "Bucky" O'Connor, a sprinter on the track team, into duty as a fullback that week. Come game time, O'Connor was unstoppable on the reverse, and Notre Dame crushed the Trojans 27–0. Then there were the times the media came to the Irish's aid more directly. According to a 1994 *Sporting News* article, Rockne would often hire friendly and influential writers, like the *Chicago Tribune's* Walter Eckersall, to officiate the very same Notre Dame games they were covering. For a modern comparison, try picturing Kirk Herbstreit spending three hours making holding and pass interference calls, then running back to the GameDay set to comment on what happened. Eckersall, in fact, was the referee in that famous 1928 Army game, which he happened to whistle dead with the Cadets standing at the Irish 1-foot line, poised for the winning score. Modern Notre Dame haters would undoubtedly consider that story to be absurdly fitting—favoritism from both the media *and* the rule-makers on the same play!

No matter his methods, Rockne became so revered over the course of his career that his tragic death at the age of forty-three in a 1931 plane crash* was treated like the passing of a head of state. Members of the national press accompanied the train carrying his body back to South Bend, and by the time it arrived at the station, an estimated ten thousand mourners—many of them having made the pilgrimage from hometowns far and wide—had lined the streets leading to the funeral home. His memorial service was broadcast on national radio. "You died one of our national heroes," eulogized Will Rogers, the famous comedian and a close friend of Rockne's. "Notre Dame was your address, but every gridiron in America was your home."

The legions of newfound Notre Dame fans that had sprouted up across the country during Rockne's tenure did not abandon the Fighting Irish following his death. If anything, their loyalty to the school only grew stronger. There's no denying the fact that for most of the twentieth century, Notre Dame was the one school in the country with a truly national following. For many fans, the national radio broadcasts of Fighting Irish games in the days before television served as their only link to college football. Those Domers passed their allegiance on to their sons and daughters, who in turn passed it on to their offspring, and so on, and the next thing you knew you couldn't walk into a watering hole in Sandusky, Ohio, or Albion, Michigan, without seeing a Notre Dame pennant on the wall.

The subway alumni had plenty to cheer about, too. From the beginning of Rockne's tenure in 1918 through the end of Dan Devine's in 1980, the Irish won more than 75 percent of their games and captured ten national championships, and the ever-adoring national press ensured that the public heard all about it. Though there were plenty of other stars on plenty of other teams playing in plenty of other big games, the ones involving gold helmets always seemed to take precedent in the minds and typewriters of the nation's scribes. Only a

---

*Rockne was traveling from Kansas City, where he'd visited his two sons in boarding school, to Los Angeles to assist in the production of a film entitled *The Spirit of Notre Dame*. The plane's wings separated shortly after takeoff and crashed into a wheat field in Bazaar, Kansas. A memorial to Rockne and the seven other passengers who perished was erected on the site of the crash in 1935 and remains there today.

Notre Dame quarterback, Paul Hornung, could have captured the 1956 Heisman while playing for a 2–8 team. Only the 9–0–1 Irish could have finished number 1 in the polls in 1966 ahead of 11–0 Alabama despite backing its way into a tie against Michigan State in the teams' season-ending "Game of the Century" that year. *Sports Illustrated*'s Dan Jenkins, the nation's most prominent college football writer of the time, let the Irish have it over their conservative decision to run out the clock in the final minutes of what was easily the most hyped college football game in decades. He led his story that week with a parody of the "Notre Dame Victory March": "Cheer, cheer for old Notre Dame, *Equal* the echoes, *deadlock* her name. . . ." Brainy Notre Dame students, not accustomed to such unfavorable press, responded by burning twelve hundred copies of the magazine—but only after analyzing the articles' proper grammar and verbiage.

It's hard to say when exactly the transformation occurred, but at some point during the course of all those triumphs, the Fighting Irish went from being the sport's lovable underdogs to its most resented villains. Part of it, of course, is that people naturally tend to root against dynasties. But in the case of the gaping dichotomy regarding Notre Dame that exists to this day, it wasn't just the winning that sprouted so many critics but the school's holier-than-thou approach to said winning. Not only did the Irish win more than their share of championships under renowned coaches like Frank Leahy and Ara Parseghian, but also, if you were to believe their backers, they did so while holding true to a different set of ideals than the Ohio States and Nebraskas. They did so while maintaining rigorous admissions requirements for their players and making sure they didn't skip out on their philosophy and modern language courses. They did so while refusing to yield to such common practices as redshirting freshmen or participating in bowl games. They did so while attending Mass on Saturday mornings before taking a licking to Michigan State or Purdue. And they did so without spoiling the players with amenities like athletic dormitories or special training tables. Notre Dame football players were good, upstanding *student*-athletes, by golly, who did everything short of taking communion at the 50-yard line.

In his 1976 book *The Joy of Sports*, acclaimed Catholic author Michael Novak wrote, "The very words Notre Dame mean a certain kind of spirit: a spirit of never quitting, of using one's wit, of playing with desperate seriousness and intense delight, of achieving not just excellence, but a certain kind of flair that must be thought of as gift and grace." Is one to infer that Fighting Irish players catch passes and make tackles more cerebrally and gracefully than those of Michigan or USC? I doubt it. The concept of a "spirit of Notre Dame," however, has become a common refrain among generation upon generation of Notre Dame students, faculty, alumni, and fans who view their football team as not only powerful, but special. From the Golden Dome (the majestic crown that sits atop the school's administration building) to Touchdown Jesus (the 62-foot mosaic of Christ, arms raised above his head, that adorns the side of the Notre Dame library facing the stadium) to the Leprechaun (the school's real-life student mascot, complete with green suit and hat), nearly everything about Notre Dame football carries with it a mystical quality. Notre Dame Stadium itself is said to house the "ghosts" of Rockne, Leahy, and all those other past greats. Who do you think cleans up all that popcorn on Sundays?

But while Notre Dame may present itself as a sacred castle, it has not been immune to the ills of a typical football factory—particularly during the Lou Holtz era (1986–96). A devout Catholic with an aw-shucks personality, an endless arsenal of one-liners ("It's ironic, I wasn't smart enough to go to Notre Dame, but I'm smart enough to coach at Notre Dame"), and a professed love and encyclopedic knowledge of Fighting Irish football, Holtz endeared himself to the ND herd before ever coaching a single game. And then, in just his third season, he assured himself a spot in Irish lore right alongside Rockne, Leahy, and Parseghian by leading Notre Dame to the 1988 national championship. He did it partially by preaching fundamentals, instilling discipline, and outscheming his opponents. However, according to the 1993 exposé *Under the Tarnished Dome* by Don Yaeger and Douglas S. Looney, he also did so by convincing the once-impregnable university to admit a few less-than-stellar scholars who happened to be gifted football players. Among the stars of that 1988 title team was quarterback

Tony Rice, an NCAA "Prop 48" athlete who had to sit out his first season because he failed to achieve the NCAA-minimum 700 on the SAT. He told the authors of *Under the Tarnished Dome* that he had a 2.3 GPA coming out of high school. Future All-Americans Chris Zorich, Todd Lyght, and Michael Stonebraker were also reported to have fallen well below the typical ND admission standard, though, to their credit, all three, along with Rice, wound up graduating. "What the school did was say, 'Let's get all the alumni off our backs,'" former Irish offensive lineman Tom Freeman told the book's authors. "'We will lower our standards and try to get the best athletes rather than the best academic athletes.'"

They may have been doing it, but they weren't exactly admitting to it. As Holtz continued to build his budding dynasty, one that would go 64–9–1 and finish in the AP top 6 all but one year from 1988 to 1993, both he and university administrators continued to insist it was business as usual within Notre Dame's ivory towers. "Notre Dame is not going to lower its standard for anybody," he liked to bark. All the while, according to *Under the Tarnished Dome*, Irish officials were not only looking the other way in the realm of low SAT scores but also at an alarming rash of suspensions and academic casualties, rampant steroid use, and an unspoken end to the program's longtime policy against redshirting. It wasn't until Notre Dame started regressing on the field, going 6–5–1 in 1994, that the faithful finally started to tire of Holtz's blatant hypocrisy. He "retired" 2 years later, having failed to get the team back into national title contention.*

There was, however, one area where Notre Dame managed to leave its competitors in the dust and in doing so reinforce its separatist— albeit financially driven—values. In 1990, the school stunned college football officials by defecting from its peers in the College Football Association to sign a five-year, $30 million deal with NBC, becoming

---

*Holtz went on to coach South Carolina from 1999 to 2004. In a similar pattern, he engineered a dramatic turnaround from 0–11 to consecutive New Year's Day bowl berths—and the school wound up on probation.

the first sports team in history to have its own network television contract. Its share of the CFA contract over the same time period would have been closer to $20 million. The deal, pulled off in clandestine fashion by NBC Sports executive vice president Ken Schanzer, Notre Dame's executive VP, Reverend William Beauchamp, and athletic director Dick Rosenthal, infuriated the Irish's former CFA colleagues, who had already agreed in principle to new deals with ABC and ESPN under the assumption Notre Dame would be part of the package.* "It's been a fun year for all of us," Penn State coach Joe Paterno told *Sports Illustrated* at the time. "We got to see Notre Dame go from an academic institute to a banking institute."

For Notre Dame, the arrangement would help fulfill its longtime vision of itself as a truly national institution. Now, rather than having to share ABC's increasingly crowded airwaves—the network would often show regional broadcasts, airing multiple games at once to different parts of the country—Notre Dame fans from Alaska to Alabama would be able to tune in to every Irish home game, no matter who else might be playing that day. "It's important for us to be on the network," Reverend Beauchamp told the *New York Times*. "We don't have a regional following. We need the [national] exposure." Plus, added Beauchamp, defending his school from charges of greed and hypocrisy, "We are turning the new television money over to our [general] scholarship fund. It won't even see its way to the athletic department." Indeed, in an effort to cut down on paperwork, all the talented poets, cellists, and philosophers fortunate enough to earn financial aid from Notre Dame would now receive their scholarship checks directly from NBC's sponsors.

In truth, most of the grumbling that arose (and continues to this day) about the Irish's NBC marriage wasn't actually outrage over the school's apparent money grab but a case of jealousy, perhaps even bewilderment, that the Irish could even fetch such a deal. Why, many

---

*The networks ended up renegotiating their CFA deals, resulting in a 15 percent reduction in value.

wondered, would NBC want to surrender its airwaves to the same team every week? "If you're an advertiser," said Schanzer, "you're going to buy Notre Dame football." Was there really that much more of a national demand to watch Notre Dame games than those of, say, Penn State or Texas? "Notre Dame is the biggest thing in sports," longtime ESPN analyst and unabashed Domer homer Beano Cook told *USA Today*. "If I could own two things in television, it's the movie *Casablanca* and Notre Dame football." Cook then hung up the phone and returned to petting his Rocket Ismail poster.

In the first two seasons of the deal, 1991 and 1992, Notre Dame games on NBC averaged a 4.8 Nielsen rating—solid but not on the same level as ABC's regional broadcasts, which averaged between 6.5 and 6.8. However, when you consider that ABC had its choice of nearly every other game in the country each week while NBC was at the mercy of whoever the Irish were playing (sometimes Michigan, sometimes Air Force), and when you consider that ABC was paying about two and a half times as much in rights fees per broadcast, NBC clearly was getting its money's worth. This proved to be particularly true in 1993, when the Irish were a season-long contender for the national championship. A mid-November showdown between then number 1 Florida State and number 2 Notre Dame in South Bend garnered a staggering 16.0 rating, a number no regular-season college football game has eclipsed since. Not surprisingly, NBC extended the deal for another five years shortly thereafter. "It's been an idyllic relationship," said then-NBC sports president Dick Ebersol.

In addition to filling NBC's and Notre Dame's coffers, the deal was important to the Irish for another reason: at a time when nearly all of the nation's other unattached teams were flocking to join conferences (including Penn State to the Big Ten, Florida State to the ACC, and Miami to the Big East), Notre Dame had assured itself the financial wherewithal to remain an independent, something that had become an increasing source of pride for the institution. "We have independent status by design," Rosenthal told the *New York Times*. "It gives us a choice of where to play. By traveling, we feel this is one of the ways we can communicate with alumni."

All of this was fine and dandy as long as the Irish kept winning. From the day the NBC deal was first announced, the skeptics wondered how harmonious the relationship might be if Notre Dame ever lost its national relevance. They didn't have to wait long to find out. Starting in 1994, the Irish slipped into an extended pattern of mediocrity that continued right up until the past couple of years. From 1994 to 2004, Notre Dame had more losing seasons (three) than appearances in one of the four major bowls (two). Bob Davie, a defensive coordinator under Holtz who succeeded him as head coach in 1997, managed just a .583 winning percentage in five seasons. After going 10–3 in his first season, Davie's successor, Tyrone Willingham, stumbled to 5–7 and 6–5 seasons, leading to his unexpected ouster. Suddenly Notre Dame, the sport's reigning powerhouse for three-quarters of a century, was no more powerful than Virginia Tech or Kansas State—only those schools weren't appearing on national television every week or having movies made about them. To add insult to injury, Notre Dame incurred its first-ever NCAA sanctions in 1999 after it was revealed that a twenty-eight-year-old booster/groupie, Kim Dunbar, had lavished several players with gifts over a four-year period using money she had embezzled from her employer. Silly Kim: If only she'd directed the payola to some *better* players, maybe the Irish wouldn't have been going 6–5.

Pundits far and wide pontificated about the reasons behind the Irish's descent, but it was obvious that the overall talent level at Notre Dame had slipped considerably. Sure, Holtz and Davie were still pulling in top 20 recruiting classes, but no longer were the elite difference-makers like Ismail, Tim Brown, and Jerome Bettis—the kind of guys who now littered the rosters at places like USC and Miami—finding their way to South Bend. The reason, according to a lengthy 2000 *Sports Illustrated* article, was that the school's admissions office was no longer affording the football program the kind of leniency it had during the early years of Holtz's tenure. Among the future stars the school rejected, according to SI, were quarterback Carson Palmer, the 2002 Heisman winner at USC, who claimed to have a 2.6 GPA and 970 SAT; running back T.J. Duckett, a standout at Michigan State and first-round draft choice by the Atlanta Falcons; and David Terrell, an eventual All-American receiver at Michigan. Future all-pro receiver Randy Moss originally signed with the Irish in 1995 before getting into legal troubles back home and was denied admission. "The admissions process at Notre Dame eliminates a whole bunch of people who you could really use," a former Irish assistant told SI. Meanwhile, other elite prospects who could get into the school simply chose not to because, quite frankly, there were any number of other glamour programs (Florida State, Ohio State, Florida, Michigan) more enticing to the modern era's typical seventeen-year-old. "They [the Irish] had their glory back in the old days," explained 2000 offensive line recruit Max Starks, who signed with Florida over Notre Dame despite his father, Ross Browner, having starred for the Irish in the 1970s. Maybe in the days of Rockne or Parseghian, the chance to bring glory to ol' Notre Dame was motivation enough, but the new-age blue-chip recruit had his sights set on a grander goal: reaching the NFL. And while those other football factories were churning out high draft picks by the bushel, Notre Dame's track record had become abysmal: just three first-round selections from 1995 to 2005,* this after producing seven in the 1993 and 1994 drafts alone. "In the last three or four years, I've not graded one player from Notre Dame and gone, 'Oooo—wow!'" an NFC personnel director told SI.

The competitive landscape changed for everyone in the 1990s. Between new scholarship limitations (eighty-five per team), more TV exposure, and increased financial investments, it was now possible for even the most tradition-starved programs, like Wisconsin and Louisville, to compete at the highest level. On the flip side, with increased competition it became harder for any school—much less one with stringent academic standards—to consistently compete for national titles. Add to that the fact that Notre Dame continued to eschew conference affiliation in favor of a rigorous, often brutal national schedule, and most outside observers came to believe the Irish

---

*By comparison, during that same time period Miami had twenty-eight first-rounders, Ohio State and Florida State seventeen.

were dooming themselves to failure. While there would always be a certain type of player for whom the Notre Dame mystique would hold influence—mainly Midwestern Catholic boys or 4.0 scholars from the Chicago suburbs—the more typical modern athlete, many from black, urban households, wanted to go play in the Big Ten or SEC, or mingle with other future NFLers at Miami or Florida State. Some of the linemen at those schools were running faster 40 times than Notre Dame's receivers.

It seemed the only remaining people still in denial of this new reality were Golden Domers themselves. As the Irish slipped further and further from their traditional perch under the reigns of Davie and Willingham, the outrage among Notre Dame alumni, both the real and subway variety, grew louder and louder. They'd heard all the excuses about academics, tough schedules, and lack of conference affiliation, and quite frankly, they weren't buying it. In fact, when the school briefly considered joining the Big Ten in 1999, its constituents came out vehemently against it, writing angry letters to university administrators and hanging anti–Big Ten banners in dorm windows. "I'm not saying that the Big Ten is weak," defensive end Tony Weaver told the *South Bend Tribune*, "but joining the league will make us just like everyone else—it will make us average." Somehow Weaver had failed to notice that had already happened. At a special meeting that February in that noted bastion of college football, London, the school's board of trustees formally voted against pursuing membership. "As a Catholic university with a national constituency," said Notre Dame's president, the Reverend Edward "Monk" Malloy, "we believe independence continues to be our best way forward, not just in athletics, but first and foremost in the fulfillment of our academic aspirations." Apparently, administrators felt that by joining the Big Ten they'd not only be forced to share their TV and bowl revenue with the likes of Indiana and Minnesota, but their library books as well.

Though school officials denied it, there was another big motivation for the Irish to remain independent: money. Not only had NBC recently renewed its deal with the school for another five years, but with the advent of the BCS in 1998, the Orange, Sugar, Rose, and Fiesta bowls were now offering staggering payouts in excess of $14 million—and unlike teams from the conferences, Notre Dame didn't have to share their loot with anyone. There was only one little itty-bitty problem: the talent-depleted Irish were no longer fielding good enough teams to get there, earning just one BCS bowl invite (the Fiesta in 2000) in the first seven years of the system. This was cause for increasing consternation among Domers. To them, there was no reason why Notre Dame shouldn't be the same type of powerhouse today that it was in the days of Rockne and Gipp, Leahy and Lujack.

Obviously there could be only one possible explanation for why the Irish weren't still churning out national championships: bad coaching. Davie, a first-time head coach with a vanilla offense to match his personality,* was the subject of pretty much constant criticism throughout his five seasons. "The one word they don't have in their vocabulary here is rebuild," Davie said of the school's notoriously impatient fans. "You look at the dictionaries on this campus and that word is not in there." His successor, Willingham, was a controversial choice to begin with both because he was the school's first African American head coach in any sport and because he was tabbed only after Notre Dame's original choice, Georgia Tech coach George O'Leary, was forced to resign less than a week into the job due to discovered inaccuracies on his résumé. Willingham got off to a roaring start, winning his first eight games in 2002 by upsetting the likes of Michigan and Florida State, thus briefly shaking the thunder and waking the echoes. The eerily stoic Willingham, revered by his players and acclaimed as an educator and disciplinarian, had been fortunate to inherit a senior-laden team, however. When his younger second edition struggled to a 2–6 start, his popularity plummeted quicker than a tech stock. A little more than a year later, having amassed an unacceptable 21–15 record in three seasons—and having failed to utter a single interesting thought in three years of press conferences—Willingham, impeccable character and all, was ousted.

---

*Davie mysteriously became much more loquacious upon becoming a network television analyst in 2002 and is now a far more respected commentator than he ever was a coach.

The Notre Dame board's unprecedented decision to terminate its coach with two years left on his contract (See "FireMyCoach.com" chapter for more detail), a practice previously frowned upon at the school (even the hapless Gerry Faust got his full five years) would prove to be a watershed moment for the Irish. For one, it extinguished once and for all the naïve notion that Notre Dame was any different from the nation's other football powerhouses in the way it operates. "We'd always looked at Michigan, Oklahoma, Miami, Florida State as the 'football' schools," former All-American Zorich told the *Chicago Sun Times*. "Now you can throw Notre Dame's name in there because we no longer care about the integrity of the coach. We care now more about wins." Meanwhile, the search for Willingham's replacement would prove unexpectedly humbling to proud Domers. The school's clear first choice, Utah coach Urban Meyer, seemed like a no-brainer to take the job. A Catholic-raised Midwesterner named after a pope, Meyer had grown up worshipping the Irish and had coached there as an assistant under both Holtz and Davie. Just two days after Willingham's firing, a plane bearing the Notre Dame logo and carrying athletics director Kevin White and other school officials swooped down from the Salt Lake City skies, presumably to pick up their man. Only Meyer wasn't a passenger on the flight back to South Bend—the next day, he opted to accept an offer from Florida instead. "At the University of Florida," said Meyer, "you have everything in place to make a run at the [national title], and that was a factor." Translation: Notre Dame did not.* The ensuing weeks would prove just as disheartening to all those Irish loyalists still caked in the delusion that Notre Dame trumps all, as one attractive candidate after another—Cal's Jeff Tedford, Louisville's Bobby Petrino, Boise State's Dan Hawkins, Buffalo Bills offensive coordinator Tom Clements—kindly tendered their "Thanks, but no thanks."

In the end, however, those chaotic few weeks in December 2004 proved well worth it for Notre Dame football because of the man they

---

*Meyer did in fact go on to lead the Gators to the national title in his second season.

did end up hiring: a Notre Dame grad (Class of 1978) from New Jersey who never played for the Irish but did pull pranks on star quarterback Joe Montana and road-tripped with classmates to the 1978 Cotton Bowl. In the two decades since, Charlie Weis had furiously worked his way up the coaching profession, from assistant high school coach in New Jersey to chief lieutenant for NFL heavyweight Bill Parcells to offensive coordinator for the 2001, 2003, and 2004 Super Bowl–champion New England Patriots. Weis's hiring by Notre Dame was met with much enthusiasm in South Bend, where the natives always look favorably upon a Notre Dame guy, but drew mixed reviews in other football circles. Yes, Weis was a noted offensive guru whose Super Bowl rings would give him instant credibility with today's NFL-thirsty players. But he was also a gruff, obese (he underwent gastric bypass surgery in 2002), atypical coaching figure with no college coaching experience. A man who'd spent his entire career poring over X's and O's, his job duties would now include working the room at booster functions, leading pep rallies, and charming recruits' mothers. "He seemed a little arrogant," outgoing defensive end Justin Tuck said of his first impression of Weis. Wherever would Justin have gotten that idea? "If it comes down to everything being even and it's X's and O's," Weis said at his introductory news conference, "I have to believe we're going to win most of the time." Wow.

It didn't take long, however, for Weis to back up his words, opening his debut 2005 season with upsets over nationally ranked Pittsburgh and Michigan, followed shortly thereafter by offensive explosions against Michigan State (albeit in a 44–41 loss) and Purdue. Brady Quinn, the strong-armed junior quarterback who had struggled during his first two seasons, was suddenly throwing with the poise and confidence of another Weis protégé, Tom Brady. The Irish offense, so inept under Willingham, was suddenly among the most productive in the nation. Then came the game that would raise excitement in South Bend to its highest levels since the days of Holtz and officially seal Weis's savior status. On October 15, 2005, two-time national champion USC came to town riding a twenty-seven-game winning streak and boasting stars Matt Leinart and Reggie Bush. In the three previous seasons, the Trojans had beaten their rivals by scores of 44–13, 45–14, and 41–10. This time was different, as the Irish, donning special green jerseys and executing Weis's masterful ball-control game plan to a tee, engaged in a back-and-forth thriller with the Trojans. They would have pulled off the upset if not for a pair of miraculous plays by Leinart (a 61-yard completion to Dwayne Jarrett on fourth and 9 and a controversial, do-or-die touchdown sneak in which Bush appeared to push him into the end zone) in the final minute. Notre Dame, in the eyes of its long-suffering believers, was finally "back."

So, too, was another famous national pastime: hating Notre Dame. Not that it had ever gone away, but the Irish hadn't provided their haters much cause for backlash over the past decade. In 2005, fans of the nation's other college football teams watched with increasing incredulity as Weis's team soared from unranked in the preseason to as high as fifth in the AP poll despite beating just one major-conference team with a winning record. They were downright baffled when the Irish, despite giving up 617 yards to Ohio State in that season's bowl game, started the 2006 campaign ranked as high as second in the country. And they rolled their eyes as one gushing story after another anointed Weis as the second coming of Rockne, particularly after Notre Dame, looking to fend off potential NFL suitors, tapped into its seemingly bottomless, Ft. Knox-like reservoir (perhaps the Vatican treasury?) to sign Weis to a ten-year extension worth a reported $30 to $40 million just seven games into his tenure. Weis did his part to perpetuate the animosity with his cocky, Parcells-like demeanor and condescending attitude toward the college coaching fraternity. "Weis is arrogant as hell," an opposing coach told the *Sporting News*. "I couldn't even talk to him before [our] game last year. I tried to. It was a one-sided conversation. After asking him six different questions and getting little to no answer, I went to the other side of the field." Others, meanwhile, were indignant that one 9–3 season had suddenly launched the Irish back into the national media's favor. As one opposing coach said to me during the 2006 preseason, "They gave up 600 yards in their bowl game and now they're supposed to contend for the national title?"*

The national backlash over Notre Dame's supposed resurgence reached its peak on September 16, 2006, when Michigan humiliated the Irish 47–21 in South Bend, causing my in-box to overflow with e-mails from readers wondering why media dopes such as myself bought into Weis's hype in the first place. Notre Dame would go on to win its next eight games before suffering another blowout in its season finale at USC, by which time it was apparent the national-title talk regarding Weis's program had been premature. Still, thanks to Weis engineering Notre Dame's best two-year run (19–6 in 2005 and 2006) in thirteen years, interest in Irish football had been restored—which meant that so, too, had the interest of bowl suitors. Notre Dame was invited to BCS bowls following both the 2005 (Fiesta) and 2006 (Sugar) seasons.† Those of us who follow such things for a living know it's pretty much a given that no bowl in its right mind passes up a chance to host Notre Dame, which is why when Web sites like mine issued their projected bowl lineups over the final month of the 2005 and 2006 seasons, the Irish were automatically slotted into one of the BCS bowl games. To many fans, this treatment seemed . . . well, unfair. "How come anytime Notre Dame has a shot at being anything above horrid the whole country lines up to kiss their backside?" wrote one of my e-mailers, Curtis from Birmingham, Alabama.

I can't speak for the whole country, but I think I can tell you why it likely took the Fiesta Bowl committee about fifteen seconds of deliberation before deciding to invite 9–2 Notre Dame to face 9–2 Ohio

---

*I was guilty of falling into that trap myself, not only voting the Irish number 2 in the country in the preseason but devoting an entire column to the "myths" being perpetrated by Notre Dame's critics. Only most of these myths turned out to be facts.
†The Irish were throttled by Ohio State and LSU in those games, extending a streak of nine straight bowl losses, the last five coming by an average margin of 22.4 points. There's a simple explanation: because Notre Dame is often selected by a better bowl than its record would merit, it is almost always matched up against a stronger opponent.

State in its January 2, 2006, game (a decision that became a formality when the Irish moved up high enough in the final BCS standings to automatically qualify). While 10–1 Oregon, 10–2 Virginia Tech, and 9–2 Auburn were probably all more deserving, none would have delivered the month-long buzz and 12.9 Nielsen rating (the Fiesta's highest ever for a nonchampionship BCS game) the Irish–Buckeyes showdown (which Ohio State wound up winning 34–20) generated. In explaining his game's potential choice to the *Columbus Dispatch* in the days leading up to the announcement, Fiesta Bowl CEO John Junker said, "There are some things in the marketplace, if you do a side-by-side comparison, that make [the Irish] different."

If you want a simple explanation as to why Notre Dame gets treated differently, it's contained right there in Junker's words. College football, unlike any other sport, is basically one big open marketplace, and Notre Dame is its Microsoft. This isn't the egalitarian NFL, where one indisputable authority (the commissioner) sets the rules for all thirty-two teams, which share the league's TV revenue equally, abide by the same salary cap, and follow the same playoff qualifications. As has been the case throughout the sport's history, the spoils of college football are open to whoever can offer the most attractive product. Notre Dame, through 80 years of history and tradition, has asserted itself as the industry leader, creating a brand powerful enough to withstand the various on-field struggles of the past decade, one that remains as coveted as ever by television executives, bowl committees, and media types. Tom Hanks has had his share of stinkers, too, but he's had enough good ones that people keep buying tickets. "When Notre Dame plays, you sell every ticket you have," Gator Bowl president Rick Catlett told the *New York Times*. "When they're good, it's great for business and great for college football."

The Irish's recent resurgence under Weis has only served to further convince the school of its ability to remain a national, independent power. Its NBC deal is in place through at least 2010 at a value of $9 million per season (up from $6 million at its inception). The BCS, while reducing the school's golden ticket (Notre Dame now pockets a reduced $4.5 million share per appearance but nets an additional $1 million annually from the BCS's revenue pool), has assured the independent Irish a continued place in its hierarchy, guaranteeing them a berth with a top-8 finish (other major-conference schools must win their league or finish in the top four to be assured automatic entry). In the years Notre Dame doesn't qualify for the BCS, it always has the Gator Bowl and other Big East–affiliated partners (the Irish compete in that conference in all other sports) to fall back on. And in 2006, the school announced it would be altering its future scheduling philosophy to include more neutral-site games around the country in places like Orlando and Dallas. "Over time we've really begun to behave like a wannabe conference member," said athletic director White. "It was real important for us to go back to our roots and behave more like an independent, go back to the Coach Rockne barnstorming era if you will."

In other words, all the pieces are in place for a return to perennial national prominence, and this time, if it doesn't happen, Domers won't be able to blame the coaching. In just a short period of time, Weis has brought the program a level of credibility unlike anything Davie or Willingham ever demonstrated. His ability to lure top-rated high school quarterback Jimmy Clausen in 2007—dubbed the "LeBron James of football" by some—shows the lure his NFL background has over aspiring phenoms.

It remains to be seen whether Weis will be able to deliver the national championship Irish fans have been craving now for nearly twenty years. If he does, Notre Dame will be able to officially reassert itself as one of the sport's reigning powers. If he doesn't, the Irish will continue to be just one in an army of good-but-not-great programs that litter the national landscape . . . but one that just happens to have its own TV network and conference of one.

Imagine the confusion there will be in Belgium.

6

Invasion of the Recruiting Geeks

It is the worst problem to hit college
football in my lifetime.

—*Anonymous ACC coach to* ESPN the Magazine
about the influence of recruiting Web sites

———————

When I announce [my commitment], I want it to be
more low-key. Like *SportsCenter*, maybe.

—*All-America high school quarterback
Ryan Perrilloux, January 2005*

I t was one of those life-defining moments experienced by millions of seventeen-year-olds every year, that fateful day when a soon-to-be young adult chooses the institution of higher learning where he or she will spend the next four to five years. For this particular seventeen-year-old, however, the moment would be shared with not only his friends and family but also a packed restaurant full of screaming football fans— and a national television audience. Decked out in a black suit and red tie—Maryland Terrapins colors—Antonio Logan-El, the state of Maryland's top-rated high school offensive lineman for 2006, chose to announce his college choice in front of more than a hundred spectators at Baltimore's ESPN Zone, including Gloria Friedgen, the wife of Terrapins head coach Ralph Friedgen. The proceedings were beamed live to the rest of the nation on ESPNews. As described by the *Baltimore Sun*, the 6-foot-6, 320-pounder first reached into a bag at his side and pulled out a baseball cap from the University of Florida. After a few kind words, he tossed it aside, eliciting cheers from the Terrapins faithful. Next came a Tennessee cap, which received the same treatment and a similar response. Finally, Logan-El held up a familiar-looking cap from the University of Maryland, a school whose coaches first offered him a scholarship way back before his sophomore year of high school— an offer which, at the time, he verbally accepted. Once the fans' initial cheers had died down, Logan-El delivered his spiel about the Terps— then promptly dropped the cap on the ground, sending much of the room into a stunned silence. At that point, Logan-El held up a picture of himself with venerable Penn State coach Joe Paterno, signifying his decision to play for the tradition-rich Nittany Lions.

Upon sharing his momentous decision, one that will undoubtedly shape the course of his life for years to come, Logan-El was greeted by the sound of a lone voice in the back of the room shouting: "TRAI-TOR!"*

Such spectacles have become commonplace in the weeks and months leading up to college football's national Signing Day in early February. Regular followers of the sport have long since become numb to such proceedings. A less jaded observer, however, might find himself wondering which part is more absurd: that an increasing number of ego-inflated seventeen-year-olds are turning their college decisions into made-for-TV events, or that there are actually grown men and women who care enough about those decisions to show up at a restaurant and heckle a kid they've never met.

Welcome to the warped world of college football recruiting in the twenty-first century. Over the past decade, Internet recruiting services like Scout.com and Rivals.com† have helped transform a process that once took place almost entirely behind closed doors into a full-blown spectator sport followed nearly as intently and obsessively as the games themselves. For the true diehard, waiting for that first Wednesday in February—when recruits are first allowed to sign binding letters of intent with their chosen teams, and coaches are permitted to publicly comment on their latest batch of fine scholar-athletes—is not only intolerable but unnecessary. For $9.95 a month, he can log on to one of the Internet sites any time of year and find out not only the names of those scholar-athletes, but also their hometowns, high school stats, heights, weights, 40 times, video clips, summer camps they've attended, assistant coaches who have recruited them, dates and destinations of campus visits, dates of the coaches' visits to their homes, and dates they've had with their girlfriend. The reader will also be one of the first to know when a certain prospect "commits" to a school, football's

---

*After all that fuss, Logan-El spent just one season at Penn State, where he never saw the field. The following spring, he announced his intent to transfer to I-AA Towson.
†In the interest of full disclosure, my employer, SI.com, has had working partnerships with both Scout.com and Rivals.com over the past few years. I have made a conscious effort in this chapter not to endorse or highlight one over the other.

equivalent to accepting a bid to a fraternity (though not much about this particular initiation rite is secret anymore).

All of this information is updated continually anytime a new development occurs in a player's recruitment ("He just got back from his Oklahoma visit!" "An LSU assistant was in his home last night!"), and promptly fed to an audience whose members often speak their own language, casually tossing around terms like "camped," "de-commit," and "soft verbal." For the person who lives, eats, sleeps, and breathes his favorite team, it's the closest thing to actually sitting in the coaches' offices while they call the kids. "You literally don't need to know anything about recruiting," said *SuperPrep* publisher Allen Wallace, one of the early pioneers of recruiting coverage, in explaining its appeal. "You can sit down and read about it, and instantaneously you can feel like you're involved in it."

But why, one might wonder, would any self-respecting adult willingly immerse himself in such a seemingly unsatisfying hobby? Seeing that only eleven players from a team can be on the field at any given moment, common sense tells us that at best roughly half the members of a given recruiting class will go on to have any sort of a meaningful career, and even then might not start a game until their third or fourth year on campus. The true recruiting junkie, however, does not let himself be affected by any such buzz-kill. Few things in life represent as much dreamy possibility to such a large number of people as that of a coveted football recruit. At the time of his choosing a fan's favorite school, there's no reason *not* to think he won't be the next big thing.

Taken together, the twenty-five or so recruits who comprise a team's signing class each February invariably represent the same thing to fans of all teams, be they from West Virginia or Wisconsin, Ohio State or Oklahoma: hope. If your team has had a couple of bad years, then by golly this is the class that will turn things around. If they haven't been able to get over the 7–4 hump lately, then this is the class that will take things to the next level. And if your team is one of those already winning championships regularly, then this is undoubtedly the greatest class yet, the one that will inevitably deliver another title 3 years from now. Having a bad day? Life got you down lately? There's no need for

Prozac when your favorite team just signed eleven four-star recruits.

Having spent quite a bit of time observing the people who observe recruiting, I've found that the only bad recruits are the ones who sign with someone else's team. Following months and months of nothing but unabashed praise, these previously coveted prospects suddenly develop a mystery weakness or character flaw the minute they decide the Iowa Hawkeyes or Georgia Bulldogs aren't for them. Take Louisiana's Joe McKnight, the nation's top-rated running back in the Class of 2007, whom home-state LSU fans turned on the moment he signed with USC. "He's a glorified thug with a head full of bull$hit," wrote one message-board poster. "I hope he gets AIDS from a transvestite out in L.A. in the middle of an earthquake." Recruiting offers fans an opportunity to stoke their competitive fires beyond just the twelve or thirteen games that make up a season. It's not simply that the highly touted linebacker decides to sign with Oklahoma that thrills the recruiting-obsessed Sooners fan—it's that the player chose the Sooners over rivals Texas and Oklahoma State. "I can't tell you why," Florida State fan and Rivals.com subscriber Eric Shane said to the *South Florida Sun-Sentinel*, "but if we win the battle and a kid picks us over Florida, it feels really good."

Information about recruiting wasn't always as easily accessible as it is today. While the ritual of college coaches wooing high school superstars is as old as the sport itself, the business of chronicling such endeavors didn't formally arise until the latter part of the twentieth century. Joe Terranova, a Ford Motor executive in Dearborn, Michigan, was widely credited as the first recruiting expert. For years, Terranova had been compiling information about the all-state high school players in each state as a personal hobby dating to the early 1970s.* Upon realizing he could use this knowledge to reasonably assess which college teams were accumulating the most talent, Terranova began writing a recruiting column for his local paper and publishing a report—priced

---

*Here's guessing his wife kept the basement tightly locked whenever they had company.

at two dollars a copy—detailing the nation's top college prospects and ranking teams' recruiting classes.

Following closely in Terranova's footsteps, Chicago native Tom Lemming began publishing *Prep Football Report* in the early 1980s. Each spring, Lemming traversed the country by car to scout, interview, and take photographs of the nation's top prospects, as did former Texas high school coach Max Emfinger for his newsletter, *National High School Recruiting Service*. Wallace, a Southern California native, joined the fray in 1985. Shelving a successful career as an attorney, Wallace started his own magazine, *SuperPrep*, which, by drawing on an extensive network of regional high school writers and college coaches, soon became viewed as the industry's bible. By the early 1990s, Wallace had added both a daily fax service and a 1-900 line for the truly obsessed.

While there was no questioning the demand for such products (several fanatics paid Wallace $250 for a lifetime subscription within the first year of *SuperPrep's* existence), they still catered mostly to a small, niche audience. At their peak, *SuperPrep* and *Prep Football Report* each garnered about 4,000 subscribers—which is only about 203,000 less than *Cat Fancy*. The majority of Wallace's exposure came from quotes and appearances in mainstream newspapers and on radio talk shows, which rarely covered recruiting much before Signing Day. College football recruiting's metamorphosis from cottage industry to a countrywide obsession came about when all that information found itself a superhighway.

"The Internet and recruiting coverage were the perfect marriage," said Jamie Newberg. In 1996, Newberg, then working as a producer for the regional television show *Countdown to Signing Day* in Atlanta, decided to start *Border Wars*, a publication covering college recruiting in the South, and launched a corresponding Web site to accompany it. BorderWars.com netted about 80,000 page views during its first year of existence. Within 4 years, it would garner 1.8 million page views on Signing Day alone. This, of course, was the heyday of the Internet boom, when fifteen-year-olds were getting stock options, startups were advertising during the Super Bowl, and every entrepreneur under the sun was trying to get a piece of the action. One such man, Seattle-based

Jim Heckman, raised more than $70 million in 1998 to launch Rivals.com, a loosely formed conglomeration of niche sports sites like Newberg's, covering nearly every team and sport imaginable. Whereas a metropolitan newspaper might provide only one or two stories a day about the local college team (and almost none at all once the season ends), sites with names like Dawgman.com (Washington), Warchant.com (Florida State), and WeAreSC.com (USC) could churn out a nonstop flurry of team-specific content—albeit amateurish and decidedly partisan—with an emphasis on insider recruiting news.

While not quite as disastrous as that sock-puppet dog, Heckman's incarnation went bankrupt by 2001, but not before revolutionizing the recruiting industry. In the era of twenty-four-hour news cycles, Rivals.com spawned tens of thousands of new-wave recruiting junkies by providing them around-the-clock updates, a searchable database of nationwide prospects, video clips, and rankings as well as message boards, where fans could interact with the network's recruiting analysts and with one another. It didn't take long for Rivals.com to resurrect itself, this time under the leadership of longtime Texas recruiting analyst Bobby Burton, and for Heckman to reenter the game with his own competitor, TheInsiders.com (since renamed Scout.com), featuring Newberg as its lead analyst. Only this time the two services wouldn't be giving away their information for free—by then, the true diehards were as hooked on the stuff as a meth addict and didn't think twice about handing over their credit card information.

Today, Rivals.com and Scout.com boast a combined 350,000 subscribers (at a rate of $9.95 per month or $99.95 a year), nearly all of whom are desperate to know whether that four-star running back from Pennsylvania has narrowed his list of potential colleges or whether or not their favorite team has "offered" that three-star receiver from California. For example, on the Tuesday afternoon in December 2005 when heralded quarterback Tim Tebow was to announce his final choice between Florida and Alabama, nearly seven thousand users logged on to the main message boards of each team's Scout.com sites, where enthusiasts received hourly updates ("His dad has arrived at the school!" "He just finished sixth period math!") leading up to the

5:00 P.M. press conference where Tebow pledged his services to the Gators. Florida fans immediately began celebrating their now-certain string of four straight national championships, while Alabama fans immediately channeled Tony Soprano, declaring of Tebow, "He's dead to me."

Whether Tebow will actually live up to the substantial expectations placed on him before he ever took a college snap is another matter altogether.* As any coach or analyst will tell you, the job of trying to predict which raw, largely undeveloped seventeen-year-olds will one day morph into Heisman winners and All-Americans and which will become benchwarmers or washouts is about as scientific an endeavor as dating. Just as the average red-blooded American male, upon meeting a gorgeous, curvy brunette who shares the same taste in movies, laughs at the same jokes, and can open a beer bottle with her teeth will invariably conclude, "She and I have a bright future together," the average college coach sees a 6-foot-3 receiver with sticky-glove hands and track-sprinter speed and thinks, "Oh yeah, this is going to be good." Just as our dreamy-eyed bachelor has no way of predicting that in three years' time his womanly gem will have packed on twenty pounds, sent him spiraling into credit card debt, and spent one too many late nights screaming over the phone at her overbearing mother, the coach has no way of knowing that his can't-miss receiver will struggle to learn the playbook, get drunk at a frat party and punch out an unsuspecting freshman, or suffer a devastating leg injury while running a basic crossing pattern in a largely meaningless game against Akron.

No matter how carefully a recruit is scrutinized, there's absolutely no way to guarantee he will successfully make the transition to college. Therefore, it's always a fun and enlightening exercise to take a look back at a list of the top-ranked recruits from four or five years earlier to see which ones panned out and which ones didn't. For instance, using

---

*Those expectations grew even larger after a freshman season in which Tebow, as the Gators' backup quarterback, saw extensive action as a runner, scoring eight touchdowns during Florida's 2006 national title season.

SuperPrep's top twenty-five prospects in the high school class of 2002 (the most recent class to have completed its college eligibility), one could divide the list into three classifications:

- The superstars: number 1 Vince Young (QB, Texas), number 2 Haloti Ngata (DE, Oregon), number 4 Marcedes Lewis (TE, UCLA), and number 16 Tamba Hali (DE, Penn State).

  All four players turned out to be college All-Americans (with Young finishing second in the 2005 Heisman voting and earning MVP honors in that year's national title game) and all were selected in the first round of the 2006 NFL draft. If every top-ranked recruit delivered this much return on their potential, I would have long ago asked one of the recruiting pundits to start handling my stock portfolio.

- The starters: number 3 Lorenzo Booker (RB, Florida State), number 6 Devin Hester (WR/CB, Miami), number 7 Mike Nixon (LB, Arizona State), number 8 Darnell Bing (S, USC), number 10 Ben Olson (QB, UCLA), number 11 Chris Davis (WR, Florida State), number 12 Reggie McNeal (QB, Texas A&M), number 13 Ahmad Brooks (LB, Virginia), number 15 Ciatrick Fason (RB, Florida), number 17 Ricardo Hurley (LB, South Carolina), number 18 Ryan Moore (WR, Miami), number 19 Pat Watkins (S, Florida State), number 21 Julian Jenkins (DE, Stanford), number 23 Isaiah Stanback (QB, Washington), and number 25 Zach Latimer (LB, Oklahoma).

  This group included several all-conference performers and mid-round NFL selections (Hester, Bing, Brooks, Fason), while all started at least one or two seasons for their teams (in Hester's case, as a return specialist). However, Booker, the top running back in the class, never rushed for 1,000 yards in a season, and McNeal didn't have nearly as much success as his cross-state rival Young. They can't all be superhuman.

- The busts: number 5 Mike D'Andrea (LB, Ohio State), number 9 Brian Pickryl (DE, Texas), number 14 Dishon Platt (WR, Florida State), number 20 Hershel Dennis (RB, USC), number

22 James Banks (QB/WR, Tennessee), and number 24 Marcus Vick (QB, Virginia Tech).

These are the ones you can't predict. Banks and Vick had one impact season each before getting booted from their respective teams for disciplinary problems, Platt never qualified academically, D'Andrea, Dennis, and Pickryl were victimized by repeated major injuries.

Interestingly, D'Andrea was in the same class as another Ohio State linebacker, A.J. Hawk, who wound up becoming a three-time All-American and top-five NFL draft pick. Hawk was rated the nation's thirtieth-best linebacker that year by Scout.com, one spot behind Texas A&M signee Nurahda Manning, who, as a senior in 2006, made a whopping twelve tackles, and one spot ahead of UCLA signee Xavier Burgess, who was booted from the team his sophomore year following a run-in with a campus parking attendant. The officer should have given Burgess a ticket for taking up parking space on the Bruins' roster.

The pattern of unpredictability continues as you comb through prospects 26 through 50. For every D'Brickashaw Ferguson (an All-American at Virginia) or Troy Williamson (a first-round receiver out of South Carolina), there's a Curtis Justus (a tight end who became Miami's long-snapper) or Aaron Kirkland (if anyone knows of the former Tennessee tight end's whereabouts, please, alert the authorities).

In truth, most recruiting followers don't spend a whole lot of time revisiting the past, or even living in the present, for that matter. Recruiting is all about getting a leg up on the future, and each year, on the first Wednesday in February, fans officially usher in that future. National Signing Day is the culmination of a year's worth of rumors, speculation, and intrigue, a day when college football fans of all allegiances can agree on at least one thing: their whacked-out priorities. In the South, where recruiting is generally followed the most intently, it is not uncommon for rabid fans to skip work, bars to open early, and the schools themselves to set up telephone hotlines for fans to find out which signatures have arrived. At Georgia, for example, hundreds of diehards crowd into Butts-Mehre Heritage Hall around 8:00 A.M. to watch a TV screen fill up with names as each fax arrives. Some of them even tailgate in the parking lot. No, that was not a joke.

For years, Signing Day didn't garner much play in the mainstream media. The local TV station might send a camera crew over to a high school to show off one of its hometown heroes signing on the dotted line. And the beat writers for a college team would likely show up at the coach's signing day press conference and rehash his glowing comments in the next day's paper. In the hierarchy of that day's news, however, Signing Day ranked somewhere between an annual charity golf tournament and an area resident bowling a 300 game. But ever since the Internet turned recruiting into its own pastime, Signing Day has become a full-fledged media event across the country. In 2006, ESPN's college sports network, ESPNU, broadcast six straight hours of live coverage, with parts of it simulcast on ESPN2 and ESPNews. USA Today devoted eight stories to the subject in the next day's paper. Rivals.com and Scout.com both boasted upwards of fifty million page views. And at my site, SI.com, Signing Day content generated almost as many eyeballs as the site's Super Bowl coverage would 4 days later.

All that interest might seem a tad puzzling considering that for about 90 percent of the nation's top prospects, Signing Day is merely a formality. By that point, most have already announced which school they'll be attending. But rarely does a Signing Day go by without at least some unforeseen drama. In 1999, heralded Charlotte quarterback C. J. Leak shocked the recruiting world by spurning Notre Dame to sign with perennial doormat Wake Forest.* In 2002, California running back Booker, regarded by some as the top prospect in the country, announced his decision to sign with Florida State instead of Notre Dame live on ESPN's prime-time *SportsCenter*. And in 2006, USC fans were left in suspense when the father of top-rated receiver Vidal Hazelton, who had verbally committed to the Trojans, refused to sign his son's letter of

---

*And after all that hoopla, Leak started one season at Wake Forest before transferring to Tennessee, where he started one game, then sat on the bench for three years.

intent, hoping the youngster would change his mind and choose closer-to-home Penn State (Hazelton eventually stuck with USC).

Also that year, Scout.com did its best reenactment of the 2000 presidential election controversy, declaring at about 6:00 P.M. EST that Florida had claimed the nation's number 1 recruiting class, only to realize about 4 hours later that it had called the race too soon when number 2 USC suddenly picked up several last-minute additions. This was no small occurrence, seeing as for most fans, these rankings are the most eagerly anticipated aspect of the entire recruiting season. Once the official signatures are in and each team's class is complete, the recruiting pundits attempt to figure out whether one team's collection of raw, largely unproven prospects is more or less impressive than another's. After all, where's the fun in following a competition where you don't find out who won until four or five years down the road? Recruiting junkies demand an instant measuring stick, and the various pundits deliver them. Scout.com and Rivals.com have even devised automated computer rankings that update daily throughout the season as each new commitment pours in.

But what does it really mean to net the number 3 class in the country versus, say, the number 8 or the number 18? "The difference between the number 1 class and the number 20 class," said Wallace, "is probably two or three players. Any school that recruits a top-20 class every year has enough talent to win the national championship." Cynics love to say that the annual recruiting racket is a bunch of bunk and that the rankings are meaningless, but they're actually a better indicator of future success than one might think. If you calculate the average *SuperPrep* ranking of the five recruiting classes that comprised each of the past 15 national champions' rosters, you'll find that all but one (Oklahoma in 2000) averaged a top-20 ranking. Nine of the fifteen garnered an average in the top 10, including five of the past six (2002 Ohio State, 2003 and 2004 USC, 2005 Texas, and 2006 Florida) national champions.

Of course, there were presumably countless other teams over the same time period that fared even better in the rankings yet did not capture any national titles. Heck, in 2005, Tennessee scored the number 1 class in the country according to most services, only to put up its worst record in seventeen years (5–6) the following fall. And there have been plenty of other teams that far exceeded the success one might have expected based solely on their recruiting rankings. For example, Kansas State posted six 11-win seasons in seven years under former coach Bill Snyder despite rarely registering a peep on the recruiting scene. Virginia Tech reached the 1999 national championship game without ever posting a top-30 class. And only a handful of players on Boise State's undefeated, 2006 Fiesta Bowl team even registered on the recruiting sites' radars. In some cases, the analysts severely misjudged the talents of a particular class's signees. In others, the talent was there but the coaches didn't properly develop it.

There are some flaws in the rankings, however, that seem to repeat themselves nearly every year. Having covered the past nine Signing Days for SI.com, I've noticed the following four patterns when it comes to recruiting rankings:

1. *Major program favoritism.* If on-field performance mirrored the recruiting rankings, Florida State, Florida, Michigan, and Ohio State would field a top-10 team every season. The annual recruiting top-10 lists are almost exclusively the domain of the game's most storied programs, which makes sense, seeing as one of the main benefits of being a Michigan or Florida State is that you're able to attract top-level prospects. Strangely, however, teams like Iowa, Cal, and Auburn have been appearing in the AP top 10 just as frequently during the past few years despite rarely getting the same kind of props from the recruiting guys. Maybe they send out prettier brochures.

   The popular theory is that the coaches at the less heralded programs simply do a better job evaluating and developing talent than their more celebrated colleagues, in large part because they have no other choice. There's certainly some truth to that, but might it also be possible that the recruiting pundits aren't taking these programs' recruiting targets seriously enough to begin with? For instance, say you're a recruiting analyst, and say the

Florida receivers coach tells you that the Gators are going after receivers X, Y, and Z. Seeing that Florida pretty much has its pick of the litter when it comes to receivers, you might reasonably conclude that the Gators' staff feels that X, Y, and Z are among the very best in the country and therefore your own rankings should probably reflect that. So you rank all three among the top 10 in the country, and come February, when the Gators wind up landing two of the three, it reflects well on their overall signing class. In the meantime, however, Rutgers may have found a stud receiver of its own, receiver W, who's just as good as X, Y, and Z. But because he wasn't on Florida's board, he isn't taken as seriously, and, in turn, Rutgers' class doesn't get the same kind of boost. Not that Rutgers fans are going to lose any sleep over it.

2. *If you sign a QB, they will come.* In a world based entirely on potential, no individual embodies the promise of greatness more than the classic golden-boy quarterback. Depending on the school he signs with, an elite quarterback prospect often takes on a saviorlike status, boosting the expectations surrounding himself and his fellow signees to astronomical proportions. *SuperPrep's* Wallace readily admits that the presence of at least one elite QB greatly boosts his opinion of a team's signing class, a dangerous yet largely unavoidable flaw considering that many times the game's very best quarterbacks (Ben Roethlisberger, Alex Smith, and Aaron Rodgers, to name a few) weren't regarded that highly coming out of high school. The fact is, QB prospects are by far the hardest to project, because so many different variables enter into his chances of success. Will he be able to master a more complicated playbook? Will he adjust to reading faster, more athletic college defenses? Will the coach call the right plays to best utilize his skills? Will his offensive line protect him? Will he start spending too much time with his groupies?

It's no coincidence that nearly all of the most memorable recruiting flops over the past decade have involved these supposed savior quarterbacks. Names like Ron Powlus (Notre

Dame), Dan Kendra (Florida State), Brock Berlin (Florida and Miami), Josh Booty (LSU), and Chris Simms (Texas) are known to most college football followers not for what they achieved on the field but for the things they didn't—mainly, win a national championship. Powlus, whom longtime ESPN pundit Beano Cook famously predicted would win multiple Heisman trophies, finished his career as the school's all-time passing leader but amassed a very un-Notre Dame–like 29–16 record as the Irish starter. Berlin, the centerpiece of Steve Spurrier's lone number 1-ranked class in 2000, failed to win the Gators' starting job and wound up transferring to Miami, where he had two undistinguished seasons. Simms, the son of former NFL star Phil Simms, whose signing helped then second-year Texas coach Mack Brown land the nation's top recruiting class in 1999, went 26–6, but is remembered primarily for his interception-tinged meltdowns in the Longhorns' three consecutive losses to archrival Oklahoma and in the 2001 Big 12 championship game against Colorado. Basically, if you're a highly touted quarterback in a top-ranked class, there's no such thing as middle ground. Either you're going to get a street named after you like Peyton Manning, or you're going to get flicked off by a passing driver while walking down someone else's street.

3. *The bigger, the better.* Division I-A football teams are allowed to award up to twenty-five scholarships for each entering class, and some sign even more than that with the intention of delaying a few players' enrollment until the spring, or under the assumption that a few won't qualify academically. However, teams are also restricted to a maximum of eighty-five total scholarships at any given time. So, depending on how many returning upperclassmen a team has, there may be far fewer than twenty-five scholarships available for its recruiting class in any given year. Without question, the recruiting rankings tend to favor those teams that sign larger classes, particularly the computer-driven formulas used by Rivals.com and Scout.com. In some cases, this might not

do justice to a team that only signed, say, sixteen players, but landed a higher percentage of elite-level prospects, or did a better job than most at filling its most pressing needs.

For example, Penn State's 2005 recruiting class included one of the nation's top receivers, Derrick Williams, and a boatload of other skill players—receiver Jordan Norwood, cornerbacks Justin King and Devin Fentress, running back Lydell Sargeant—who all gave the Nittany Lions a much-needed infusion of speed and significantly impacted a 2005 team that finished 11–1 and third in the country. But because the class consisted of just nineteen players, Penn State registered just twenty-fifth in that year's Rivals.com rankings and twenty-eighth on Scout.com. Joe Paterno would undoubtedly have been miffed if he actually knew how to log on to one of those sites.

4. *The second-year boost.* Tell me if you've heard this story before: Proud program fallen on hard times goes out and hires a big-name new coach. The coach immediately pledges to pound the pavement and find some talented young players willing to "jump on board" and "get this thing back on the right track." Seeing that he's been hired just a month or so before Signing Day, he and the staff chalk up that year's class as a lost cause and instead focus on getting a head start on the following year, inviting the nation's top juniors to come in for a visit in the spring. By summer, one blue-chipper after another is committing, each one speaking more giddily than the last about how he can't wait to be part of the class that brings pride and glory back to ol' State U.

Over the years, I've watched this movie play out almost as many times as I have *Anchorman*. Nearly every year, the so-called hot recruiting schools are the ones directed by freshly hired coaches, because let's face it, the excitement surrounding a program is rarely higher than when the coach is 0–0. Texas's Brown (1999), LSU's Nick Saban (2001), Georgia's Mark Richt (2001), Ohio State's Jim Tressel (2002), USC's Pete Carroll (2002), Virginia's Al Groh (2002), Florida's Ron Zook (2003), Nebraska's

Bill Callahan (2005), Notre Dame's Charlie Weis (2006), and Florida's Urban Meyer (2006) all "took the recruiting world by storm" with their second signing classes (their first following a full recruiting calendar). It's become so cliché that on the days they were hired in December 2004, I was able to successfully predict that Weis and Meyer would land top-five classes 14 months later (on Scout.com, Florida finished number 2, Notre Dame number 5). This was months before even a single player had committed.

Speaking of which, according to Miriam-Webster's online dictionary, one of the definitions of the verb "commit"—presumably the one that was intended by whoever started using the term for recruiting purposes—is "to obligate or pledge oneself." However, the verbal commitments many recruits make to coaches and programs in the months leading up to Signing Day don't seem to carry nearly the same sense of obligation as, say, a military commitment or lavaliering your girlfriend. Increasingly, many of the biggest stories on the recruiting scene each year involve a player "de-committing" from one school to sign with another. This practice causes no shortage of headaches for coaches, who not only lose out on that player but also don't get a chance to find a replacement at his position, seeing as most of the top candidates will have found another school by then. Of course, chances are that many of these same coaches have been busily wooing other schools' committed recruits at the same time.

No one demonstrated the commit/de-commit trend more vividly in recent years than Ryan Perriloux, one of the two highest-rated quarterbacks in the high school class of 2005. The summer before his senior year of high school, the Louisiana native announced his commitment to Texas. In the months that followed, Perrilloux—clearly enjoying the attention of being a highly sought-after recruit—continued to insist he was committed to the Longhorns, while at the same time entertaining other suitors like LSU, Mississippi State, and Miami. At that January's U.S. Army All-America game in San Antonio, Perrilloux toyed with local Longhorns fans, at one point donning a cowboy hat while flashing the "Hook 'em 'Horns sign." But then at other points in the week he would tell reporters things like, "Anyone who wants to make an offer, I'm listening."

In the end, Perrilloux ended up signing with his home-state school, LSU. In explaining his decision, the unabashedly cocky quarterback said he didn't want to "sit on the bench for two years" behind Texas star Vince Young. Instead, he opted for Baton Rouge, where, he said, "I can come in and play next year. JaMarcus [Russell] struggled last year, and Matt Flynn is definitely not a better quarterback than me." Two years later, Russell was on the verge of becoming a number one NFL draft pick, Flynn had earned MVP honors in the 2005 Peach Bowl, and Perrilloux had yet to see the field.* Meanwhile, Young turned pro a year early, leaving the Horns with two unproven freshman quarterbacks, neither of whom was rated as highly as Perrilloux. Humble pie can be so darn inconvenient sometimes.

Amidst the backdrop of today's recruiting circus, the idea that a seventeen-year-old kid would have the seeming audacity to manipulate millionaire coaches and legions of college fans shouldn't be considered altogether surprising. You, too, might develop a slightly overinflated ego after being swooned over for twelve months by pretty much anyone with whom you come into contact. It's one thing to get the *Johnny Be Good*† treatment when a particularly sought-after prospect visits a campus. The keggers, the lobster dinners, the pretty recruiting "hostesses"—that stuff has been going on for as long as recruiting itself, and for the most part is contained to a single weekend. These days, however, recruits are subjected to an entire year of daily adulation in the form of Internet recruiting "reporters."

---

*Perrilloux did see significant TV time during the 2006 season: Eevery time the camera panned to LSU's sideline, there was Perrilloux, wearing a baseball cap and signaling in the plays.
†If you never saw it, *Johnny Be Good* was a hilarious 1980s high school movie starring Anthony Michael Hall as a hotshot quarterback recruit who has college recruiters camping out in his front lawn and engaging in every unethical recruiting tactic imaginable.

As mentioned previously, the advent of the Internet has spawned an endless array of recruiting-oriented Web sites that feed off fans' insatiable appetite for recruiting updates. In most cases, the primary source of these updates is telephone "interviews" with the prospects, conducted not only by reputable national writers like Scout.com's Newberg or Rivals.com's Mike Farrell, but also by representatives from the hundreds of regional and team-oriented fan sites that exist within those companies' networks or that operate independently. While the NCAA has specific rules regulating the dates and frequency with which college coaches can contact recruits, there's no such oversight for recruiting Web sites. Writers for those sites can dial up the nation's top prospects as often as they do their closest buddies, and in some cases are deluded enough to think the recruits *are* their buddies. Depending on how highly they're regarded, recruits have reported receiving as many as ten to twenty calls a night from these reporters in the weeks leading up to Signing Day. "We kind of created a monster," said Newberg. "We're calling these kids way too damn much."

The most alarming aspect of the Internet recruiting business is that many of these so-called reporters often cross the ethical line from observer to participant. Very few of the writers who cover recruiting for fan sites have any prior journalism experience. In many cases, their biggest job qualification is their allegiance to the team their site covers. While both Scout.com and Rivals.com lay out ethical guidelines for their network of publishers to follow, it's impossible for their editors to constantly police the hundreds of sites within their networks. In 2004, the University of Kentucky banned one such fan-site publisher from buying season tickets for twenty-seven years after it was revealed that he was using his role as interviewer to put a sell job on potential Wildcats recruits.

While few such extreme cases have been documented, it is not at all uncommon for writers to either frame their questions in a way that will elicit positive responses about a certain team, offer up suggestive information, or criticize one of the other schools recruiting the player. And in many cases the writers don't even realize they're doing anything wrong. As fans of a particular team—ones who happen to be writing to an audience of like-minded people—they're simply incapable of approaching the subject matter from a detached perspective. "Interestingly, the Internet has proven there's a very large market for the acceptance of hugely biased work," said Wallace. "Most of the fan sites that make up these networks are not interested in the truth—their readers just want to hear the good stuff." Take, for example, this January 2007 "report" on GatorCountry.com by a writer named Bob Redman regarding a surprise visit to Florida by highly ranked defensive end and standing USC commit Everson Griffin. The opening sentence: "It looks like one of the benefits of winning a decisive National Championship game is the attention on the Florida Gators now shines like a beacon to top prospects that were not otherwise considering them." Redman conducted an interview with Griffin, who spoke highly of the coaches and players who hosted him. Wrote Redman: "Like in most reports, it seems the people on the campus and on the team are what make the University of Florida a good place to be to top recruits." Florida's PR department immediately called Redman about a potential job opening.

In a 2005 *ESPN the Magazine* article, top-rated high school safety Myron Rolle, a 4.0 student and class president at New Jersey's prestigious Hun School, spilled the dirt on this not-so-secret side of the recruiting biz. He talked about a writer for Oklahoma's Scout.com site trying to trick him into praising OU's academics in comparison to one of his other suitors, Michigan. "He kept saying, 'There's no difference academically, right?'" said Rolle. Meanwhile, when Rolle's brother, McKinley, who had been filtering Myron's interview requests, failed to return a call from Michigan's Rivals.com site, he received an e-mail from the writer saying, "I just feel hurt. I thought we were friends."

These sort of conflict-of-interest tales aren't limited just to the Internet guys, either. Rolle's strongest comments in the story were directed at Lemming, one of the early recruiting pioneers, who has been accused for years of trying to steer recruits to his favorite team, Notre Dame. "He kept saying to me, 'You know they have a great coaching staff. You know Charlie Weis is Mr. NFL. You're an academic guy. That place is for you.' Then he killed Florida State. He said, 'You're stupid if you go there.'"

Rolle, who wound up signing with FSU anyway, raised similar accusations against Lemming at a reform summit for college athletics the following January, saying Lemming promised to showcase him in the U.S. Army All-America game (for which Lemming chooses the participants) if he "kept a certain school on his list." Lemming vehemently denied Rolle's claims, but they echo others made against the guru by Booker, the former Florida State running back, who also chose the 'Noles over the Irish, and former Colorado coach Gary Barnett, who accused Lemming of trying to steer recruits to his old Chicago buddy Bill Callahan after the coach took over at Nebraska in 2004.*

When asked about the current state of recruiting, Penn State coach Joe Paterno made a couple of thinly veiled references to Lemming when he said, "One of the coaches [in the Big Ten] complained that some kids were supposed to visit his school but canceled because one of these recruiting gurus told them they needed to be at another campus that weekend so he could take their picture for his magazine. We have recruiting guys say to a kid, 'Don't commit yet, I want you to announce it at my all-star game.'"

With all the attention heaped on elite recruits, it's easy to see why some come to believe that their college decisions are a matter of public interest on a par with the State of the Union address. As a result, when recruits finally are ready to announce their decisions, they often feel the need to do so in the most overblown fashion possible. It's no longer enough to simply tell someone where you're going and let the word get out. There has to be a press conference, usually at the prospect's high school, but often somewhere more glamorous than that. If you can get a television network to air the proceedings, even better. It's also become increasingly fashionable for many of the participants in the annual U.S. Army All-America game in San Antonio to announce their choice live on the sideline during NBC's game broadcast, often pulling the worn-out baseball-hat act while doing so. This

---

*It just so happened that Lemming was the only analyst to rank the 'Huskers' 2005 signing class number 1 in the country; no other prominent pundit had them higher than fifth.

prestigious national high school all-star game sprouted up almost overnight in 2001, and disclosing one's college commitment there became the hip thing to do after star quarterback Chris Leak announced his pledge to Florida during the 2003 game. I have covered two of these games, and while it's a great promotional tool for the Army, the extent to which these high school kids are coddled during the week leading up to the game—there is a dinner and a parade down the River Walk in their honor, among other things—is mind-boggling. It is also easier to get an interview with the Heisman Trophy winner on the field after his bowl game than it is to get access to the recruits there. In essence, the game itself has become a microcosm of the direction recruiting as a whole has taken—extravagant and ego-inflating.

In April 2006, Jimmy Clausen, a California quarterback phenom who had been drawing comparisons to John Elway since before he could drive, managed to trump all previous comers in the area of commitment announcements. His father hired a Los Angeles PR firm to organize a press conference at the College Football Hall of Fame in South Bend, Indiana, where Clausen announced his commitment to Notre Dame the morning of the Fighting Irish's spring game. Clausen, not yet a senior in high school at the time, showed up for the event in a white stretch Hummer complete with police escort. "[Clausen] is not a showboat," the player's PR guy, Jeff Freedman, insisted to CBS SportsLine.com. Of course not—he presumably passed on the chance to don a Notre Dame jersey made of solid gold.

Maryland coach Friedgen, whose return to the college game in 1997 following a five-year stint with the NFL's San Diego Chargers coincided with the birth of the Internet sites, said the impact they've had on recruiting is unmistakable. "I see these recruiting rankings, and some of these guys, you're like, Huh? I've watched the tape," he said. "But now all your fans want to know why you're not going after the guy just because some Internet site has them ranked." Coaches also bemoan the preponderance of incorrect or misleading information on the sites that the recruits themselves then read, making the coaches' jobs that much more difficult. "About 40 percent of it you can't believe," Arizona recruiting coordinator Dan Berezowitz told the *Tucson Citizen*.

For all the complaints raised by coaches about the recruiting services, however, the reality is that they themselves are among the sites' most loyal customers. Nearly every coaching staff in the country has at least one subscription to either or both Rivals.com and Scout.com. In fact, I've been in coaches' offices when they were perusing the sites, using them to keep up on the latest recruiting developments in much the same way a Tennessee or UCLA fan would while procrastinating at work. For them, however, the information is a little more relevant. "You can learn a lot from the Internet," said Berezowitz. "What a kid says he likes and doesn't like on one visit, we can use [on ours]." Even the age-old line that coaches don't pay any attention to the recruiting rankings is beginning to ring hollow. At his Signing Day press conference in 2006, Florida coach Meyer said, "I hate to [admit] this, but I actually hit Rivals.com a little bit ago and saw where we were ranked. The competitive part of me wants to see where we end up." That same year, Dexter Hazelton, the aforementioned father who initially refused to sign son Vidal's letter of intent to USC, complained to Scout.com about "getting calls from coach Carroll telling me that he's worried about his rankings."

And that, my friends, says everything you need to know about the ever-growing influence of Internet recruiting services on the landscape of college football. No longer is it just for the most obsessed, hard-core fans or merely a niche group of people in desperate need of a hobby. Even Meyer and Carroll, two wildly respected coaches who between them make more than $5 million a year and are as qualified to evaluate future potential as nearly anyone else in the business, occasionally seek validation from the panel of self made experts who decree who's number 1 and who's number 10. Today, you no longer need to spend decades toiling as an assistant coach, or get rich enough to be one of the program's most valued boosters, to feel like an insider. These days, all you need is an Internet connection and a credit card.

7

How Boston College and Clemson Became Neighbors

I think this might be a move that's going to trigger changes to the face of college athletics.

—*Penn State athletic director Jim Tarman announcing the school's decision to join the Big Ten, June 1990*

This will be the most disastrous blow to intercollegiate athletics in my lifetime.

—*Big East commissioner Mike Tranghese on the ACC's decision to raid three teams from his conference, May 2003*

T he following is a reenactment of a conversation believed to have taken place inside the office of Virginia govenor Mark R. Warner sometime in the spring of 2003:

ADVISER A: Govenor Warner, sir, we've just gotten our latest surveillance report on the ACC. I'm afraid the situation is worse than we imagined.

GOVENOR WARNER: Worse? How?

ADVISER A: Sir . . . I'm afraid they've annexed Miami.

GOVENOR WARNER: Great Scott! Miami?? Have you any idea what this means? My god, they'll wipe the Big East right off the map!

ADVISER B: I'm afraid there's more, sir. They've cut off all talks with Virginia Tech.

GOVENOR WARNER: That can't be! The Hokies are our constituents, too, you know. Can you imagine what will happen if they get stranded in a post–Miami Big East?? They'll never make it back to the BCS!

ADVISER A: What do you suggest we do, sir?

GOVENOR WARNER: There's only one thing we can do. Get President Casteen on the phone!

ADVISER A: John Casteen? The president of UVA? With all due respect, sir, you can't possibly be serious.

GOVENOR WARNER: I'm dead serious. Get him on . . . now!

ADVISER B: Whatever you say, sir.

(Adviser B places the call)

PRESIDENT CASTEEN: Governor? To what do I owe the pleasure?

GOVENOR WARNER: John, I need you to do me a favor on behalf of our great commonwealth. I understand your conference will be holding an expansion vote soon?

PRESIDENT CASTEEN: You betcha. There's going to be a Hurricane sweeping through the ACC. Do you know how much TV money we're going to get? I already went out and bought new ties.

GOVENOR WARNER: John, listen to me carefully. I need you to block the vote until they agree to let in Tech, too.

PRESIDENT CASTEEN: (Sound of cackling laughter audible for several seconds.) That's a good one, Governor. You think those country-club fuddy-duddies from Duke and Carolina are going to agree to be in the same conference with a school from Blacksburg? You crack me up, governor.

GOVENOR WARNER: Oh it's going to happen, John. And you're the one that's going to make it happen.

PRESIDENT CASTEEN: But Mark . . . they're our archrivals! I'm supposed to hate those guys, not help them!

GOVENOR WARNER: Well, maybe this will you help you get over your hatred. Remember that budget hike you asked for to pay for that new computer lab?

PRESIDENT CASTEEN: Oh no . . . you wouldn't.

GOVENOR WARNER: I heard it's about to stall on the House floor.

PRESIDENT CASTEEN: (Sighs, then is silent for a moment.) You'll have your vote.

GOVENOR WARNER: Excellent! Adviser A—bring me my cigars!

ADVISER A: Coming, sir.

For nearly as long as college football has been played, teams have been dividing themselves into geographical alliances known as conferences. As far back as the late nineteenth century, Midwestern schools like Illinois, Michigan, and Minnesota were joining together to form what would later be known as the Big Ten; Southern schools like

Auburn, Alabama, and Vanderbilt were hammering out the first incarnation of the Southeastern Conference; the likes of Texas, Texas A&M, and Arkansas were constructing the Southwest Conference; and West Coast schools California, Oregon, and Washington were forming the precursor to today's Pac-10. These conference alliances would soon become entrenched in the fabric of college football, helping shape the familiar rivalries and championship races generations of fans set their calendars by each fall. The entire economic infrastructure of Ames, Iowa, was built around Nebraska fans caravanning into town every other year.

But if a college football fan from as recently as, say, 1985 could borrow Marty McFly's DeLorean to transport himself to the present day, he would find the sport's current conference landscape about as familiar to him as a Starbucks Venti Mocha Lite. He'd be more than a little surprised to learn that the Big Ten now has eleven teams; that the Big 8 is now the Big 12; that Texas Christian plays in the same conference as Brigham Young; that Louisville and Cincinnati are considered part of the (Big) East; that Louisiana Tech is considered part of the West(ern Athletic Conference); and that the ACC now cares as much about football as basketball. And if our time traveler was to stop and ask someone how this all came to be—why it is that sixty-one major college teams have joined or changed conferences (some more than once) over the past twenty years—he would be handed the one explanation that a person from any era would understand: a dollar bill.

University presidents, athletic directors, and football coaches offer a variety of explanations when their school chooses to align itself with a new set of conference partners. Reasons include everything from shared academic ideals to cultural commonalities, travel budgets to competitive spirit. It's all pretty much baloney. College football's mass conference realignment over the past two decades has been almost entirely Darwinian in nature, each program looking to assure its own survival in a rapidly changing environment, sometimes going so far as to invoke the help of state governors and other politicians. All parties are chasing the same interest: money. And in the modern sports landscape, there's no more important revenue stream than that of television.

The event that opened the floodgates to the age of conference musical chairs took place not on a football field or even on a college campus, but rather in the hallowed halls of the United States Supreme Court. In 1984, the highest court in the land, the same judicial body that has ruled on such important societal matters as civil rights, gun laws, and national security, was asked to settle a dispute involving televised football games. When television first became popular in the 1950s, the NCAA placed tight restrictions on its network football packages, stemming from its mistaken belief that airing too many games would have an adverse effect on ticket sales.* For decades, teams were limited to a certain amount of television appearances per season, networks were required to show teams from all levels and regions, and rights fees were distributed in a largely egalitarian fashion. For example, on September 26, 1981, ABC aired a much-anticipated game between number 1 USC and number 2 Oklahoma to most of the country. Viewers in certain parts of the South, however, were treated to a different showdown between the Citadel and Appalachian State—with all four schools receiving the same $200,000 appearance fee. Even some of the Citadel and Appalachian State fans were ticked. For comparison's sake, picture the Screen Actors Guild telling NBC in the early 1990s that it could only broadcast *Seinfeld* the same number of times per season as *Blossom*, and to top it off they had to pay both casts the same salary. There'd be a whole bunch of thirty-somethings walking around today quoting the character Six instead of the Soup Nazi—which would just be plain wrong.

Feeling they were being deprived of the opportunity to receive their true market value, administrators at reigning powerhouses Oklahoma and Georgia in 1982 filed an antitrust suit against the NCAA, which the Supreme Court upheld by a 7–2 vote two years later. Suddenly the NCAA was powerless to stop the nation's college football-playing

---

*Interestingly, it was by taking the exact opposite approach and showing all its games on television, albeit with blackout restrictions, that the NFL was able to eventually surpass the longer-standing collegiate brand of football in national popularity.

schools from negotiating their own TV deals. Apparently feeling some separation anxiety, however, sixty-one major conference teams (excluding the Big Ten and Pac-10) and high-profile independents joined together to form a collective negotiating body called the College Football Association. It was a mostly harmonious operation until 1990, when all hell broke loose. That's when Notre Dame, ever the contrarian, made the stunning decision to break off on its own, signing an exclusive five-year, $30 million deal with NBC to televise all Irish home games just days after ABC had agreed to a five-year million extension with the CFA. The reaction? "I wasn't surprised by this," Georgia athletic director Vince Dooley told *Sports Illustrated.* "I was shocked." Across the sport, administrators like Dooley chided the Irish's supposed greediness, knowing full well that every last one of them would have done the exact same thing if afforded the opportunity. With Notre Dame out of the mix, observers knew it would be only a matter of time before there were other defectors, and that networks would soon be negotiating with individual conferences rather than one big conglomeration. Suddenly the race was on among conferences to assemble the most attractive lineups for prospective television suitors.

Penn State, the Northeast's lone remaining independent power and one of the most dominant teams of the era under longtime coach Joe Paterno, was the first domino to fall. Having attempted unsuccessfully for years to form a coalition with other Eastern schools like Syracuse, Pittsburgh, and Rutgers, the Nittany Lions became the first new team to join the Big Ten since Michigan State in 1950. The decision was couched largely as a marriage of academic convenience, with the invitation coming from the conference members' presidents* rather than its athletic directors. "Not one athletic director was consulted on this matter," then Wolverines athletic director Bo Schembechler groused to *Sports Illustrated.* "How can they do that?" Not yet grasping the bigger picture that would soon envelop the sport, officials both within the conference and around the country expressed bewilderment as to why

---

*The leaders of Michigan, Michigan State, and Indiana voted against the move.

the Big Ten would want to add a school so geographically isolated from its other members.*

Behind the scenes, however, there were two particularly visionary men spearheading the whole thing: Paterno and newly appointed Big Ten commissioner Jim Delany. A shrewd, power-hungry executive, Delany was the first of his colleagues to view the collegiate sports landscape first and foremost as a television entity, often referring to his league's members as "inventory." He therefore coveted the Nittany Lions because of their reach into the major New York, Philadelphia, and Pittsburgh television markets, along with the league's existing footholds in such metropolitan areas as Detroit, Minneapolis, Milwaukee, and Cleveland. Delany would now be able to sit across the negotiating table from an ABC or ESPN and offer up more potential eyeballs than any other conference. Meanwhile, Paterno, a man who had witnessed the transformation of college football into big business firsthand over a nearly forty-year career, could see the next train leaving the station and wanted to be absolutely sure he was on board. "I've been concerned about two or three schools getting together and doing something like Notre Dame did," Paterno said at the time. ". . . We were afraid we might be left out of some arrangements that would be put together by other people."

Paterno's foresight would prove correct. Within a year of Penn State's move, independent power Florida State joined the ACC, the SEC added Arkansas and South Carolina, and the Big East launched a new football conference with previously independent Miami as its centerpiece. By 1994, when the Big 8 had morphed into the Big 12, annexing longtime Southwest Conference schools Texas, Texas A&M, Texas Tech, and Baylor, and the SEC had rendered the CFA extinct by brokering its own deal with CBS, the age of autonomy in college football was officially dead. "There's no question in my mind that independents have become an endangered species," Fred Gruninger,

---

*If you've ever flown on a Pittsburgh-to-State College puddle jumper, you'd wonder the same thing.

Rutgers' athletic director, said at the time. With the exception of Notre Dame, no one school could garner the same kind of television revenue as it could by sharing in the riches of a beefed-up superconference like the revamped ACC, Big Ten, SEC, and Big 12.

The impact for those involved was immediate and enormous. In 1994, the penultimate season for the CFA, ACC teams shared about $13 million in football television revenue. Starting in 1996, the league was able to cut its own deals with ABC, ESPN, and regional distributor Raycom worth more than $17 million annually. Clearly, there was no shortage of viewers eager to spend their Saturdays watching Florida State beat up on Duke and Wake Forest. Other leagues got even richer: the SEC's deal with CBS netted $85 million over five years, while the newly formed Big 12 secured $100 million through ABC and Liberty Sports. By now the beneficiaries had to be thinking: Why didn't we sue the NCAA sooner?*

Interestingly, this new era of college football was instigated not by the obvious parties, like coaches, athletic directors, and conference commissioners, but by a wide range of movers and shakers who, on the surface at least, would seem to have little connection to athletics. Their involvement shows how the impact of conference realignment decisions are felt far beyond the realm of just sports, by such "real-world" sectors as business and politics. According to a 1990 *Orlando Sentinel* article, the impetus for expansion first hit former SEC commissioner Harvey Schiller while trying to sell corporate sponsorship to a Florida-based retail drug chain. "They were interested but reasoned that creating a tie-in with the SEC to gain Florida Gators fans might be a turnoff to Florida State and Miami fans," said Schiller. "A light went on. I thought, 'Well, there's certainly a way to fix that.'" Under the direction of Schiller's successor, Roy Kramer, the conference had no trouble landing Arkansas as its

---

*Actually, it couldn't have happened that much sooner. The NCAA is somehow considered a nonprofit organization, and prior to a 1975 Supreme Court case, nonprofits were not subject to antitrust laws.

eleventh member,* but struck out in its attempt to land Florida State. Seminoles coach Bobby Bowden, who by then was on the cusp of building an annual national championship contender, opted for the less rigorous competition of the ACC, a decision that paid off handsomely. FSU spent most of its first decade in the conference treating the other league members the same way the Harlem Globetrotters do the Washington Generals. The SEC plucked South Carolina instead.

The birth of the Big 12 was a tad more complex, seeing as it basically involved killing off the eighty-year-old Southwest Conference. By the late 1980s, the regal days of the Sammy Baugh–Davey O'Brien SWC had long since been supplanted by a far less endearing era of cheating (seven of the league's nine schools were placed on probation, including SMU, which received the NCAA's first and only "death penalty"), poor attendance, and national irrelevance. Representatives from nearly every school had been bickering with one another for years. By the time Notre Dame deserted the CFA and Penn State joined the Big Ten, the writing was on the wall for the antiquated conference. "[The SWC] didn't have enough TV sets," former commissioner Steve Hatchell told the *Express-News*. ". . . The economics of TV is leverage—it wasn't going to work." Arkansas was the first to officially jump ship, but Texas and Texas A&M had been putting out feelers for years, and at one point in late 1993 it appeared that Texas and the Big 8's Colorado would jump to the Pac-10, Texas A&M to the SEC. Eventually the two Texas schools set their sights on the Big 8 instead. Under Hatchell's direction, ongoing discussions had been held about potentially merging the Big 8 with the entire remaining SWC, but truth be told, the Nebraskas and Oklahomas had little interest in anyone besides the two Texas heavyweights. Suddenly the scramble was on among Texas's remaining SWC schools (Texas Tech, Baylor, Rice, Houston, TCU, and SMU) not to get left in the dust. The ones who would succeed had friends in high places.

---

*According to the *San Antonio Express-News*, Arkansas athletic director Frank Broyles had told Schiller during a round of golf in 1987, "If you ever want to expand, just ask us."

On February 12, 1994, the SEC announced it was breaking away from the CFA to sign with CBS, sending the nation's other conferences on a mad dash for television cash, and Texas and Texas A&M, faced with an imminent decision over their futures, were dragged into the center of a nasty political firestorm. From what I've been told over the years by sources with firsthand knowledge, the late Texas governor Ann Richards, a Baylor grad, made it her personal mission to ensure that the two Texas heavyweights did not leave her alma mater out to dry. As detailed by the *Express-News* ten years later, when word spread around the Texas state capital in Austin of Texas' imminent departure that February, Lieutenant Governor Bob Bullock, himself a Baylor graduate, summoned Texas chancellor William Cunningham, A&M interim president Dean Gage, and A&M chancellor William Mobley to an emergency President's Day meeting. State Senate Finance Committee member David Sibley, a Baylor grad, and State Senate President Pro Tempore John Montford, a Texas Tech grad, also attended. Sibley threatened major cuts to UT's funding if the Red Raiders weren't included. Bullock promised to deliver the necessary votes from a higher education committee to seal funding for A&M's new basketball arena if his beloved Bears could be part of the new conference. Wouldn't you know it, four days later—and just twelve days after the SEC's defection from the CFA—UT, A&M, Texas Tech, and Baylor were officially invited to join the Big 8. "Candidly, if not for the [political] influence, it'd be the Big 10—that's taken, so some other name," said former Tech AD Bob Bockrath. "I don't think Texas and A&M saw Tech and Baylor as equal partners."

Not that it was the worst thing in the world for the former Big 8 to suddenly find itself with twelve teams. Only a couple of years earlier, SEC commissioner Kramer had taken advantage of an obscure NCAA bylaw to create a fantastic new revenue stream for his own twelve-team conference. In 1987, the Pennsylvania State Athletic Conference, a fourteen-team Division II league and home to such juggernauts as Slippery Rock and Shippensburg, petitioned the NCAA for permission to hold an end-of-season championship game without it counting against its teams' regular season schedules. The organization agreed, stipulating that any conference with at least twelve teams and two divisions could hold one such extra game. The PSAC never did get around to implementing such a game, but Kramer did. Upon the arrival of Arkansas and South Carolina in 1992, he divided the SEC into East and West divisions and staged Division I-A's first conference title game that same year at Birmingham's Legion Field. By 1994, the game had moved to Atlanta's brand-new 71,000-seat Georgia Dome, where it has sold out every season and now generates more than $12 million annually. Upon its inception in 1996, the Big 12 created its own title game, which has rotated among several Midwestern cities. There's no truth to the rumor that PSAC officials were given lifetime tickets to both.

It was Kramer's brainchild that loomed large in the minds of ACC presidents and athletic directors when, in the spring of 2003, the conference set in motion a dizzying, often stupefying chain of events that would once again rock the collegiate sports landscape. Those of us who cover college football for a living were looking forward to a nice, uneventful off-season before Big East commissioner Mike Tranghese lobbed the first grenade in what would soon become an all-out feud, tipping off the *New York Daily News* that the nine-team ACC was secretly wooing Big East members Miami, Syracuse, and Boston College in an attempt to stage its own championship game. "I have no use for the ACC right now," said Tranghese. "They're a bunch of hypocrites." Clearly, it was going to be a long summer.

The rhetoric would only grow louder in the weeks that followed as it became clear that the ACC, despite its initial denials, was proceeding exactly as Tranghese described. By mid-May, conference presidents had voted 7–2 to begin expansion proceedings and quickly sent delegations to visit each campus. The remaining Big East schools (Pittsburgh, Rutgers, West Virginia, Virginia Tech, and Connecticut), with the support of Connecticut attorney general Richard Blumenthal, filed a lawsuit in the state against both the ACC and the three expected defectors, accusing the parties of engaging in "a backroom conspiracy, born in secrecy, founded on greed, and carried out through calculated deceit." We can only speculate as to whether said "backrooms" were also "dingy" and "smoke-filled."

Tranghese made it clear that the primary hypocrite on his radar was Miami president Donna Shalala, who had reportedly assured her Big East colleagues during a closed-door meeting in 2001 that the Hurricanes weren't going anywhere. "At the end of the day, President Shalala is going to have to look at . . . the integrity issues that she has been involved in with [the] other [Big East] presidents," said Tranghese. Clearly, he had forgotten that Shalala was a former White House cabinet member, serving as secretary of Health and Human Services during the Clinton administration, and therefore couldn't be held accountable for any lapses in integrity.

Considering that by this point conferences had been pilfering teams from one another for years, many observers wondered why the ACC's own imperialistic ambitions were causing such a fuss. Business is business, right? Well, in the case of this business, the stakes had risen considerably in the decade or so since the game's previous expansion wave. No longer was realignment solely about regular season television contracts. Since that time, three little letters, B-C-S, had changed the face of the sport completely, drawing a distinct line in the sand between the sport's rich (the six conferences with automatic BCS bowl bids) and its poor (everyone else). By this time, the financial benefit for a conference of sending one team to a BCS bowl game ($14–$17 million) had come to dwarf that of qualifying six teams to the NCAA basketball tournament.* You can understand, then, why the ACC was eager to assert itself once and for all as something more than a basketball league—and why the Big East was so desperate to avoid becoming just that.

With those stakes in mind, the golden carrot for the ACC was unquestionably Miami, which, along with Florida State, would give the conference two of the game's preeminent football programs. Any additional schools would essentially be window dressing to get to the requisite twelve teams, which explains why the conference of Tobacco

---

*The NCAA uses a formula so complex to determine these things that I can't even speculate as to a hypothetical figure. Just know that it's somewhere between $13.50 and $13 million.

Road would suddenly be interested in the land of snow and clam chowder. Miami, with its large East Coast alumni presence, pushed hard for the inclusion of B.C. and Syracuse, though it certainly didn't hurt that they represented two of the nation's top five television markets. Longtime Syracuse athletic director Jake Crouthamel basically admitted that his school wasn't exactly foaming at the mouth to part ways with its East Coast brethren but that it might have no choice but to ride the Hurricanes' coattails. "Without Miami, the Big East will probably lose its Bowl Championship Series status," he told the *Hartford Courant*. Boston College coach Tom O'Brien expressed a similarly dire view to the *Boston Globe*. "If we don't stay with Miami, in 20 years we will be what people thought BC should have been 20 years ago—a team that people thought should be at the I-AA level."

And so the fate of the free world—or at least that of college football teams along the Atlantic seaboard—rested squarely in the hands of Miami and the ACC. Big East officials trotted out one last-ditch plan to appease the Hurricanes, offering a revamped, heavily pro-Miami revenue-sharing arrangement during a presentation to athletic director Paul Dee—who reportedly fell asleep during the meeting. In early June, with everything seemingly moving full speed ahead, I departed on a preplanned three-week vacation, fully assuming the whole thing would be resolved by the time I returned. But three weeks into June—more than two months after Tranghese's initial accusation—the ACC's expansion plans were suddenly falling apart. To understand why, allow me to re-create another likely conversation, this one set in a country club dining room somewhere along Tobacco Road.

UVA PRESIDENT CASTEEN: I'm sorry, fellow presidents, but I can no longer support any expansion plan that does not include those orange-and-maroon gobblers from up the road.

ACC COMMISSIONER JOHN SWOFFORD: But John, you were one of the seven that voted to start this process in the first place. Without your vote, we don't have enough to pass this thing. What changed?

PRESIDENT CASTEEN: Let's just say the decision was made for me.

SWOFFORD: Very well, then. We'll just add Virginia Tech, too. No biggie. We're still getting Miami.

PRESIDENT CASTEEN: Good.

SWOFFORD: Great.

PRESIDENT CASTEEN: Grand.

SWOFFORD: Then it's settled.

OTHER ACC PRESIDENT: Umm . . . excuse me, fellas? There's just one little problem. If we do that, we'll have thirteen teams. You can't have two divisions with an odd number of teams.

SWOFFORD: Hmm, odd indeed. Here's what we'll do. We'll throw out BC and Syracuse. We didn't really want them anyway.

OTHER ACC PRESIDENT: Excellent idea, if I do say so, sir.

SWOFFORD: Yes, I agree. PR lackey—send out a press release pronto.

PR LACKEY: Already done, sir.

SWOFFORD: Good.

CASTEEN: Great.

SWOFFORD: Grand. Then it's settled.

ANOTHER ACC PRESIDENT: Umm . . . excuse me, PR lackey? Did you really send out that press release already?

PR LACKEY: Yes. Why?

ANOTHER ACC PRESIDENT: Well . . . I don't mean to be nitpicky, but now we only have eleven teams, which means we can no longer hold a championship game, which is kind of why we started this thing in the first place.

SWOFFORD AND PR LACKEY (simultaneously): . . . Ooops.

That might not be exactly how it went down—but it probably wasn't far off. The ACC's foolproof expansion plan hit a snag when Virginia politicians, including the governor himself, began applying pressure on behalf of Virginia Tech, a more geographically sensible choice that had been coveting ACC membership for decades but had only recently developed a major football program. Following a series of futile conference calls and meetings, it became apparent to ACC presidents they weren't going to get the necessary seven votes unless Tech was included.* So the ACC, whose image had gone from imperialistic to incompetent in a matter of weeks, hammered out a bizarre eleventh-hour compromise. Syracuse and B.C., part of the discussions from day one, were suddenly out, and Virginia Tech, the same school that had sued the ACC just weeks earlier, was in. The Hokies brass withdrew from the lawsuit and accepted the invitation quicker than you can say "Vick." "It has been a bizarre, strange, and goofy process," conceded Shalala. Like a jilted lover, Syracuse officials blasted the ACC's handling of the situation and vowed never again to give the league the time of day.

B.C., on the other hand, remained conspicuously quiet, and would be rewarded three months later when it finally became the ACC's twelfth member. As O'Brien said, where Miami goes, so too do the Eagles. One could make the argument that no team in the country better illustrates how drastically conferences have veered from their traditional geographical roots than Boston College. Penn State may have been the first to buck regional boundaries in favor of big-conference glamour, but at least its university and football history were similar in profile to that of the other Big Ten members. Boston College, by contrast, is a small, private Jesuit university nestled in the heart of the Northeast best known for its hockey team. It would seem almost spiritually linked to such like-minded Big East schools as Villanova, Georgetown, and St. John's. But because those teams don't field BCS-conference football programs, B.C. now finds itself in a conference where its nearest competitor, Maryland, is 430 miles away. Not to mention that its colleagues now include one of the nation's most renowned party schools (Florida State), one of the greatest embodiments of the Deep South (Clemson), and the model for Oxford-and-khaki-wearing preppies (UVA). To nearly any observer, it's a union that makes about

---

*Duke and North Carolina, far more concerned with the start of Midnight Madness, opposed expansion throughout.

as much sense as Arnold Schwarzenegger and Maria Shriver. But don't bother telling that to the two parties themselves—B.C. is too busy counting its BCS money, and the ACC is preoccupied counting all of those Boston television households. In fact, the ACC's new lineup proved even more lucrative than imagined: in 2004, the conference signed a seven-year, $258 million football deal with ABC and ESPN, nearly doubling its previous annual revenue from $20 million to $37.6 million. Sometimes it pays to be hypocrites.

The ACC's expansion set off a massive domino effect that resulted in college football's most dramatic makeover to date. Splintered by the defections, the Big East very nearly split apart ("We were dead . . . we didn't even know if we were going to have a league," Tranghese said in 2006), but once the initial panic died down, the league was able to retain its BCS status—barely—by swiping upstart power Louisville, Cincinnati, and South Florida from Conference USA.* In turn, C-USA (which also suffered the loss of basketball-only members Marquette, DePaul, and Charlotte) reinvented itself entirely, adding SMU, Tulsa, Rice, and UTEP from the WAC and Marshall and Central Florida from the MAC, splitting into two divisions and staging its first championship game in 2005; TCU also left the now watered-down C-USA for the upstart Mountain West and promptly won a league title in its first season there; and the WAC picked up the Sun Belt's Idaho, New Mexico State, and Utah State, giving reigning power Boise State three new schools to beat up on. The only thing that could have possibly been more confusing than this mass game of musical chairs was if the schools had all swapped mascots as well.

By the time the dust had settled, only four of the eleven Division I-A conferences had been unaffected by realignment. Two, the SEC and Big 12, already had twelve teams and faced no particular urgency to

---

*In an ironic twist, the reconfigured Big East has thus far upstaged the beefed-up ACC in the rankings. The Big East's 2005 (West Virginia) and 2006 (Louisville) champions both finished in the top six nationally, while the ACC's, Florida State and Wake Forest, finished twenty-third and eighteenth.

expand. But what about the Big Ten and Pac-10? Considering the substantial trouble the ACC went through to secure a championship game, fans of the two conferences—at least the ones who flooded my in-box—began to wonder, understandably, what are we missing out on? Shouldn't we be doing the same thing? Conference realignment fever had taken the nation by storm, creating a fun new pastime for imaginative football fans: devising new conference lineups. Why wouldn't the Big Ten want to add a Syracuse, Pittsburgh, or Missouri and split into two divisions? Why on earth hadn't the Pac-10 called Utah, BYU, Fresno State, or Boise State? These are questions that continue to linger to this day as many fans wait almost expectedly for the next shoe to drop.

It isn't going to happen.

Flying in the face of its colleagues, the two conferences haven't developed even the initial symptoms of expansion fever. The fact is, what made sense for the SEC, Big 12, and ACC doesn't necessarily make sense for the Big Ten and Pac-10. Here are three reasons why:

1. *They love their tradition too much.* In an age of Sidekicks and Blackberrys, the Pac-10 is the one conference that still uses a rotary telephone. Like a true California beach bum, the league is content to sit back and block out the craziness of the ever-changing world around it. The conference hasn't added a new team since Arizona and Arizona State joined the fold nearly thirty years ago and hasn't seriously entertained the idea since flirting with Texas and Colorado in the early 1990s. In fact, the league's commissioner, Thomas C. Hansen, one of the sport's last remaining dinosaurs (he began working at the Pac-10 in *1960*), would love nothing more than to return to the days before the BCS when the Rose Bowl was the conference's ultimate destination. A telling sign of the conference's old-fashioned priorities came when the NCAA approved a twelfth regular season game for all teams starting in 2006. The Pac-10, unlike its counterparts, used the opportunity not to pad its teams' schedules with another meaningless, money-making home game but to bump its conference schedule up to nine games (no other league plays more than

eight) so that the champion could be determined by a true round robin. "We are not going to be directly or indirectly affected by what happens in the ACC or the Big East," Hansen told the *Los Angeles Daily News* in 2003. "In addition, our members are very comfortable with our configuration and have no desire to change." Suffice to say, rocking the boat is not high on the Pac-10 priority list.

And while the Big Ten, in the spirit of its uncompromising leader Delany, is on the opposite end of the spectrum when it comes to trendsetting (its Penn State invitation touched off this whole charade in the first place), the conference is also meticulous when it comes to preserving tradition. For instance, Ohio State and Michigan always meet the Saturday before Thanksgiving come hell or high water, often to decide the conference championship. What would happen, then, if the league was to split into two divisions and stage a championship game in early December? Surely the divisions would be unbalanced if the Buckeyes and Wolverines were placed on the same side. So would the Buckeyes and Wolverines meet again two weeks later if they both won their divisions? Or would the league feel compelled to move their game to the beginning of the season, like the ACC did with Miami and Florida State from 2004 to 2006, to give both teams the best possible chance to remain in BCS contention? Needless to say, the two schools wouldn't be keen to any of those possibilities. Meanwhile, how would a twelve-team conference possibly be able to devise a schedule capable of maintaining all of its many annual trophy games? Minnesota alone has three of them—the Little Brown Jug (Michigan), Paul Bunyan's Ax (Wisconsin), and the Floyd of Rosedale (Iowa), the nation's only competitive sporting event in which the prize is a bronzed pig. You can bet the Big Ten won't be willing to muck up these traditions for just anyone.

2. *There's no added value.* As stated previously, the Big Ten's Delany is a man who views the world through Nielsen ratings. If his con-

ference was to add a team, it would almost assuredly be one that commands more television leverage, and none of the most commonly mentioned possibilities do that. The Big Ten is already considered a New York City market (ABC almost always airs its Big Ten regional telecast in the Big Apple), eliminating the need for Syracuse. Penn State already carries Pittsburgh, and Illinois has nearly as much reach into St. Louis as does Mizzou. The one available team that would not only boost the Big Ten's TV contract but send it into another stratosphere is Notre Dame. Let me make it perfectly clear that *if* the Irish were to suddenly come calling, this entire chapter section would become moot, because the Big Ten would sign them up faster than ND alum Regis Philbin can talk. The Big Ten already invited the Domers once, in 1999, and got a big 'ol Heisman stiff-arm—but you better believe that a place mat will remain permanently set for them. Notre Dame will always be the Big Ten's dream girl, and the conference isn't about to go settling for just any old floozy in the meantime. But Notre Dame has given no indication that it intends to join a conference anytime soon.

The Pac-10 has a similar problem in that there's a dearth of attractive expansion candidates in the West. All of the teams mentioned as possibilities—mainly Utah, BYU, Fresno State, and Boise State—are so-called mid-majors from leagues like the Mountain West and WAC. All four have fielded highly competitive football programs recently, and in fact all four have kicked the snot out of at least one Pac-10 foe in recent seasons.* Despite the narrowing competitive gap, however, there's not yet any evidence that mainstream football fans want to watch these teams regularly on television. On the one hand, the Pac-10 adding a Utah or Boise State would be no less logical a step for those programs than when the Big East plucked upstart Louisville out of

---

*Utah beat Cal and Oregon in 2003 and routed Arizona in 2004, Fresno State pummeled Washington in 2004, Boise State crushed Oregon State in 2004 and 2006, and BYU beat Oregon by 30 in the 2006 Las Vegas Bowl.

Conference USA. But then again, the Pac-10 isn't under nearly as much urgency to add warm bodies as the Big East was following its ACC raid. There's also the ever-delicate matter of cultural compatibility. The Pac-10 is made up almost entirely of highly respected academic institutions* and would frown on admitting lesser-regarded Fresno State and Boise State. As for the two Utah schools, Hansen told the *Tucson Citizen*, "BYU is not a research institution, and that was the first criterion of our presidents the last time it was brought up. Utah is pretty good academically, but the Salt Lake City TV market isn't all that great." In other words . . . eh.

3. *Championship games aren't all they're cracked up to be.* Give ex-SEC boss Kramer his due—there's no question the SEC title game has been an unqualified success. With the conference's rabid fan base and the game's convenient location (Atlanta) in the epicenter of the South, the title game sells out every year long before the participants are even known. In 2004, the game brought in $12.4 million in extra revenue, which was split equally among the league's members.[†]

But what works for the SEC doesn't necessarily work for everyone. The Big 12's title game has been a mixed bag at best. Yes, it produces more than $9 million in annual revenue. But because of the league's far-flung membership, the site constantly rotates between cities like San Antonio, Kansas City, and Dallas, leaving it lacking an identity, and attendance varies greatly depending on both the location and the participants. For instance, when Texas played Colorado in the 2001 game in Dallas, the league had no problem selling out 65,675-seat Texas Stadium. A year later, however, when the Buffaloes met Okla-

---

*Eight of ten Pac-10 schools were ranked among *U.S. News & World Report's* top 120 national universities in 2006. The other two: Oregon State and Arizona State. The latter, however, consistently ranks high in rankings compiled by another periodical—*Playboy*.

[†]Even Kentucky and Vanderbilt.

homa at Houston's Reliant Stadium—not exactly convenient to either campus—there were close to twenty thousand no-shows. Then there are the on-field disasters. On three separate occasions, 1996 (Texas over Nebraska), 1998 (Texas A&M over Kansas State) and 2001 (Colorado over Texas), the Big 12 missed out on placing a team in the national-championship game because that squad lost in the conference finale.* Not surprisingly, the Big 12's coaches, foreseeing a disadvantage versus teams whose conferences didn't require such an extra hurdle, voted unanimously *against* the title game when it was initially proposed. But then football coaches aren't the ones who have to worry about funding the cross-country team.

Admittedly, none of the potential negative consequences—like the fact that no team (besides Oklahoma in 2003) has ever received a BCS bowl berth after losing in its conference championship game—dissuaded the ACC from joining the party in 2005. The inaugural game, pitting Florida State against Virginia Tech in Jacksonville, Florida, achieved its desired goal, attracting 72,749 spectators to 77,000-seat Alltell Stadium and producing nearly $11 million in revenue. But that's to be expected whenever Florida State is playing in nearby Jacksonville, be it for the ACC title game or for the Gator Bowl. A year later, when surprise participants Wake Forest and Georgia Tech met, the announced attendance was 62,850, though reporters who covered the game placed the actual crowd at closer to 50,000, about two-thirds of capacity. In a league with far fewer glamour programs than the Big 12 or SEC, one that hasn't produced a serious national championship contender since 2000, it remains to be seen whether the ACC's game will ever become a truly marquee event.

With that in mind, try picturing the following scenario: It's early December in Chicago, the wind blowing off Lake Michigan is sharp enough to leave permanent indentations in your

---

*A fourth, Oklahoma in 2003, lost the game 35–7 to Kansas State but still somehow finished number 1 in the BCS standings.

face, and 10–2 Minnesota and 9–3 Indiana are playing for the Big Ten championship at Solider Field. That'll pack 'em in. Or worse, 11–0 Ohio State goes to Ann Arbor and knocks off 10–1 Michigan in one of the rivals' epic late-November matchups. But instead of wrapping up a bid to the national championship game, the Buckeyes must then go to Ford Field in Detroit to face a 9–3 Wisconsin team. By pulling off the upset, the Badgers not only knock OSU out of the title game but also take the Buckeyes' place in the Rose Bowl. How attractive does a Big Ten title game sound now? "If we expand—and that's not in the front or the back of our minds right now—there's a 50- to 60-percent chance there wouldn't even be a title game," Delany said in 2005. "Our viewpoint is, you expand because you're ready to expand, not because you want to have a title game." Ditto for the Pac-10, where the schools are even more spread out and any logical championship site—Los Angeles, Phoenix, Seattle—would mean a plane ride for at least one of the teams' fan bases. It's hard enough to get Los Angelenos excited about their own teams, much less a Cal–Oregon State game at the Rose Bowl. Besides, the perennially snake-bitten Pac-10 has had enough trouble getting its teams into BCS games without the additional obstacle. "It's hard to have a team that has won a very difficult conference race have to put it all on the line one more time," Hansen told the *Hartford Courant*. "We would just as soon see our team get off to the BCS game with one fewer exposure." Translation: We're a bunch of wusses—and we're not about to apologize for it.

So with the Big Ten and Pac-10 both content to ride the status quo, life is quiet once again on the conference realignment front. Barring a drastic change in leadership and/or philosophy at one of these two conferences, or a sudden change of heart by Notre Dame, it's tough to foresee another major ripple occurring anytime soon. Why? Because for one thing, the primary impetus behind all that movement in the first place—television revenue—has just about maxed out. Regular season TV ratings for nearly every major sport, college football included, have been stuck in neutral for years, making it unlikely that the networks will be throwing more money at the conferences the next time their contracts come up. In fact, the conferences have already begun taking up the TV cause on their own—both the Mountain West and Big Ten recently started their own networks. Commissioners and athletic directors seeking new revenue streams in the coming years will also likely turn to emerging markets like the Internet and wireless technology. It's only a matter of time before fans will be able to watch live games on their cell phones and other handheld devices. The money at stake, however, will likely be minuscule in comparison to traditional broadcast deals, so there won't be the same kind of urgency to bolster their lineups that conferences felt in the past. You're not going to see Verizon telling the SEC, "We'd love to do business with you, but only if you add Marshall."

It's my belief that the next major wave of changes to affect conference membership will be directly linked to changes in the sport's postseason structure. As long as the BCS retains the same basic format (the current contract runs through the 2009 season), there won't be much motivation for conferences to expand. As it stands now, no one league can send more than two teams to a BCS bowl, and with the recent loosening of eligibility requirements for at-large berths, teams from outside the six major conferences will be claiming berths on a more regular basis. If the sport were ever to adopt a full-fledged playoff, however, there could very well be a massive realignment among conference lines. Just like with the NCAA basketball tournament, leagues would vie to place as many teams in the field as possible. At that point, it might behoove the Pac-10 to absorb a Boise State or the Big Ten to absorb a Pittsburgh. One could even envision a more sweeping consolidation where the six major conferences devolve into four superconferences (East, South, Midwest, and West), with the top four teams in each advancing to a playoff. It would be like the NBA's playoffs, only with about 273 less games.

Finally, there have been rumblings dating as far back as the early 1990s that the power conferences, knowing full well their ability to dominate the marketplace, could flat-out secede from the rest of the

NCAA one day, ridding themselves of any obligation to their less attractive competitors and freeing themselves to dictate their own postseason destiny. "The direction is clear," CBS basketball analyst Billy Packer told the *Washington Times* in 2003. ". . . The group of five [major] conferences made up of 60 teams will play for the football national championship and eventually for the basketball championship."

While such Armageddon scenarios are fun to discuss, they're not exactly caked in reality. Although it certainly seems sometimes as if major college football teams are their own autonomous enterprises, they're still just one facet of a larger university. While the NCAA has almost no oversight when it comes to BCS bowls and television contracts, it still plays a huge role in such issues as amateurism, academics, and enforcement. It's hard to imagine college presidents signing off on an arrangement that would essentially turn major college football into a de facto pro league. Plus, you can be sure Congress would hold hearings.

If anything, the sport seems to be headed in the *opposite* direction. In addition to making the BCS more inclusive, administrators in recent years have been quietly working to reduce the distinctions between the sport's marquee programs and its more obscure programs. In 2006, the NCAA's membership voted to eliminate the nearly thirty-year-old monikers of "Division I-A" and "Division I-AA," replacing them with the less stigmatizing, albeit more confusing, Football Bowl Subdivision (formerly I-A) and NCAA Football Championship Subdivision (formerly I-AA).* A year earlier, a sweeping set of new I-A eligibility requirements (attendance minimums, scholarship totals, etc.) aimed at slowing the recent migration of teams from the lower level to the higher level was met with so much resistance that the final, watered-down version is unlikely to have any meaningful impact.† In addition,

---

*I have continued to refer to them as I-A and I-AA, as have most media outlets.
†In the most controversial aspect of the new standards, teams must average 15,000 fans per home game at least once every two seasons. In 2006, eight schools fell short of this mark. However, it's yet to be determined how strictly, if at all, these standards will be enforced, and it would likely take several years of poor attendance before a school would be in danger of losing its I-A status.

an old bylaw that restricted I-A teams from counting wins over I-AA opponents toward bowl eligibility has been lifted, thus opening the floodgates for the scheduling of such contests. In 2006, 74 of the nation's 119 Division I-A teams played at least one game against a I-AA opponent. "I kind of feel like, why not just open it up and let anyone who wants to call themselves [I-A]," said Delany, who recognizes that the marketplace, much more than an arbitrary label, will ultimately determine who gets the TV dollars and bowl bids.

So to all of you out there dreaming up the next big conference shakeup—TCU to the Big 12! Hawaii to the Pac-10!—do yourself a favor and take a couple of deep breaths. The seas of change have calmed for the foreseeable future, which is probably for the best. After all, the governor of Virginia has other work to do.

8

Tonight, It's the MPC Motor City Car Care Credit Union Bowl

News item: Jan. 1, 2000—The NCAA announced today that there are enough sanctioned college football bowl games to permit every college football team to appear in a bowl game after the 2001 season.

—*Satirical* Los Angeles Times *column, 1985*

———

I think we will have pizza [in the stadium] in future years. It certainly makes sense to have it.

—*Mark Meadows, executive director of the inaugural PapaJohns.com Bowl, 2006*

On December 29, 2005, 25,742 spectators—about a fourth of the typical Saturday crowd at a Michigan or Tennessee home game—filed into San Francisco's SBC Park, normally the home of baseball's San Francisco Giants, to watch college football's Emerald Bowl. This momentous contest, broadcast nationally on ESPN for the viewing pleasure of anyone sitting idly at home at 4:30 on a Thursday afternoon, pitted the third-place team from the ACC's Coastal Division, 7–4 Georgia Tech, against the fourth-place finisher out of the Mountain West, 6–5 Utah. Considering that the Yellow Jackets had defeated nationally ranked Auburn and Miami during the season while the Utes had needed an overtime victory in their regular season finale against BYU just to become bowl-eligible, most of the so-called experts (including this one) assumed that Georgia Tech would win in a cakewalk. Instead, defying all reasonable logic, Utah rolled up 550 yards of offense against one of the nation's most highly regarded defenses to steamroll the Jackets 38–10. Asked afterward to explain the puzzling disparity, Utah cornerback and Emerald Bowl defensive MVP Eric Weddle said of his defeated adversaries, "You could tell they didn't want to be here."

What? Why wouldn't the Yellow Jackets want to be there? Wasn't this a bowl game? You know, the season-ending goal every college player dreams of from the time they first strap on the helmets in August? Surely the Georgia Tech players were elated to be spending the holidays playing in a windy, half-empty baseball stadium three thousand miles from home against a team from one of the non-BCS conferences.

Maybe not.

Welcome to the strangest, most confounding, most unique postseason in all of sports. After twelve to thirteen weeks of heated rivalries and conference showdowns, grueling practices, and road games played in front of ninety thousand hostile fans, two teams are tapped to play for the national championship while sixty-two others face off in what are essentially glorified exhibitions. Some, like the Rose Bowl and Orange Bowl, Cotton Bowl and Sugar Bowl, have traditions dating back three-quarters of a century or longer. Others, like the PapaJohns.com Bowl, International Bowl, and New Mexico Bowl, might not have existed a year earlier. From the Pioneer PureVision Las Vegas Bowl to the Bell Helicopter Armed Forces Bowl, nearly all carry a clunky sponsor name in the title, meaning that two teams of college athletes—NCAA-regulated amateurs strictly prohibited from receiving compensation or endorsing products—wind up participating in 3-hour televised adver-tisements for various products. Often the teams have gone a month or longer since playing their last game, and in some cases their coach has already taken a job at another school—like Brian Kelly, who coached Central Michigan through its entire 2006 regular season, left for Cincinnati, and coached the Bearcats for the first time in their ensuing bowl game.*

Taking all that into consideration, I often find myself wondering how bowl games continue to survive in today's championship-driven, win-at-all-costs sports world. In fact, each year when the bowl pairings come out, I, like a lot of people, find myself rolling my eyes and groan-ing at most of the matchups. I see that South Carolina and Houston are playing each other in the 2006 Liberty Bowl and I think to myself, "If this game were on a regular Saturday it wouldn't even be televised; why should I watch it?" But then, inevitably, I, like 5 million other football fans, not only end up watching the game but ooohing and ahhing at one big play after another in a 44–36 South Carolina victory. I break a smile watching jubilant Boston College players mob their kicker after he hits a game-winning field goal to beat Navy in the next day's Meineke Car Care Bowl. And just hours after covering the Rose Bowl, I sit riveted in front of the television, mouth agape, watching another bowl, the Fiesta, where Boise State running back Ian Johnson

---

*In doing so, Kelly became the first coach in history to beat the same opponent, West-ern Michigan, twice in the same season with two different teams.

dashes into the end zone on a trick play to beat Oklahoma in one of the most exciting football games ever played. It's the kind of scene that could happen only in a college bowl game. "When you see people so happy, some of them not from the biggest schools, it reminds you why we do this," said Fiesta Bowl CEO John Junker. "The celebrations—no matter how small the bowl game—you would have thought what they just won was the greatest thing in the world."

Not everybody thinks bowl games are the greatest thing in the world. In fact, college football fans spend more time grumbling come bowl season than any other time of the year. Most of them want to see a playoff system to determine the national champion. And nearly all of them agree that there's too many damn bowls. Once upon a time, playing in a bowl game—any bowl game—was the highest possible reward a college football team could hope for. For all those coaches, players, and fans stuck in cold-weather climates, a New Year's vacation in Florida or California meant the culmination of a highly successful season. In fact, for most of the twentieth century, qualifying for such an event was an accomplishment of the highest order. Prior to 1975, for example, the only bowl game available to Big Ten schools was the Rose Bowl, which meant that only the conference's champion earned a post-season trip in any given year.* As of that year, there were only eleven bowl games total.

Today there are thirty-two such contests, assuring berths for more than half the nation's major college teams. Amidst such a drastically diluted postseason landscape, where every city from Boise to Birmingham has a game and it takes only a pedestrian 6–6 record to get there, the enthusiasm of the participants can vary drastically depending on the game and the team's own circumstances. If you're an Akron, Rutgers, or any number of other tradition-starved programs, a trip to the Motor City Bowl or Texas Bowl is cause for celebration. If you're a USC or Florida State, however, a season ending in anything short of the four

---

*Actually, from 1946 to 1971, the Big Ten also prohibited the same team from participating in the Rose Bowl in consecutive seasons—in which place the second-place team got to go.

BCS bowls (Rose, Orange, Sugar, and Fiesta) or the national championship game is often considered an abject failure. "Rule of thumb," wrote *Orlando Sentinel* columnist Mike Bianchi. "If your season is so disappointing that you actually fire your coach, you probably haven't earned [your] bowl bid." In a December 2006 column entitled "Pardon Us for Our Bowl Boredom," John P. Lopez of the *Houston Chronicle* wrote: "Bowls are neither what they once were nor what they should be. That is, they are neither something special nor part of a playoff."

The college bowl game was born in 1902, when organizers for the twelve-year-old New Year's Day Tournament of Roses festival in Pasadena, California, having had great success with their popular parade of flower-covered floats but continually whiffing with other entertainment options such as ostrich races, broncobusting demonstrations, and tug of war, invited Michigan and Stanford to stage a football exhibition. The powerful Fielding Yost-coached Wolverines beat the Cardinals 49–0. The football idea was promptly scrapped the next year in favor of chariot races. In 1916, however, New Year's Day football returned to Pasadena. Washington State beat Brown 14–0, ushering in one of the sport's most beloved annual traditions. Other cities like New Orleans (Sugar), Dallas (Cotton), and Miami (Orange) would soon follow suit, sensing the potential boon for tourism with thousands of out-of-town fans buying up hotel rooms, consuming restaurant meals, and running up bar tabs. In later years, televised broadcasts would allow host cities to show themselves off to audiences around the country thanks to those obligatory shots of surfers catching waves at the beach and revelers mingling on Bourbon Street. The organizing committees that staged the bowls were nonprofits that engendered goodwill by donating extra revenue raised by the games to local charities and the community. It was a win-win for everybody.

For the teams involved in these exhibitions, the benefits were also obvious. For one, every winner gets to hoist a trophy. Besides getting the chance to play an extra game and to measure your abilities against a quality opponent from another part of the country, participating coaches and players are treated like visiting royalty—delegations greet them when they get off the plane, buses whisk them away to their ritzy hotels and chauffeur them through a week's worth of events and festivities leading up to the game. At the Rose Bowl, for instance, teams visit Disneyland and chow down at the annual Lawry's Beef Bowl, where they also have the pleasure of mingling with the always dashing Rose Queen. Bowl participants through the years could also be assured that a whole lot of people would be watching. For decades, college bowl games were the nation's most popular form of New Year's Day entertainment. In 1987, for example, the six New Year's Day games (Orange, Rose, Cotton, Fiesta, Sugar, and Citrus) garnered a combined Nielsen rating of 88.9, nearly twice that of a typical Super Bowl. Bowl games were as much a slice of Americana as the Fourth of July, apple pie, and beer guts.

So what happened? Why, in 2005, was the combined rating of those same six games down 43 percent from that of 2 decades earlier? Why, during the 2005–06 bowl season, were only eleven of that season's twenty-eight bowl games able to sell out their stadiums? Why, over the years, have one-time mainstays such as the Bluebonnet (Houston), Aloha (Honolulu), and Freedom (Anaheim, California) bowls gone out of business, along with flashes in the pan like the Seattle, Silicon Valley and GalleryFurniture.com bowls? Because somewhere along the way, the college football public decided, "You know, all these glorified exhibition games are fun and all, but we'd kind of like to know who the national champion is."

It's tough to pinpoint when, exactly, college football's postseason began its transformation from a recreational entertainment vehicle into a serious, full-blown sporting matter. We do know, however, that prior to 1969 (with the exception of two seasons), the AP conducted its final poll of the season *before* the bowl games, making bowl results irrelevant to the then mythical national championship race. Even after that change, the various conference tie-ins with the major bowls (the Big Ten and Pac-10 with the Rose, the Big 8 with the Orange, the SEC with the Sugar, and the Southwest with the Cotton) made it rare that the number 1 and 2 teams wound up in the same bowl game (only three times from 1969 to 1985). In fact, with back-room deals often being brokered between bowls and schools as early as October, there was no way to predict where the participants in a bowl game would be ranked at the end of the regular season. If anything, the ambiguity of the process added more drama to the bowl season. With the right matchups and with enough upsets, it was possible for the final number 1 team to emerge from any number of bowl games.

In 1986, however, the Fiesta Bowl in Tempe, Arizona—a relative newcomer to the scene, having been born in 1971 and moved to New Year's Day just five years earlier—changed the bowl business forever. Unencumbered by conference partnerships like so many of their more venerable competitors, shrewd Fiesta execs started brokering a deal in mid-October to pit potential undefeated independents Penn State and Miami against each other. By offering to double its previous high payout to $2.4 million per team and convincing NBC to move the game to its own exclusive prime-time window on January 2, a day later than the other major bowls, the Fiesta was able to land one of the most hyped bowl matchups in history pitting the brash, star-studded Hurricanes of Jimmy Johnson, Vinny Testaverde, and Michael Irvin against Joe Paterno's brutish, buttoned-down Nittany Lions.

When second-ranked Penn State pulled off the gigantic upset, picking off Testaverde in the final seconds to seal the win, the game not only achieved classic status but gave the college football world an irresistible taste of what a true national championship game could be. "Bless you, Fiesta Bowl Committee," wrote *Sports Illustrated*'s Rick Reilly, "for delivering us from Poll Day trauma, from 119-pound sportswriters* picking national champions." At that point, there was no turning back. The demand for an annual number 1 versus number 2 game was too enticing to ignore, yet at the same time nearly impossible to facilitate within the traditional bowl structure, because every bowl operated independently of the others and major conference champions had obligatory tie-ins to certain games. In 1992, the Cotton, Fiesta, Orange, and Sugar bowls united to form the Bowl Coalition, with the objective of creating a national championship game whenever possible.

---

*Apparently Reilly's colleagues at the time weren't hitting the media buffets as recklessly as today's sportswriting crowd, many of whom weigh at least twice that.

It worked the first two years, with Miami playing Alabama in the Sugar Bowl and Florida State and Nebraska in the Orange. But when Big Ten champion Penn State finished number 2 in 1994, there was no getting around the Nittany Lions' obligation to the Rose Bowl. Number 1 Nebraska was left to face number 3 Miami in the Orange Bowl. In 1995, the Bowl Coalition was replaced by the Bowl Alliance, which first kicked out the Cotton Bowl because its longtime partner, the Southwest Conference, was about to disband, and eliminated the constraints of traditional conference tie-ins. As a result, the 1996 Fiesta Bowl was able to pit number 1 Nebraska, which in the past would have gone to the Orange Bowl, against number 2 Florida, which normally would have played in the Sugar.

Still, the system was plagued by a giant asterisk, in that there could still be no championship game if the Big Ten or Pac-10 champions finished number 1 or number 2. Finally, in 1998, those two conferences reluctantly agreed to release their fifty-year-old stranglehold on the Pasadena game, opening the door for the Bowl Championship Series. The Rose, Sugar, Fiesta, and Orange Bowls, as well as the six major conferences and Notre Dame, all signed off on an arrangement in which the number 1 and 2 teams would meet every year, regardless of conference affiliation. While there had always been an unofficial hierarchy to the postseason landscape, the BCS created a demarcation that has irreparably changed the public's perception of various bowl games. No longer is reaching a bowl game the ultimate goal; for the nation's preeminent powers, it's national championship game or bust. No longer is it enough to play on New Year's Day; there's a considerable prestige gap between playing in the BCS-sponsored Sugar Bowl, with its staggering $17 million payout, and the plain old Gator Bowl, with its more modest $2.5 million offering. While many of the pre-New Year's games, like the Holiday, Alamo, and Chick-fil-A (formerly Peach) bowls, still garner a certain level of respect, others, like the Music City Bowl, MPC Computers Bowl, or New Orleans Bowl, have become college football's equivalent to the basketball NIT, games that interest very few besides the fans of the teams involved—and, of course, degenerate gamblers. You haven't lived until you've spent a night in the Bellagio sports book watching grown men stomp and curse over a blocked extra point in the waning seconds of the Champs Sports Bowl.*

Betting on bowl games, mind you, is a highly risky proposition. While I consider myself to be a fairly decent college football prognosticator, I gave up long ago trying to make any sense whatsoever about nonchampionship bowl games. The problem is, the teams that play in them often bear almost no resemblance to those of the twelve games preceding them. Think about it. Teams play their regular season games in a highly controlled environment. The players go to classes, practices, the training room, and meeting rooms for six days, then on the seventh get on a bus or plane, play a game, and come back. Besides injuries, there are very few non-football variables that factor into the equation. Coaches may vary their game plans from week to week depending on the opponent, but by the fourth or fifth week of the season, most teams take on a fairly consistent identity. Running teams can be expected to run a lot, defensive-minded teams can be expected to play in low-scoring games, and so on. This goes on for twelve or thirteen weeks, with maybe one bye week interruption, and as a result teams fall into a largely predictable routine.

And then, suddenly, they stop playing—sometimes for as long as five or six weeks preceding their bowl games. The coaches go off recruiting. The players go home for Christmas. Eventually everyone reconvenes, only this time it's in some far-flung locale devoid of the familiar comforts of campus, where they squeeze in practices and meetings between luaus, amusement park visits, and watermelon-eating contests. Often the coaches use the extra time to experiment and install new plays or try out new players they never got a chance to use during the regular season. Suddenly, the same offense that could barely complete a forward pass during the season goes out and puts up 45 points on the same defense that was previously as stingy as it could be

---

*I in fact witnessed this very scene when Clemson, favored by nine points over Colorado in the 2005 Champs Sports Bowl, scored a late touchdown to go up 19–10, then had its extra-point try blocked, turning what would have been a win for Clemson bettors into a push. This is why gambling is bad for you, children.

but, after five weeks off, is suddenly all out of synch. Case in point: the 2006 Emerald Bowl between Florida State and UCLA. The 6–6 Seminoles, closing out their worst season in 31 years, had fielded a woeful offense all year, one that had been shut out by Wake Forest and gained just 251 yards against Western Michigan. Their offensive coordinator, Jeff Bowden, had already announced his resignation. The 7–5 Bruins, meanwhile, were coming off a season-ending 13–9 upset of number 2 USC in which their nationally acclaimed defense had held the Trojans to their lowest scoring output in 5 years. So of course, predictably, FSU's offense chose the occasion to suddenly explode for 430 yards in a 44–27 victory. Asked afterward where that night's Florida State team had been all season, quarterback Drew Weatherford told the *Orlando Sentinel*, "I have no idea."

A year earlier, in the 2005 Peach Bowl, an LSU team that had scored 16, 19, and 14 points in three of its last four contests and was playing with its backup quarterback, Matt Flynn, due to an injury to starter JaMarcus Russell, racked up 468 yards in a 40–3 victory over a Miami team that had led the nation in defense for most of the season. "I don't know that the team quit," Hurricanes coach Larry Coker said afterward. "We just didn't match their energy." What Coker didn't say, but what was fairly obvious to anyone who watched, was, "Our team didn't give a rat's ass about this game, and it showed." Miami is a program accustomed to BCS bowls and national championships. The Peach Bowl, while a perfectly desirable destination for most teams, doesn't exactly stoke the Hurricanes' competitive fire. That's the other thing that makes nonchampionship bowl games so wildly unpredictable. You can't just break down the teams' respective strengths and weaknesses and conjure up a probable result like you can in the regular season. As with the Georgia Tech–Utah game at the beginning of this chapter, you never know which team will come out playing like its life depends on it and which team will come out playing like it's got dinner reservations it'd really like to keep. Such is the reality of the BCS era, in which each bowl takes on varying significance to the respective participants. In both 2004 and 2005, for instance, a pair of top-five teams from the Pac-10, Cal and Oregon, failed to garner bids to one of the four BCS bowls—

despite their only losses of the season each coming to top-ranked USC—and instead wound up in the Holiday Bowl against 7–4 Big 12 teams Texas Tech and Oklahoma. "It's difficult to swallow," Oregon coach Mike Bellotti said when his team's bid was announced. Excuse me? A late-December trip to San Diego difficult to swallow? It's warm, it's gorgeous, and you get to see Shamu. But the disparity in cachet between the five BCS bowls and everyone else has become so immense that if you're a 10–1 team from a major conference, playing in the Holiday Bowl can feel pretty anticlimactic. Not surprisingly, both Pac-10 teams got upset by their hungrier, lower-ranked opponents.

Gripes about injustices in the bowl selections have become an annual December tradition. Due to the confusing and often haphazard manner in which the non-BCS bowls select their participants, several deserving teams find themselves at a less desirable destination than they figured to have earned. Nearly every bowl is locked into partnerships with certain conferences, guaranteeing those leagues a certain number of bowl berths each year; however, just because, say, the Capital One Bowl is number 2 on the Big Ten's pecking order doesn't mean the team that finished second in the conference automatically gets slotted there. All it means is that the bowl has second choice among eligible Big Ten teams, and while record is certainly a big factor, the bowl also must consider which team is likely to sell the most tickets, fill the most hotel rooms, garner the highest TV ratings, and so on. If that team happens to be 9–3 Michigan rather than 10–2 Purdue, the bowl has every right to select the Wolverines.

Unlike the NCAA basketball tournament, where one can reasonably guestimate where a team will be seeded based on its on-court performance during the season, football teams are often at the mercy of completely uncontrollable factors. For instance, in 2003, the Outback Bowl in Tampa, Florida, elected to take an 8–4 Florida team over a 10–2 Tennessee team that had beaten the home-state Gators during the season. Think there weren't a few Florida fanatics on the bowl's selection committee? The Vols slipped to the Peach Bowl, where they promptly laid an egg against 8–4 Clemson. In 2005, Boston College fell victim to a bad case of, well, geography, when it got shipped to the MPC Computers

Bowl in Boise, Idaho, despite finishing 8–3 and tying for first in the ACC's Atlantic Division. Among the other bowls with ACC ties, the Champs Sports Bowl in Orlando chose 7–4 Clemson because it knew more Tigers fans would travel there, and the Charlotte-based Meineke Car Care Bowl elected to go with local fave N.C. State despite its 6–5 record.* "I'm sure [the players] are disappointed [about the destination]. They felt they played their way into one of the Florida games," said Boston College coach Tom O'Brien. "But sometimes you don't get out of life what you give." See—who says college doesn't teach valuable life lessons?

In the bowl business, however, one man's trash can be another man's treasure. While Michigan and Michigan State fans live in fear of being invited to the home-state Motor City Bowl, the 2005 game was a big enough deal to participants Akron and Memphis to draw a respectable crowd of 50,616, most of them highly appreciative fans of the two teams. According to the *Detroit News*, traffic was backed up off I-75 coming into the city and at least one nearby restaurant reported an hour-and-fifteen-minute wait on what might otherwise have been a slow Monday the day after Christmas. "This is a big deal [for us]," said Akron fan Christianne Craig, whose team was making the first bowl appearance in school history. The crowd was even bigger the next year (54,113) when home-state Central Michigan made its first bowl appearance since 1994. "People laughed at us when we started this bowl," said Motor City Bowl founder George Perles, the former long-time Michigan State coach. "I don't think people can do that anymore." No way—there are at least ten others out there much easier to laugh at.

Filling seats remains a problem for many of the nation's lower-tier bowls. Among the attendance figures for the 2006–07 bowl games: 24,791 for the Rice–Troy New Orleans Bowl, 29,709 for the TCU–Northern Illinois Poinsettia Bowl, and 28,652 for the Miami–Nevada MPC Computers Bowl. You can find more people at your local Whole Foods on a Sunday night. Convincing football fans to take off work and

---

*The ACC instituted a rule the following year that said a bowl cannot select a team that finished more than one game below another available team in the standings.

shell out the money for what is often a cross-country trip can be a tough sell in today's bowl climate. It's not that fans aren't loyal to their team. It's just that they're not altogether different from the players—they need motivation. Any number of extenuating circumstances can quash that enthusiasm.

In 2005, the Capital One Bowl (formerly the Citrus Bowl) in Orlando, generally considered the most desirable of the non-BCS bowls due to its location and New Year's afternoon time slot, figured it had struck gold by landing 9–3 Wisconsin. The Badgers would be playing their final game under revered coach Barry Alvarez and are known for their horde of traveling fans. Wisconsin, however, had ended its Big Ten season with blowout losses to Penn State and Iowa and played in another Florida game, the Outback Bowl, a year earlier. The school sold just eight thousand tickets. "I would have thought Wisconsin would have blown it through the roof," late bowl director Tom Mickle told the *Birmingham News*. "If I had guessed coming in, I would have thought 16,000 to 18,000, no problem." And that's for a major New Year's Day bowl. You can imagine some of the turnouts the further one goes down the postseason pecking order. That December, Missouri sent a whopping 2,500 supporters to the Independence Bowl in Shreveport, Louisiana. The *El Paso Times* estimated there to be about 300 to 400 UTEP fans—including the band—at the GMAC Bowl in Mobile, Alabama. And Nevada, despite making its first bowl appearance in nine years, sold exactly one hundred tickets to its Hawaii Bowl matchup with Central Florida (total attendance: 16,134). The Wolf Pack probably could have drawn a bigger cheering section by staying home and holding a scrimmage. "With airplane ticket prices being higher and the airlines running fewer flights," Fort Worth Bowl executive director Tom Starr told ESPN.com, "more and more people either want to drive or sit down in front of their TV or watch a game at a bar."

So why, then, amidst such a seemingly unfavorable climate, do so many cities keep clamoring to get into the bowl business? The last decade alone has seen an explosion in the number of bowl games, from eighteen in 1996 to thirty-two today, and that doesn't count the handful that have already come and gone during that time. The latest entrants to the field came in 2006 with the arrival of the International Bowl in Toronto, the New Mexico Bowl in Albuquerque, New Mexico, and the PapaJohns.com Bowl in Birmingham, Alabama, as well as the BCS's new stand-alone national championship game. Birmingham's first bowl game since the 1990 All-American Bowl pitted South Florida and East Carolina and drew a modest 32,023 spectators to 71,000-seat Legion Field. To make the crowd look bigger, ESPN2 producers made sure fans were seated on the same side of the stadium, according to the *Birmingham News*. Meanwhile, Canada's first-ever bowl game, pitting Cincinnati against Western Michigan, attracted 26,717 curious onlookers to Rogers Centre, home of the CFL's Toronto Argonauts. Scalpers outside both venues were spotted hawking tickets for half-price the day of the game.

The bowl market's mass oversaturation is made possible by the NCAA's lax standards for attaining bowl certification. All an aspiring bowl host has to do to get rubber-stamped is pay a $12,000 licensing fee to the NCAA, get at least one commitment from a partnering conference, and convince a bank to guarantee a $2 million line of credit. No word on whether it also needs to show two proofs of ID. To maintain certification, the bowl must pay at least $750,000 to each participating team and average at least 25,000 in attendance over a three-year period. The bowl certification committee claims to keep a close watch on the total number, wanting to avoid a potentially embarrassing situation where not enough eligible teams are available.* But it hasn't invoked a moratorium on new games since 2001, when the NCAA's Football Study Oversight Committee recommended that the Bowl Certification Committee exercise an "open market" philosophy.† In other words, if aspiring organizers for the Peoria Bowl can come up with the cash and an interested conference, then by golly, the Peoria Bowl could become a reality.

---

*This very nearly happened in 2004, when Clemson and South Carolina removed themselves from consideration as punishment for an ugly brawl in their season-ending rivalry game and 6–6 teams were not yet eligible. In the end, there were fifty-seven eligible teams for fifty-six spots. Akron was the unlucky loser left out.

†In case you're curious, the NCAA has more committees than Congress.

Of course, the Peoria Bowl couldn't just be the Peoria Bowl. In today's bowl world, it would almost certainly be the John Deere Peoria Bowl. Or the Jim Sweeney New & Used Chevrolet Peoria Bowl. Maybe, if Jim was having a particularly good year, he could afford to cut out the Peoria altogether and go straight for the Jim Sweeney New & Used Chevrolet Bowl. I can already picture the Northern Illinois Huskies holding up the trophy.

The now-ubiquitous tradition of bowl sponsorship began with the Florida Department of Citrus, which in 1983 paid an undisclosed amount to change the name of Orlando's 35-year-old Tangerine Bowl to the Florida Citrus Bowl, more commonly known as the Citrus Bowl. As it is not uncommon for bowl games to be named after fruit, and because the name didn't have a particularly corporate feel to it, the real ripple effect wouldn't come until 1985, when the Fiesta Bowl struck a five-year, $10 million deal with Sunkist Growers Inc. to change the name of its event to the Sunkist Fiesta Bowl. Both the bowl industry and corporate America reacted as if they'd just struck gold. Suddenly bowl games, many having seen their television and ticket revenue hit a ceiling, had discovered a new way to offer participating teams more money. And the sponsors stumbled upon what was essentially a three-hour, nationally televised advertisement for their brand, thanks to the announcers constantly repeating their name and their logo painted on the field and stitched on players' jerseys. "There's no way we could buy this kind of publicity with the kind of advertising budget we have," Sunkist marketing executive Ray Cole told the *Washington Post* in 1988. By the early 1990s, the bowl world had given birth to the John Hancock Sun Bowl, the USF&G Sugar Bowl, the Sea World Holiday Bowl, the FedEx Orange Bowl, the Mobil Cotton Bowl, and the Mazda Gator Bowl, among others. In one of the more amusing sponsorships of the day, the venerable Independence Bowl in Shreveport, Louisiana, spent six seasons (1991–96) as the Poulan/Weed Eater Independence Bowl. If nothing else, it established a legacy—to this day, many fans still use the derisive term "Weed Whacker Bowl" as a common reference point when mocking some mediocre team's bowl possibilities.

In 1990, video rental behemoth Blockbuster took the inevitable next plunge, teaming with regional television network Raycom to form a new game in Miami that would be known solely as the Blockbuster Bowl. No longer would there need to be a formal name wedged between the sponsor's brand and the word "bowl." In 1993, the Blockbuster Bowl renamed itself the Carquest Bowl, and a year later the Hall of Fame Bowl in Tampa, Florida, became the Outback Steakhouse Bowl (later shortened to Outback Bowl). While such monikers certainly drew no shortage of snickers from college football fans ("Someday in the not-so-distant future, New Year's Day football fans may wake up to the IBM-Exxon-Publishers' Clearinghouse Bowl" carped the *Washington Post*), the trend didn't turn truly cheesy until the dawn of the dot-coms. In 1997, the already awkward Weiser Lock Copper Bowl in Tucson, Arizona, elected to discard whatever shreds of dignity it had left and allow itself to be renamed the Insight.com Bowl. Keep in mind, in 1997, the Internet was still a fairly new concept to most Americans, nonetheless the idea of companies with dot-com in their names, nonetheless football games allowing themselves to be named after them. "'All right, team, you know what's at stake in this game!'" wrote *Charlotte Observer* columnist Ron Green. "'Win this one and we go to the Insight-Dot-Com Bowl!' Makes you want to pull on your cleats, doesn't it?"

By this point, the last remaining floodgates had been obliterated, and it was clear that bowl organizers would now sell their souls to just about anyone if the price was right. The ensuing decade has treated us to such classics as the MicronPC.com Bowl, the Diamond Walnut San Francisco Bowl, the OurHouse.com Florida Citrus Bowl,* the MPC Computers Bowl, the Continental Tire Bowl, and the Meineke Car Care Bowl. The last two were both played in Charlotte, which means no Charlotte resident will ever have an excuse for not knowing where to take his car for a tire change or muffler installation. Even the ever-snooty Rose Bowl, which resisted conforming to the trend toward corporate sponsorship longer than any other bowl ("We believe the values of intercollegiate athletics are noncommercial values," insisted

---

*Bonus points to anyone who actually visited OurHouse.com during its brief life span.

Tournament of Roses director Jack French in 1988), finally caved in the late 1990s, becoming the Rose Bowl presented by AT&T (since replaced by Citi). In 2005, the San Diego County Credit Union made history when it became the first credit union to tack its name to a bowl game, this one the startup Poinsettia Bowl. Try saying "San Diego Country Credit Union Poinsettia Bowl" ten times fast.

And then there's the story of Jim "Mattress Mac" McIngvale. In 2000, McIngvale, the kind of wacky salesman who stars in his own late-night TV commercials dressed as a mattress and waving a bundle of cash at the camera, plopped down $500,000 to turn a newly formed Houston bowl into a national advertisement for his local furniture store's online retail site, naming the game the GalleryFurniture.com Bowl. "How else can I get our name into newspapers around the country the day before and the day after the game?" McIngvale told Bloomberg News. Indeed, for the two years McIngvale's sponsorship lasted, his store's name became part of the college football lexicon, and fans around the country presumably assumed (I know I did) that Gallery Furniture was some sort of national chain. Unless you were actively in the market for a new ottoman or recliner, you never would have guessed that one of the nation's bowl games was actually named after a lone store in Texas. "We learned our lesson," McIngvale said in explaining his decision to pull the sponsorship in 2002. "Delivering furniture across the country costs more than it's worth." Remarkably, the Houston Bowl managed to find an even more obscure sponsor, EV1.net, before losing its certification in 2006 (it has since been replaced by the Texas Bowl).

The constant turnover in title sponsors among the nation's second-tier bowl games indicates the low return most of the participating companies get from their investments. Both games and sponsors are learning that you can't just throw a new, random company in front of a bowl name every few years and expect it to magically resonate with the buying public. Such quirky partnerships "take away from the mystique of the games," Jim Andrews, editorial director of *IEG Sponsorship Report*, told the *New York Times*.

So why do so many companies keep trying? Because once in a blue moon, one of them hits the jackpot. Since 1995, the Fiesta Bowl has become synonymous with the tortilla chip Tostitos in the minds of most college football followers. When the game first hosted the BCS national championship in 1998, ABC announcer Brent Musburger made regular references to the teams "playing for all the Tostitos." Ohio State players, upon clinching their 2002 Fiesta berth with a win over Michigan, were seen walking off the field clutching bags of Tostitos, and in 2005, Notre Dame fans, anticipating a Fiesta invitation, threw tortillas on the field after their final home game. Obviously there's a natural connection between "fiesta" and a brand of party food, but bowl organizers also went to extraordinary lengths to promote the brand, painting a huge Tostitos logo at midfield and lining the walls with Tostitos-colored bunting, creating the effect of the stadium as a giant bowl of Tostitos when viewed aerially. According to a study by Image Impact, Tostitos, which pays an estimated $8 million a year for its sponsorship, received approximately $30.4 million worth of exposure during the 2006 game broadcast, with its logo appearing more than five hundred times. Meanwhile, Chick-fil-A, the Southern fast-food giant, has seen its profile rise so dramatically since partnering with Atlanta's Peach Bowl in 1997 that in 2006 the company signed a five-year, $22 million deal to rename the game the Chick-fil-A Bowl. Since first signing on with Chick-fil-A, the game has seen its per-team payout nearly triple, to $3 million. "There is no doubt that this bowl is where it is today because of Chick-fil-A," said bowl president Gary Stokan. Who knew a chicken sandwich could be more important to a bowl game's success than a Tennessee or LSU?

It's good to know someone's making money off the bowl racket, because it certainly isn't the participating teams. In fact, in many cases, reaching a bowl game can actually be a losing proposition financially. A 2000 *USA Today* study of thirty-eight bowl teams' expenditures found that more than half of them (eighteen) spent more money participating in the game than they received from the bowls. Between the cost of flying several hundred players, coaches, support staff, cheerleaders, band members, family members, and, in some cases, boosters to a remote location, plus a week's worth of meals, lodging, and entertainment, the NCAA-mandated $750,000 minimum payout—the amount offered by more than a third of all bowls—simply is not enough. On top of that, the schools are also obligated to buy a certain amount of tickets and wind up eating the cost of any they don't sell.* An *Atlanta-Journal Constitution* study of Georgia's 2000 trip to the $750,000 Oahu Bowl in Hawaii revealed expenses totaling $971,963, resulting in a $221,963 net loss. While the BCS bowls pay between $14 and $17 million per team, only eight others pay even $2 million.[†]

Most major conferences have revenue-sharing plans, where the combined payouts of their teams' bowl appearances are divided among all members, so a Big Ten or SEC team that winds up in a minimum-payout game will still come out ahead thanks to those leagues' lucrative spots in the BCS. In 2005, the Big Ten sent two teams to BCS bowls (Penn State and Ohio State) and five others to the Capital One (Wisconsin), Outback (Iowa), Alamo (Michigan), Sun (Northwestern), and Music City (Minnesota) bowls. The appearances netted a record $35 million (of which nearly $23 million came from the BCS), so each league team pocketed a little over $3 million whether they were one of the bowl teams or not. However, for a WAC or Conference USA team, whose bowl partnerships are limited almost entirely to low-level bowls, the monetary incentives are somewhere between negligible and non-existent. Of the six Conference USA teams that reached bowl games in 2005, five played in minimum-payout bowls, with the league netting a combined $5.7 million in revenue (about $1 million of which came from a token BCS handout). The league's participating bowl teams lost a combined $578,494. One of those teams, Central Florida, spent approximately $1 million on its first-ever bowl trip to the Hawaii Bowl,

---

*Starting in 2006, the NCAA eliminated the formal minimum while allowing bowls to structure their own financial arrangements with the teams that may include a lower payout but cover the cost of tickets they have to purchase or other travel expenditures instead.

[†]The highest-paying non-BCS bowls in 2006–07 were the Capital One ($4.3 million), the Chick-fil-A ($2.4–$3.3 million), the Outback ($3 million), and the Cotton ($3 million).

which pays $750,000. "We will lose some money," UCF president John Hitt acknowledged to the *Orlando Sentinel* before the game. "We're looking at it more of as a positioning and exposure than as a chance to make money." Indeed, Hitt was last seen on a pool chair at the Sheraton Waikiki positioning himself for just the right exposure.

Apparently, normally budget-conscious conferences believe such financial setbacks are a worthy investment, because it is they who are increasingly becoming the driving forces behind the inception of new bowl games. Each November and December, conference commissioners engage in furious lobbying efforts in hopes of ensuring bowl berths for as many of their eligible teams as possible; what better way to make that happen than to create your own bowl game? The Big East, which saw several of its existing bowl partners lose interest following the exodus of Miami, Virginia Tech, and Boston College, was instrumental in the creation of the International Bowl. The WAC, hoping to ensure a perennial bowl spot for league member Hawaii, teamed with Conference USA to start the Hawaii Bowl in 2002 and was a key player in the formation of the New Mexico Bowl in 2006. "We've had teams in the past . . . that definitely deserved to be in a bowl game that didn't get an opportunity," WAC commissioner Karl Benson told the *Idaho Statesman.* "From the WAC's standpoint, we don't have to apologize for sending non-deserving teams to bowl games." No, but the Big 12 sure owes a couple of apologies.

How important is the relationship between bowls and conferences? Look no further than the Meineke Car Care Bowl in Charlotte, which averaged an impressive 64,000 spectators and generated two sellouts in its first 4 years of existence because most of the game's participants had come from within easy driving distance. On the flip side, San Francisco's Emerald Bowl entered the market in 2002 without the backing of its most logical conference partner, the Pac-10, and often featured teams (Virginia Tech, Boston College, Georgia Tech) from the other side of the continent. Not surprisingly, attendance was tepid, averaging around 26,000, before the bowl partnered with the Pac-10 in 2006.

The other major entity driving bowl expansion is television, namely ESPN, which airs twenty-two of the twenty-seven non-BCS bowl games and whose subsidiary, Charlotte-based ESPN Regional, actually owns and operates the Las Vegas, Hawaii, Fort Worth, Birmingham, and New Mexico bowls. "Different communities continue to have a thirst for hosting college football postseason play and teams absolutely enjoy the participation in these extra postseason events," Pete Derzis, the ESPN Regional exec who spearheaded four of the aforementioned games' formations, told the *Statesman*, "so I don't see any downside." For ESPN, such games can usually be counted on to provide reliable, if unspectacular, ratings. The December 21, 2006, Las Vegas Bowl between Oregon and BYU drew a 2.0 Nielsen rating (approximately 3.3 million viewers), which, while barely a third that of the network's highest-rated game, the Texas–Iowa Alamo Bowl (5.99*), nearly doubled the Duke–Gonzaga basketball game airing on ESPN2 at the same time (1.2) or the Cavaliers–Nets NBA game (1.3) it showed a night earlier. Even a seemingly dreadful New Mexico Bowl matchup between the hometown Lobos and San Jose State two days later garnered a 1.8 rating (3 million viewers). That 3 million people tuned into a New Mexico–San Jose State game is perhaps the ultimate proof that Americans are obsessed with all things football. Either that or they're really, really bored.

Of course, the idea of bowl games as television properties would seem to run contradictory to their original mission as philanthropic, community-centered events. "It runs contrary to the image that those who defend the bowl system like to convey, that it's a civic enterprise, to promote tourism, etc.," UCLA researcher John Sandbrook told the *San Diego Union-Tribune*. "I'm not sure that image holds up as well under the microscope today as it might have as recently as 10 years ago." Said former NCAA president Cedric Dempsey: "We've moved away from the two main objectives of the bowl system. One is to reward excellence. It's hard to say a 6-6 record is excellence. Secondarily, it was supposed to be a celebration of the game by the community.

---

*Strangely, this game between the 9–3 Longhorns (which came in on a two-game losing streak) and the 6–6 Hawkeyes, played on the Saturday afternoon before New Year's, drew the most viewers of any bowl game in ESPN's history.

Many are now just television-driven." Bowl advocates counter that they're still giving plenty back, not only to their host communities* but to the participating schools, which pocketed a reported $210 million in payouts during the 2006–07 bowl season. They're also quick to point out that the bowl experience is about more than just money—it's a heck of a lot of fun for the participants, too. The players get treated to a week in a posh hotel and $500 (the NCAA allowable amount) in gifts like portable DVD players and IPod Nanos. Coaches get in an extra three weeks' worth of practices with their teams. Athletic directors get wined and dined by the bowl committees. University presidents get to espouse about the egalitarianism of a system in which thirty-two teams end their season on a high note. And admissions departments get to enjoy free advertising to a national audience of prospective students.

Needless to say, there aren't a whole lot of vested parties in college football eager to see the demise of bowl games. "The bowl system is what it is all about," said Florida coach Urban Meyer[†] following a week of pampering by the Fiesta Bowl committee when his team won the 2007 BCS championship game there. "I watch every bowl I can[‡], and to see those young people enjoy themselves and to experience a different part of the country, that can never be changed." "That the bowl structure has endured for so long is a testament to its benefits and the unique role that it plays in college football," Big 12 commissioner Kevin Weiberg told a congressional committee in 2005. While there's no question that the national prestige and importance of long-standing games like the Gator Bowl and Sun Bowl have been greatly diminished by the advent of the BCS, they remain of vital importance to their host communities, generating tens of millions in local economic impact. "The Sun Bowl is the strongest economic development event we have [in El Paso]," Sun Bowl director Bernie Olivas told the

---

*According to the Football Bowl Association, bowl games generate a combined $1.3 billion annually in economic impact for their host cities.

[†]It should be noted that five weeks earlier, when it appeared his team might be excluded from the title game, Meyer was screaming for a playoff.

[‡]He also admitted a week earlier to sleeping through that year's Fiesta Bowl.

Des Moines Register. "It is necessary for our economy and our charities to have the bowl because nothing else brings in as much money."

So one of college football's most time-honored traditions continues unabated, albeit in greatly modernized and indisputably clunky fashion. Of the 120 Division I-A teams that lace up the chin straps each August, only 2 can reach the sport's grandest stage, the national championship, and only 8 can bask in the glamour of the Rose, Fiesta, Sugar, and Orange bowls. However, sixty-two of them can take comfort during the searing heat of two-a-days and the grueling rigors of early-morning conditioning sessions knowing that even if they don't do their best during the season—in fact, even if they only do half their best—there will still be a Gaylord Hotels Music City Bowl or Auto-Zone Liberty Bowl invite waiting for them at the finish line.

Whether there will be any fans there to watch them is another story.

9

That's Great, Now Run a 40

The draft is about as scientific as we can make it, but
sometimes it's like throwing darts at the board.

—*Seattle Seahawks coach Mike Holmgren to the*
Orange County Register, 2003

―――――――

Everyone looks for the negatives and a lot of these
people have no idea what they're talking about.

—*Former USC quarterback Matt Leinart after slipping*
to number 10 in the 2006 draft

When the 2006 NFL draft began at around noon on an April Saturday, ESPN's cameras showed Matt Leinart, the former USC quarterback, seated at a table with his parents in the Radio City Music Hall green room, his demeanor that of a regal prince in his three-piece striped suit and metallic-colored tie. This was to be the ultimate coronation for one of the most accomplished players in college football history, who in a matter of minutes would become a top-three draft pick. As expected, the Houston Texans selected N.C. State defensive end Mario Williams and the New Orleans Saints grabbed Leinart's USC teammate, Reggie Bush, with the first two picks. Now the Tennessee Titans were on the clock. A club with no proven quarterback and Leinart's former USC offensive coordinator, Norm Chow, on the staff, Tennessee seemed like his logical destination. When NFL commissioner Paul Tagliabue announced the pick, however, it was a different quarterback, Texas's Vince Young, the same guy who had defeated Leinart's team in the previous season's Rose Bowl.

OK. It happens. No worries. The next team on the board was the hometown New York Jets, themselves in desperate need of a quarterback. Surely they'd be thrilled about Leinart falling into their hands, right? Wrong. They opted for an offensive lineman, Virginia's D'Brickashaw Ferguson. None of the next few teams on the board were in need of a quarterback, and as it became apparent that his stock was plummeting by the nanosecond, Leinart's air of confidence began to disappear. His cell phone sat in his hand, strangely silent. As a slew of other players—Ohio State linebacker A.J. Hawk, Maryland tight end Vernon Davis, Texas safety Michael Huff—had their names called, Leinart could be seen in the background slinking further into his chair, looking less and less like a Hollywood stud accustomed to hanging with the likes of Nick Lachey and Alyssa Milano and more and more like the stunned kid who just had his allowance taken away. By the time Buffalo passed on their potential quarterback of the future in favor of Donte Whitner, a modestly productive Ohio State safety who in the weeks leading up to the draft had somehow bolted from a projected second-round slot all the way up to the number 8 pick, and the perennially QB-deprived Lions opted for Florida State linebacker Ernie Sims, you could tell Leinart wanted to be anywhere else in the world at that moment besides that nightmarish green room.

Finally, more than an hour and a half after the draft had started, Leinart's smile returned. He'd received a much-appreciated cell phone call from Arizona Cardinals coach Dennis Green, who told the quarterback it was "a gift from heaven" to be able to draft him.* The two-time national champion and Heisman Trophy–winning quarterback—one with a career 37–2 record, 64.8 completion percentage, 99 touchdowns, and 23 interceptions—had somehow been deemed the tenth-best player in the 2006 draft. You would have had an easier time convincing me you saw Elvis at your local 7-eleven.

By now, the craze surrounding the annual NFL draft has swept up nearly every red-blooded football fan in the country, adding more dizziness and intensity each year. Media coverage of the event, once limited to a few weeks in April, now starts earlier and earlier, and the saturation has literally no bounds. Soon, Mel Kiper's first position-by-position rankings for the class of 2030 will be made available shortly after the prospects emerge from the womb. These days, the first mock drafts come out as soon as the previous one ends, and the speculation and analysis continue unabated from there, hitting their peak shortly after the college season ends in early January. In addition to ESPN's gavel-to-gavel coverage of all seven rounds, one can now tune in to the NFL Network to watch players go through their combine workouts. Writers file daily dispatches from the week of practices leading up to the late-January Senior Bowl. And on my site, SI.com, a new Peter King, Dr. Z, or Don Banks draft column goes up approximately every 7.4 minutes during the months of March and April—and hundreds of

---

*Green was fired eight months later, though not for drafting Leinart.

thousands of people read every single one of them. Sometimes I wonder why we even bother to cover the actual games when it seems that all anyone really cares about is who will be playing in them next year.

There's at least one person, however, who's managed to avoid getting caught up in the hoopla: me. In the interest of full disclosure, I must confess that I'm not much of a pro football fan in general. I realize this may be considered somewhat of a sacrilegious statement in our country, where the NFL manages to be in the news virtually 365 days a year and you can't walk more than three blocks in any major city without running into someone in a Pittsburgh Steelers jersey. I realize that there are probably plenty of you reading this right now whose passions for both college and pro football are not mutually exclusive, whose football weekends start Saturday morning and don't end until Monday night, and that's certainly your prerogative. If your idea of excitement is watching a football game in a sterile, spaceship-looking stadium with silicone-enhanced cheerleaders and fight songs that are piped in over the loudspeakers, more power to you. If you like watching thirty-two teams run variations of the same exact offense in games where a "big play" might be a running back bursting free for 7 yards and the turning point is invariably some referee's ill-timed "illegal use of the hands" call, by all means, don't let me stop you. If you're the type of person who finds a late-December game between two 8–7 teams fighting for the last wild-card spot as exciting as an Auburn–Alabama game with the SEC championship on the line . . . well, to be perfectly honest, you and I could never be friends. For whatever reason, I don't share your affinity. And that's okay. For the most part, I stay out of the NFL's way and it stays out of mine. Considering that I spend most of my fall Sundays flying back from a college game, then racing back to my apartment to file weekend wrap-up columns for both SI and SI.com, it's not like I have a whole lot of time to fret over Peyton Manning's passing rating.

The draft, however, is far less avoidable, seeing as it's the one time of year when the college and pro football worlds converge. And every year, it manages to tick me off even more than the last. Draft junkies like to describe the months-long process by which NFL teams identify, evaluate, and eventually decide upon the future members of their franchise as "fascinating." I choose to refer to it as one big gigantic insult to the intelligence of anyone who follows college football closely. Those of us who do like to think we have a fairly accurate measure of assessing the respective talents of various players: it's called watching the games. After three years of watching USC's Leinart slice and dice opposing defenses like a samurai chef and lead a miracle last-second comeback at Notre Dame, most of us felt reasonably certain in our belief that the frizzy-haired SoCal kid was a pretty darn good quarterback. Ah, but apparently we didn't know what we were talking about. Because shortly following the conclusion of Leinart's senior season in 2005, a bunch of NFL writers who had watched a total of two USC games in the previous three years told us about all these heretofore undisclosed flaws in Leinart's game that had somehow gone unnoticed during his thirty-four consecutive victories. And shortly after that, a bunch of NFL scouting types who had watched the significantly less accomplished Vanderbilt quarterback Jay Cutler work out in shorts for 2 hours started saying that Cutler* was a "better pro prospect" and "safer pick" than Leinart.

Among the knocks against Leinart circulating among the NFL cognoscenti in the weeks leading up to the draft: that he lacked arm strength (apparently all those long touchdown passes made their way to the receivers magically); that his success at USC was due more to the talent surrounding him (apparently winning the Heisman in 2004 while playing with all first-time starting receivers and a patchwork offensive line went unnoticed); and, my favorite, that, due to his well-known penchant for Hollywood carousing (Leinart is one of the 3,763 L.A. bachelors to have been romantically linked to Paris Hilton), he "doesn't take football seriously enough." Rrrrright. Was this the same guy who, after orchestrating a miraculous, game-winning drive against Notre Dame, went to the bench and cried his eyes out? "All the questions that teams had, I answered when I met with them," said Leinart.

---

*Cutler ended up going one pick after Leinart to the Denver Broncos and actually played quite well in his five rookie starts. Score one for the scouts.

"As far as the arm strength, I answered that. As far as the lifestyle that I have, I answered that. As far as them getting to know me as a person, I think I answered every question I could." Apparently not well enough. By the way, Leinart supplanted veteran Kurt Warner as Arizona's starter five games into his rookie season. While he made more than his share of rookie mistakes* for a 5–11 team, most expect that he'll remain the Cardinals' quarterback for many, many years to come.

Leinart's stupefying tumble was just one of many such situations that arise nearly every year in the draft, where a perfectly good college player mysteriously plummets in the eyes of NFL scouting types. The year before it was Cal quarterback Aaron Rodgers, a guy who led the Golden Bears to their best season in a half-century and, in one of the most impressive quarterbacking performances I've seen in person, completed twenty-three straight passes and came within a goal-line stand of knocking off eventual national champion USC. Early in the draft process, Rodgers was being mentioned as a possibility for his hometown team, the San Francisco 49ers, who held that year's number 1 pick; instead he slipped all the way to the Green Bay Packers at number 24. "I think one of the reasons Aaron Rodgers fell in this draft," said former NFL quarterback and ESPN guru Ron Jaworski, "was the fact that he did not throw the football from all of the platforms that [number 1 pick] Alex Smith threw from." Platforms? Are we talking about operating systems or quarterbacks? At least Rodgers fared better that year than Lofa Tatupu, the All-America USC linebacker and tackling machine who, because he was "undersized" and had "marginal sideline-to-sideline range," somehow slipped to the Seattle Seahawks in the middle of the second round, where he promptly became an impact starter for a Super Bowl defense. Or Darren Sproles, the blazingly fast Kansas State running back who, despite memorably torching top-ranked Oklahoma for 235 yards in the Big 12 title game his junior year,

---

*Leinart finished the year twenty-third in the league in passer rating—two spots behind Steelers star Ben Roethlisberger and two spots ahead of future Hall of Famer Brett Favre. Tennessee's Vince Young, who won the NFL's rookie of the year award, finished thirtieth.

didn't get taken until the fourth round, mainly because he's 5-foot-6. "If [NFL teams] are concerned about his size," said Sproles's college coach, Bill Snyder, "they should ask players on the other side of the ball about him." At least the San Diego Chargers did—Sproles instantly became their top kick returner as a rookie.

These bizarre oversights, and hundreds of others just like them, come courtesy of the NFL's scouting process, one of the nation's shining examples of what can happen when businesses make things way more complicated than they need to be. Each year, the league's thirty-two franchises spend hundreds of thousands of dollars in the area of college scouting, employing anywhere from ten to twenty full-time employees devoted exclusively to the subject, most of whom spend the majority of their year traveling to college campuses across the country to watch practices, games, and film of prospects. At this point, you may be wondering to yourself, couldn't they just save themselves the trouble and plunk down $129 for a subscription to ESPN GamePlan? Probably. But then several hundred former third-string receivers, journeyman coaches, and other general football hangers-on would have to go find real work. Scouts are to football what the third base coach is to baseball—an excuse for a whole bunch of old-timers to stay a part of the fraternity and collect a paycheck to boot.

No one in the business will ever admit to their dirty little secret, however, and in fact I'm pretty sure most of them truly believe that what they do is only slightly less challenging than performing a heart transplant. After all, the pro game is different from the college game, and not every college star is necessarily suited for it. The competition is faster (an axiom I've always found perplexing—weren't these speed demons once in college themselves?), the playbooks more elaborate, the defenses more complex. If identifying NFL talent was really as simple as poring through a list of college All-Americans, then former Washington State star Ryan Leaf would be an All-Pro quarterback today, not a famously embarrassing washout; Ron Dayne, who ran for more yards in college than any other player in the history of the game, would have spent the past seven years doing much the same thing in the NFL rather than becoming a journeyman short-yardage specialist; and Peter

Warrick, the all-everything receiver for Florida State's 1999 national title team, would have caught more than eleven passes for the Seahawks' 2005 Super Bowl team.* Nearly every draft class is littered with highly accomplished college stars who failed to pan out at the next level, which is why, before investing several million dollars in such a player, NFL franchises go to painstaking lengths to ensure they're making the best possible decision. And yet, based on their rate of success, one can't help but think they'd do just as well making their draft choices with a game of eenie, meenie, minie, mo. "It's a 50–50 crapshoot as to whether a guy will turn out or not," Baltimore Ravens coach Brian Billick told the *Chicago Sun-Times.* "You are talking about putting a lot of money into a player who may never play for you."

For a 50–50 crapshoot, NFL coaches, GMs, personnel directors, and fans take the whole process awfully seriously. The draft consists of seven rounds, so, barring trades, we're talking about an event that will add a maximum of seven players to a roster of fifty-three. More realistically, only four or five will end up making the team, and in a particularly good year, two or three will wind up starters. In order to find those three gems, a typical team may prepare and maintain files on as many as seven hundred prospects per class. Nearly any graduating senior or outstanding junior who plays football for nearly any college in the country—and some who don't even do that—receives at least initial consideration, as NFL types live in a state of perpetual fear of letting the next potential great slip through the cracks. In the case of a truly elite prospect, however, the amount of information each team will accumulate on him by the time of the draft is truly astounding. Starting with initial reports from their scouts in the field, who will likely see him in person several times throughout his career, up to the assistant coach in charge of his position, the head coach, and the general manager, who, depending on their level of interest, may well take the time

---

*Warrick, the number 4 pick of the 2000 draft by the Cincinnati Bengals, was cut by the Seahawks in 2006 before signing with the Arena Football League's Las Vegas Gladiators.

to watch tape of nearly every game he ever played (multiple times), countless different members of the organization chime in with their opinions of the prospect. This all seems a bit redundant to me, seeing as, in my experience, there are only about eight words in the entire English language that NFL types use to describe a player. He can be either or all of the following: "fast," "athletic," "physical," "strong," "raw," "savvy," "scrappy," or "versatile." In some extreme cases of hyperbole he may also be deemed "freakish." More often than not, the player is also a "hard worker" with "good instincts," somebody who's "motor is always on," has "a nose for the ball," and possesses "a lot of upside." Some combination or permutation of these clichés is used to assess pretty much every prospect in the entire draft. I've yet to see the scouting report that describes a player as "a fine young man whose unique abilities should allow him to single-handedly reinvent the sport of football as we know it."

Somewhere along the way, however, the NFL gurus decided that merely watching the prospects play football wasn't providing nearly enough of a picture to properly compile their detailed reports. In order to correctly determine whether a prospect was truly worthy of becoming a pro football player, he would have to be measured, weighed, and evaluated while doing such football-related activities as jumping up and grabbing a flag (vertical jump), lifting a set of 225-pound weights (bench press), and sprinting as fast as possible for 40 yards (the 40-yard dash). These drills and others like it are part of the workouts each draft prospect must endure to properly pass inspection. Most players go through the gauntlet at the NFL's annual scouting combine in Indianapolis, though other opportunities include all-star games like the Senior Bowl, "pro days" held on the campuses of various college powerhouses, and, in the case of truly elite prospects, in their own individual showcases either at their schools, hometowns, or an interested team's headquarters.

Descriptions of the combine, which the media is largely prohibited from watching, often sound like that of some creepy government experiment. One by one, the players are trotted in front of a room full of watchful eyes wearing nothing but their underwear to have their height, weight, and wingspans measured. There's also an army of team doctors waiting to poke and prod each player to make sure they haven't been hiding some previously undisclosed thigh injury. "You feel like a piece of meat," former Northern Illinois running back Michael Turner told *Newsday*. "Like a car or something that's going to get sold at auction." The players are fully clothed the rest of the weekend, though not necessarily in pads and a helmet. Prospects at each position are put through a battery of individual "shell" drills, with each quarterback throwing several different types of passes, blockers going one on one against opposing linemen, and so on. All the while, dignitaries from around the league watch from the stands in a bizarrely enraptured state. "You sometimes forget that these guys aren't going to play football on Sundays in shorts," Ravens GM Ozzie Newsome told the *Florida Times-Union*.

Indeed, most NFL types, like Colts GM Bill Polian, insist that the combine and subsequent player workouts are only "a part of the overall mosaic* of the scouting process. The combine is a very important part, but certainly not the only part. You do learn a lot about guys, but I think the most that you learn about players is what you see when they play." And yet every year they make decisions that seem to indicate the exact opposite—that they in fact place *more* importance on these workouts than anything else. How else does one explain why every March and April (the combine is held in late February), three months after they played their last competitive football games, a whole bunch of prospects suddenly see their draft stock rise or fall considerably? Most amusing to college followers is when a relatively unheralded player, after failing to distinguish himself throughout three or four seasons of actual football, suddenly soars over many of his more accomplished counterparts solely on the basis of an impressive 40 time or bench press. These are the guys who have come to be known as "workout wonders."

No player in recent history better personifies the phenomenon of

---

*The mere fact that he used the word "mosaic" to describe the scouting process should tell you these guys take this stuff *way* too seriously.

the workout wonder than Mike Mamula. Following two impressive seasons at Boston College in which he racked up twenty-five sacks, the defensive end dropped his name in the hopper for the 1995 draft, where he was initially projected to be a third-round pick. The 6-foot-5, 248-pound defensive end put on such a show at the combine, however, putting up a better 40 time (4.58) than some wide receivers and posting the highest vertical jump (38.5 inches) and shuttle time (4.06 seconds) of any player at his position, that by the end of the weekend, his name was being mentioned as a possible mid-first rounder. "Everybody knew he was a good football player," New York Giants scout Greg Gabriel said at the time. ". . . No one knew just how good he was until these drills." Really? So you're saying you knew he was "good" from watching tape of him playing football, but you didn't realize just how good until you saw him sprint 40 yards in a T-shirt and shorts? That doesn't seem at all like a recipe for disaster. So impressed were the Philadelphia Eagles, whose coach at the time, Ray Rhodes, was one of Mamula's most gushing admirers, that they traded up to select him with the seventh pick of the draft, taking him ahead of future All-Pros like Miami defensive tackle Warren Sapp, Michigan cornerback Ty Law, and Florida State linebacker Derrick Brooks. Mamula wound up playing just six NFL seasons and never came close to living up to his workout-inspired accolades. Rhodes was fired at the end of Mamula's fourth season.

For a bunch of guys running multimillion-dollar businesses, you would think a disaster like that would cause at least some of them to stop and say, "Hmm. You know what? Maybe we shouldn't go all gaga every time a guy runs a 4.5 40." Not exactly. Like the guy who can't help but order another chili dog no matter how much time he spent in the bathroom after the last one, the NFL suits fall for the workout wonders year after year after year. It's one thing if a player's workout is simply further validation of his on-the-field dominance. Such was the case for 2006 workout wonder Vernon Davis, an All-America tight end at Maryland whose dazzling combine performance helped him land the number 6 pick. What's truly amazing is that many NFL types put so much faith in a player's workout that, if impressive enough, it can make them overlook seemingly huge red flags from his actual playing career.

Take the case of former Cal quarterback Kyle Boller, who, for his first three seasons, struggled horrifically, completing barely 45 percent of his passes. Prior to his senior season, noted QB guru Jeff Tedford took over as the Bears' head coach and Boller showed noticeable improvement. Still, he was only the nation's forty-third-rated passer, and no sane college football follower at the time would have placed him in the same breath as quarterbacks like Florida's Rex Grossman, Miami's Ken Dorsey, or Virginia's Matt Schaub. Then came his workout on Cal's campus, in which he threw about a hundred times in front of watchful NFL eyes. "It was one of the better workouts I have ever seen," then-49ers coach Dennis Erickson raved to the *Contra Costa Times*. The Baltimore Ravens selected Boller with the nineteenth pick of the draft, higher than any other quarterback except USC's Carson Palmer and Marshall's Byron Leftwich. He started thirty-four games for the Ravens, throwing more interceptions (32) than touchdowns (31), before the franchise finally signed veteran Steve McNair to replace him.* Even more puzzling was the meteoric rise of Akili Smith (another Tedford protégé), who, after starting just one barely memorable season for Oregon in 1998, blew scouts away in workouts with his apparently stunning arm strength. The Cincinnati Bengals, desperately seeking a franchise quarterback at the time, selected him with the number 3 pick. He started just seventeen games, and four years later the Bengals went the slightly safer route, selecting Heisman Trophy winner Palmer with the number 1 pick. He's worked out a little bit better.

Why oh why, NFL wizards, do you keep falling for the same trick? "What we see [at the combine] is still an addictive drug," former New York Giants coach Jim Fassel told the *Times-Union*. "You try to avoid going for the great workout guys, but it happens." "What can you say?" said Ravens GM Newsome. "We're human." Really? I thought humans had the capacity to learn from their mistakes. These guys seem more

---

*The Ravens paid Boller a total of $6.7 million over his first three seasons, or roughly $200,000 for each interception.

like a dog who keeps running to the door yelping every time he hears the doorbell ring, despite the fact that that sound has yet to produce anything more exciting than the UPS guy.

The workouts don't just fool GMs into selecting potential busts, either. They can cause them to unwittingly pass on some future star. It's unclear when exactly the 40-yard dash became the football world's crown jewel of measuring sticks—a 1998 *Sports Illustrated* article traced its origins to legendary coach Paul Brown, who settled on the seemingly arbitrary distance because "he thought that was as far as a player would run on any play," said his son Mike. All we know is that four years of on-the-field accomplishments can get wiped away in the span of about five seconds if a prospect runs a slower-than-expected 40. Why? Because "speed is the one thing you can't coach," said Polian. Indeed, as a senior for Mississippi Valley State in 1984, wide receiver Jerry Rice caught 112 passes for 1,845 yards and 28 touchdowns, numbers so staggering that, despite playing for a Division I-AA school, he was named to the AP All-America team and finished ninth in the Heisman Trophy voting. Rice seemed like a no-brainer to become an NFL star, but when scouts timed him in the 40, they were disappointed to find he couldn't break a 4.6 (receivers are expected to run in the 4.4 or low 4.5 range). He therefore fell to the sixteenth pick—behind receivers Eddie Brown of Miami and Al Toon of Wisconsin—where he was selected by the San Francisco 49ers, for whom he would win four Super Bowls and establish himself as unquestionably the greatest receiver in NFL history. "Nobody realized his playing time wasn't his 40 time," said longtime Cowboys draft honcho Gil Brant. I don't even know what to say to that.

Rice may be the most famous example, but there are similar cases nearly every year. In 2003, Arizona State defensive end Terrell Suggs, who had set an NCAA single-season record the year before with twenty-four sacks, ran a disappointing 4.85 in his workouts, causing red flags to rise across the league. "No player's draft stock has dropped faster or further," the *Chicago Tribune* wrote in the days before the draft. Sure enough, Suggs, considered a top-three pick when he originally declared for the draft, slipped to the tenth pick, where the Ravens happily snapped him up. He notched twelve sacks his first season and was named NFL Defensive Rookie of the Year. "Happens every year," a bemused Phil Savage, the Ravens' director of player personnel, quipped to the *Contra Costa Times* following Suggs's rookie performance. Actually, it happened again that very same year. Athletic receiver Anquan Boldin, who had racked up an impressive 1,011 yards and 13 touchdowns his last season at Florida State, laid an egg at the combine, posting a reported 40 time of 4.75—atrocious for a receiver. Boldin fell all the way to the late second round, where he went to the Arizona Cardinals. That first season he caught a rookie-record 101 passes for 1,377 yards to run away with Offensive Rookie of the Year honors. So, just for the record, both the offensive *and* defensive rookies of the year that season ran poor 40 times. And yet when the scouting community reconvened in Indianapolis the following spring, you can bet not a single one of them wasn't still glued to his stopwatch.

As any good, grizzled coach will tell you, the game of football is as much mental as it is physical. Therefore, in addition to analyzing game film, 40 times, and bench reps, NFL teams also go to great lengths to get a sense of the prospects as people. For most of the players, professional football will be their first full-time job, a drastic departure from their often coddled and sheltered college existence. And like any potential employer, the teams want to make sure they have the character and mental fortitude to handle the responsibility. To that end, one of the most important steps in the process is the face-to-face meetings between prospects and team personnel (mostly the coaches, GM, and, in the case of some franchise-type prospects, the owner) either at the combine, where the players are shuttled through an exhausting series of fifteen-minute interviews with various teams, or in pre-draft visits to the teams' facilities. "I like to see if they look me in the eye. I like to see how a guy shakes your hand," Chiefs head coach Herman Edwards, then with the Jets, told *Newsday*. "That's when you can learn about a young man." You can learn a lot more, obviously, by talking to people who actually know the player, and teams do just that, calling everyone from his coaches to his teachers to his pastor for testimonials.

Of course, those types of people in a player's life tend to be a bit biased, so teams also utilize a wide array of more objective assessments. They run criminal background checks and employ private investigators to uncover any potential dirt. (In 1995, league security officials alerted teams that Miami defensive tackle Warren Sapp had failed multiple drug tests and solicited prostitutes.) They administer the infamous twelve-minute, fifty-question Wonderlic intelligence test at the combine, where 300-pound linemen sit nervously at a desk pondering questions like, "Paper sells for 21 cents a pad; What will 4 pads cost?"* They compile personality and psychological profiles.† And yet they continue to peg some players completely wrong.

Earlier in this chapter, I mentioned one of the most famous draft busts in recent memory, Washington State's Ryan Leaf. The number 2 pick in the 1998 draft, Leaf was released by the San Diego Chargers after just three seasons, one of which he missed entirely due to injury and another in which he threw just two touchdown passes and fifteen interceptions. It seems hard to believe now, but at the time of the draft, the Indianapolis Colts, which owned the number 1 pick, were actually faced with a tough decision, choosing between Leaf and the guy they wound up taking, eight-time Pro Bowler Peyton Manning. That's because while Leaf had all the physical tools necessary to succeed— finishing third in the Heisman Trophy race while throwing for a Pac-10 record 33 touchdowns—he had the maturity of a twelve-year-old. During his brief but eventful stint in San Diego, he was caught on tape both threatening a cameraman in the Chargers' locker room and confronting a heckling fan during training camp; he publicly criticized his teammates, many of whom came to despise him; he got into a shouting match with general manager Bobby Beathard, for which he was

---

*The correlation between good Wonderlic scores and NFL success? Zippo. Quarterback Drew Henson, who lasted two seasons with the Dallas Cowboys, scored a remarkably high 42; Hall of Famer Dan Marino scored a 16.
†The New York Giants are famous for their bizarre four hundred-question examination that includes such questions as "True or false, I like tall women." In 1996, former Illinois linebacker Kevin Hardy humorously responded by crossing out the "t" in "tall" and answering 'Yes.'"

suspended; and on one occasion, while injured, chose to skip a mini-camp to play golf.

For the Chargers, it was a devastating, humiliating, and expensive* lesson. And yet there was no shortage of warning signs. I've met a handful of Washington State grads over the years, and seemingly every one of them has a story about being at a bar where Leaf got in a fight with someone and/or got tossed out. The scouts had to have heard the same stories. "Ryan was always an impulsive kid at Washington State," draft analyst Joel Buchsbaum told the *New Orleans Times-Picayune* in 2000. "He was a spoiled kid; that much everybody in the league knew." "Everybody in the league knew of his work habits, his character and personality. People had concerns about the guy," said Houston Texans GM Charley Casserly. "But the guy had great ability." A year later, the Minnesota Vikings used the twenty-ninth pick in the first round to select defensive end Dimitrius Underwood, a definitive workout wonder from Michigan State who had entered the draft a year early despite missing the previous season with an ankle injury. After going through three agents in 4 months, Underwood finally signed with the Vikings on August 1, reported to training camp . . . and disappeared a day later. When he resurfaced, his behavior was erratic, and his mother claimed he'd been brainwashed by a religious cult near the Michigan State campus. Shortly after being released by the Vikings and latching on with the Miami Dolphins, Underwood attempted suicide. He was eventually diagnosed with bipolar disorder. Obviously, no one with the Vikings could have been expected to uncover the extent of Underwood's troubles beforehand, but they did choose to ignore signs that something might not be right. Even before the draft, reporters were aware that Underwood possessed "serious character . . . questions." And people close to the Michigan State program had questioned his work ethic and hinted that his injury wasn't as serious as he'd made it out to be.

What's particularly strange is how NFL teams can be so seemingly arbitrary about the seriousness with which they treat potential charac-

---

*Leaf received an $11.25 million signing bonus.

ter issues. Obviously, in the cases of Leaf and Underwood, the teams that drafted them fell under the spell of their physical attributes and chose to overlook everything else. More commonly, however, the traditionally conservative and gun-shy NFL types do the exact opposite, running for the hills at even the slightest sign of trouble—and often greatly exaggerating or even completely misrepresenting a player's character. I don't claim to know every college player I cover personally, but I know enough about the big names to be indignant when, in the weeks leading up to the draft, some high-profile prospect suddenly develops some mysterious character flaw that didn't previously exist. Such was the case in 2005 with Cal quarterback Rodgers, who in the weeks leading up to the draft was described by some NFL insiders as "too cocky." I had to laugh at that one. I spent the better part of a day with Rodgers that January while attending a college all-star event, including sharing a long round-trip car ride between the hotel and the stadium, and while he certainly wasn't lacking in confidence, he didn't say anything that you wouldn't expect from a player trying to sell himself to potential suitors. If anything, he carried a chip on his shoulder from having been completely ignored by colleges three years earlier (he attended a junior college before being discovered by Cal), which, in my experience, isn't a bad thing for a player to have.

Rodgers's slight was nothing, though, compared to the experience a year later of USC's LenDale White. The Trojans' bruising tailback throughout their thirty-four-game winning streak from 2003–05, White was considered a mid-first round pick shortly after the season. His stock plummeted in the weeks leading up to the draft, in part because a hamstring injury prevented him from working out for teams—again, apparently NFL teams needed to see him run a 40-yard dash in shorts before confirming the validity of those 3,159 career yards and 52 career touchdowns—but also because he somehow got pegged as an overweight, lazy punk with a bad attitude and work ethic. A scout attending USC's pro day told *Sports Illustrated*'s Michael Silver afterward that White "got behind the wheel of his Range Rover, got those rims spinning and took off. He looked like a guy who just didn't have a clue." Basically, the network of old white guys who run NFL teams got miffed when White wouldn't risk his health to run a 40 for them, saw him in a tricked-out SUV, and decided he must be a thug, going so far as to compare him to infamous Ohio State washout Maurice Clarett. Clearly, these guys hadn't spent a whole lot of time around the USC program the previous three seasons.

I don't know White personally, but I do know this: despite possessing the obvious talent to have been the featured back for nearly any team in the country, he spent most of his three seasons splitting carries while playing in the shadow of future Heisman winner Bush, yet never once said boo. Sounds like a real spoiled brat, doesn't it? Lazy? In the final game of the 2004 regular season, White suffered an ankle injury so serious he was still walking with a limp only days before that year's national title game against Oklahoma. He not only played, he ran for 118 yards and 2 touchdowns. Fat? White admitted he got carried away at the holiday dinner tables prior to his final college game, the Rose Bowl against Texas, ballooning from a regular playing weight of about 240 pounds to 253, yet that didn't seem to stop him from running for 124 yards (on 18 carries) and 3 touchdowns, and by the time of the draft he'd taken most of it off. Bad attitude? Bush and quarterback Matt Leinart may have been the Trojans' two superstars, but White was always the more vocal leader, urging his team on in practices and thumping his chest in the huddle. "I'm not a bad seed," White insisted to *Sports Illustrated* prior to the draft. "On Saturdays, if my college teammates had to put a million dollars on somebody coming through, I have to say they'd have taken their chances on me." NFL teams apparently weren't willing to take that chance. With an ESPN camera in his Colorado living room on draft day to broadcast his pained expression to the nation, White inexplicably slipped all the way to the forty-fifth pick, midway through the second round. There he was snapped up by the Tennessee Titans*—whose offensive coordinator, Norm Chow, happened to be a little more familiar with White than most, having

---

*White served as the backup to star Travis Henry as a rookie for the Titans, averaging 4.0 yards on 61 carries.

served as USC's offensive coordinator during White's first two seasons. "He is a misunderstood young man," Chow told the *Tennessean* upon drafting him. ". . . He comes from kind of a tough background, but the guy knows what's right and what's wrong." If only the same could be said of the so-called experts evaluating him.

In all fairness, it should be noted that the scouting types do deserve credit for occasionally discovering a previously unknown talent. While roughly 99 percent of NFL players were obvious standouts in college, there are always a few exceptions who—be it because they were late bloomers, or got stuck on the bench behind some superstar, or were simply misused by their college coaches— seemingly come out of nowhere to become NFL stars. By now we all know the story of Warner, the one-time Iowa grocery stock boy who went on to become an all-league player in arena football and, eventually, the starting quarterback for the 2000 Super Bowl champion St. Louis Rams. Terrell Davis, the Denver Broncos' star running back during the late 1990s who earned both league and Super Bowl MVP awards, was a sixth-round draft choice who spent most of his career at Georgia as the backup to Heisman finalist Garrison Hearst. Similarly, Baltimore Ravens and Kansas City Chiefs running back Priest Holmes, who led the NFL in rushing in 2001 and set the league's single-season touchdown record in 2003, was an undrafted free agent who spent the latter half of his college career at Texas stuck behind future Heisman winner Ricky Williams. Fifteen-year NFL veteran Brad Johnson, the Minnesota Vikings' starting quarterback in 2006, was a backup at Florida State whom the Vikings selected in the now-extinct ninth round. And New Orleans Saints receiver Marques Colston, one of the standout rookies of the 2006 season, was a seventh-round pick who spent his college career in obscurity at Hofstra.*

---

*I must admit to ignorance on this one. When our NFL producer at SI.com, Andrew Perloff, asked me about Colston early in the 2006 season, my exact response was, "Who's Marques Colston?" He finished the season with 70 catches for 1,038 yards and was a major reason the surprising Saints reached the NFC championship game.

In all of the aforementioned cases, some scout somewhere was smart enough to figure out each player was worth taking a chance on despite such limited track records. Heck, I'm guessing that discovering a Marques Colston is the scouting profession's equivalent of a stockbroker who recommended his client buy Netflix when it was just a startup. You probably get a gold watch and job security for life, not to mention a permanent get-out-of-jail-free card, for every Tyrone Calico* you subsequently endorse.

Of all the improbable NFL success stories over the years, none should be more perplexing to college football followers than that of Pittsburgh Steelers running back Willie Parker. In four seasons at North Carolina (2000–03), the aptly dubbed "Fast Willie" (he'd been timed at 4.28 in the 40) started a grand total of five games, gaining just 181 yards on 48 carries his senior season. In the ultimate insult, he didn't get a single carry on Senior Day. There are conflicting versions as to why the 5-foot-10, 200-pounder spent so much of his career riding the pine—particularly when the Tar Heels, which won a combined five games during Parker's junior and senior seasons, weren't exactly brimming with offensive stars. Apparently head coach John Bunting wanted Parker to bulk up and become more of a power back, and Parker, who'd always relied primarily on his speed, wasn't interested. "In retrospect, we probably could have done some things differently with Willie," UNC running backs coach Andre Powell would later tell the *Pittsburgh Tribune Review*. "But we were trying to develop our own style. We were bound and determined to be a [physical] running team. . . . For whatever reason, we [the coaching staff and Parker] never could get on the same page."

In *Pro Football Weekly's* rankings of the top running back prospects in the 2004 draft, Parker was listed forty-third, one spot behind Southern Oregon's Dustin McGroty and one spot ahead of Northern Colorado's Adam Matthews. Suffice it to say, he was not drafted. That the

---

*Calico, a receiver from Middle Tennessee State, was the small school sensation of the 2003 draft, going in the second round to the Tennessee Titans. He caught a combined forty-two passes in three NFL seasons before being released.

scouts even knew of his existence shows that they really do keep tabs on absolutely *everyone.* The Steelers signed Parker as a free agent. Not only did he make the team, but in only his second season, he supplanted longtime star Jerome Bettis as the Steelers' starter and exploded for 1,202 yards, culminating in a Super Bowl victory over the Seahawks. The same guy who couldn't even get on the field against Duke two years earlier recorded the longest run in Super Bowl history, a 75-yard touchdown that broke the game open. "You would think, with all the info we have, you can't find a diamond in the rough," New York Giants GM Ernie Accorsi told the *Washington Post.* "And then you see a Willie Parker. He didn't just make a roster. He was a star of the Super Bowl."

From the college perspective, the Parker story proves either that the since-fired Bunting was one of the biggest morons ever to wear a headset—a distinct possibility, considering that the Tar Heels went 27–45 under his watch—not to have seen what he had on his hands in Parker; that NFL players are basically glamorized chess pieces, that with the right system and a good offensive line, you can pluck pretty much anyone off the street and turn him into a 1,000-yard rusher (the Denver Broncos, in fact, have been doing that very thing for years); or, quite simply, that the process of determining which college players are best suited to become NFL stars has been and continues to be rooted heavily in the ancient art of blind luck. I would bet on the latter. After all, three-time Super Bowl champion quarterback Tom Brady of the New England Patriots, considered by many the Joe Montana of his era, was only the 199th player drafted in 2000—and hardly anyone who watched him at Michigan would have expected him to go much higher. Meanwhile, the top overall pick in that same draft, dominating defensive end Courtney Brown, notched more sacks his last two seasons at Penn State (24) than he would during the seven years (19) of an utterly disappointing NFL career that followed. "I remember what [former Steelers coach Chuck] Noll used to say about this," Bills president and GM Tom Donahoe told *Newsday.* ". . . Until you live with that draft choice and spend time with him day-in and day-out, you don't know what he's like. So you can do all the homework conceivable, but there's still an element of guesswork."

If I could, I'd like to offer a few bits of advice to the scouting folks that might help reduce some of that guesswork. For one, you might want to start putting more emphasis on a player's track record than on pure physical skills. If a quarterback doesn't have the world's greatest arm strength but was able to lead his college team to a 37–2 record, chances are he's going to be a pretty good pro. Same goes for the line-backer who doesn't necessarily run a 4.5 but still managed to make 400 tackles. While we're at it, if you're going to insist on using the 40 as your golden measuring stick, maybe try timing the guy two or three different times over a series of several weeks rather than basing his entire stock on one 4-second showcase in which he may have performed better or worse than usual. And finally, stop trying to outsmart yourself. If you're the general manager of the Houston Texans and you happen to hold the number 1 pick and the reigning Heisman Trophy winner, who happened to be the most electrifying college running back in two decades, is available to you . . . *draft him*! I'm sure you can find another athletic defensive end who had one huge half-season somewhere farther down the line.

I offer you this advice on behalf of all the other college football fans out there who can't help but be irritated, confused, and a tad bit amused by the way you guys do business, and all the suffering NFL fans who pay eighty dollars for a ticket to a game only to watch their team go out and draft Mario Williams instead of Reggie Bush.

Try it—you may just find that it works. All I ask in return is a $2 million signing bonus.

10

Everybody Cheats— Just Not My School

They take care of you down there. I know from
my brother [who plays there] they keep your
pockets full, give you plenty of money.

—*Texas A&M recruit Terrence McCoy to the* Midland
(Texas) Reporter-Telegram, *2006*

———————

There's a reason NCAA sanctions no longer
have any bite. No one really cares.

—Seattle Post-Intelligencer, *2004*

In November 2004, I wrote a column on SI.com suggesting that Ohio State president Dr. Karen Holbrook take the unprecedented step of shutting down the university's scandal-plagued athletic department for a year. Earlier that week, *ESPN the Magazine* had published a multipart investigative feature in which several former football players told of receiving phony jobs and academic favors. The most salacious allegations came from former star running back Maurice Clarett, previously dismissed from the program for lying to NCAA investigators about extra benefits he'd received. Clarett alleged that Buckeyes head coach Jim Tressel introduced him to boosters who lavished him with cash, free cars, and do-nothing jobs. Mind you, when I wrote my column I didn't actually expect the school to voluntarily shut down a $90 million enterprise beloved by hundreds of thousands of fans. My point was that Ohio State—which was already facing major sanctions against its men's basketball program at the time—had allowed its athletic culture to spin out of control and that a serious response from the school was in order. (To its credit, Ohio State has since made numerous progressive changes to its athletic department under new director Gene Smith).

Obviously, I realized Ohio State fans would not be overly pleased with my proposal—no one likes to see their favorite team portrayed in a negative fashion. What was most startling about the e-mails I received from Buckeyes' fans, however, was not their anger over the death-penalty suggestion or their creative use of profanities, but the seemingly universal belief that despite overwhelming evidence to the contrary, their school had done nothing wrong, that the disreputable Clarett had fabricated his entire story, and that writers like myself and those at ESPN had committed egregious journalistic sins. "If it weren't for a pathetic, egomaniacal street punk masquerading as a viable pro football prospect, there would be no issue with Ohio State athletics," wrote one.

"Everything that has happened at OSU has happened at every school in the Top 25, don't kid yourself, and my school will not take the fall," wrote another. And those were the nicer ones.

We'll never know whether or not Clarett was telling the truth. Shaken by the fallout from his ESPN interview, which some hare-brained adviser suggested might help his sagging NFL stock, he refused to cooperate with NCAA investigators, and eventually the matter was dropped.* What we do know, however, is that six weeks after Clarett's allegations became public, Ohio State's star quarterback, Troy Smith, a close friend of Clarett's at the time, was suspended for the Buckeyes' 2004 bowl game after an attorney for a Columbus-area health care company notified the university that the player had come into its office and walked out with an envelope allegedly filled with $500 cash from CEO Robert Q. Baker, an OSU booster—a scene exactly like the type Clarett described in the article. We also know that at Tressel's former school, Youngstown State, the coach introduced Ray Isaac, his star quarterback at the time, to a prominent booster who lavished him with more than $10,000 in illegal benefits. Ohio State officials even bolstered Clarett's claims when they admitted he had been seen around campus driving a different car nearly every week. It didn't take a rocket scientist to conclude that bad things went down during Clarett's brief career as a Buckeye, and that they probably involved more players than just him. Yet in Columbus, OSU fans believe to this day that the program was "vindicated" by the NCAA and that their school was the innocent victim of a venomous media crusade.

USC, Miami, Tennessee, and Colorado, on the other hand—now *those* guys are dirty.

When it comes to stories about malfeasance in college football, it never ceases to amaze me how fans suddenly morph into full-fledged political operatives. Anyone not directly affiliated with their program, from reporters to NCAA officials, is considered an enemy with a

---

*The troubled Clarett, his football career ruined, eventually turned to crime and was incarcerated following an attempted armed robbery.

potential agenda, while anyone within their gates can do no wrong. As soon as a negative rumor hits the message boards about one of their players, someone invariably posts the obligatory, "let's wait for the facts to come out" admonition. Such caution gets thrown to the wind, however, when a similar headline surfaces about a rival team or generally hated program. The fangs come out, and the natives become bloodthirsty. They want nothing more than to see the other team go down in a flame of rolling heads and NCAA sanctions. Of course, if the same exact headline were to be written about their own team, they'd likely accuse the author of initiating a witch hunt.

Cheating in college football is a tradition nearly as old as tailgating and letter sweaters. Tales of hundred-dollar handshakes, duffle bags, and shiny new cars date back to at least the days of legendary coach Bear Bryant, whose Texas A&M teams were placed on NCAA probation in the 1950s as a result of the coach soliciting the help of a few deep-pocketed oil men in the Aggies' recruiting efforts. Though the sport is monitored much more closely today than it was in its Wild West days, new scandals emerge on a near-annual basis, causing no shortage of shock and outrage among pundits, observers, and academics. In turn, fans of the teams involved mostly get angry at the outraged pundits, observers, and academics. "Fans would rather win a championship and later get busted for cheating than finish 8–4 or 9–3 every year with an upright program of student-athletes," wrote Ted Miller, the *Seattle Post-Intelligencer*'s college football columnist. "Media rants about the hypocrisy of college sports no longer raise hackles; they're just part of the background noise." Indeed, when allegations first come to light about a program, the most pressing concern among fans isn't the possibility of corruption at their revered institution but the potential impact the negative publicity might have on recruiting.

In the spring of 2006, USC, which had spent most of the past three seasons basking in the adulation of a thirty-four-game winning streak, was faced with an avalanche of bad press stemming from several different incidents. A report had recently surfaced that the family of former star Reggie Bush had lived in an expensive house paid for by an aspiring sports marketer looking to make the star his client, a potential

NCAA violation if true; freshman quarterback Mark Sanchez had been arrested on suspicion of sexual assault (no charges were ever filed); and the school was looking into the living arrangements of star receiver Dwayne Jarrett. All of this prompted a ticked-off fan by the name of TrojanAl to post this call to action on the fan site WeAreSC.com: ". . . We need to make all these rumors and accusations go away ASAP. . . . The first and easiest thing is to clear Sanchez. This is a USC town. If you work in the [district attorney's office] or know the DA, this is the time to apply pressure. . . . The second thing is to clear ALL these NCAA rumors. I have emailed the NCAA requesting a quick resolution to the Jarrett investigation. . . . Bush will be more difficult because of the lawsuits. Hopefully he and his family have some good Trojan attorneys working for him."

Sounds like something out of *The Sopranos*, doesn't it? Clearly, at least in this fan's mind, avoiding NCAA sanctions and ensuring that a potential star quarterback didn't wind up in jail before the season started were higher priorities than bringing any potential guilty parties to justice. This is not to say that college football fans don't believe in justice. On the contrary, many are in fact *obsessed* with the principles of fairness and justice—as long as they're being applied to somebody else's team. "After denial, the first defense you hear from anyone being investigated by the NCAA is a list of who else the NCAA should be investigating," wrote *Birmingham Post-Herald* columnist Ray Melick. ". . . It's the old 'everybody's doing it' defense."

Indeed, I get all kinds of e-mails every year from confused fans wondering why their school is getting called on the carpet by the NCAA and vilified by the media, while School B, which everyone in the free world knows to be just as dirty, appears to be getting off scot-free. In most cases, their confusion is well founded. We live in an age when all manner of misbehavior, no matter how slight or salacious, gets covered by the media. This is especially true in college sports, where something as seemingly minor as a quarterback getting caught using a fake ID gets much the same treatment as a running back selling Ecstasy out of his dorm room, where it's against NCAA rules not only to give a hotshot linebacker his own Cadillac Escalade but also to buy that same player a slice of pizza. No matter the severity, all of these various indiscretions as well as others just like them get lumped together in the public conscience as part of the perceived cesspool that is major college athletics. In an environment like this, the assumption is that anyone who's anyone has skeletons in his closet, and so if the NCAA is going to come down on my house, surely it ought to be looking into my neighbor's as well. The reality, however, is that not all indiscretions are created equal, and many of them don't even fall under the NCAA's jurisdiction (which may seem hard to believe, considering that the NCAA handbook is longer than *Ulysses*). In fact, a disparity in justice seems almost unavoidable once you come to understand the arcane way in which our nation's college athletic programs go about policing themselves.

The NCAA's enforcement division was created in 1952 and, according to its Web site, "is an integral part of the process to ensure integrity and fair play among [its] members." Much of the public is under the mistaken impression that the NCAA has an army of suits constantly digging up dirt on its members and conducting clandestine sting operations, à la the FBI or the health department. In actuality, there are just six enforcement directors and nineteen field investigators policing more than fifteen thousand sports teams at more than eleven hundred colleges. Not surprisingly, then, the NCAA is usually among the last to know when something seedy is going down at a particular campus and is almost entirely dependent on anonymous tips, news accounts, or actual police investigations to do the majority of their dirty work. In many cases schools self-report violations, in an effort to stay in the NCAA's good graces. While major infraction cases are rare, the NCAA processes hundreds of so-called secondary violations every year, nearly all of them self-reported by the schools and nearly all of them so trivial they'd make you pull your hair out.

If the NCAA does decide to investigate a school, the ensuing process is a lot like an episode of *Law & Order* gone awry. The NCAA assigns one of its field officers, most of whom are lawyers by training, to go out and interview potential perpetrators, witnesses, and other involved parties just like a real-life criminal case, only with one major caveat: unless the subject is a school employee or currently enrolled athlete, there's nothing requiring him to talk to the NCAA. Therefore, investigations are almost entirely dependent on the presence of at least one central figure who is willing to voluntarily come forward and blow the whistle, even if it means incriminating himself. Hence, when Clarett opted against sharing what he knew about potential booster violations at Ohio State, the investigation pretty much hit a wall. It's not like the corrupt boosters themselves were going to come forward and say, "All right, here's how much I paid and to whom." In many cases, the most productive NCAA investigations are the ones whose subject matter coincides with an actual court case, thus producing subpoenaed depositions and public records. "We don't have subpoena powers," NCAA spokeswoman Jane Jankowski told *U.S. News and World Report,* "and I think people get frustrated with the NCAA because our cases don't go as far as they would like them to go."

The NCAA didn't use to be saddled with that perception. On the contrary, there was a time not so long ago when coaches and administrators didn't dare breathe wrong lest they wind up on probation. Under the direction of take-no-prisoners director David Berst, the guys in enforcement spent much of the 1980s taking down perps, then handing them over to the Committee on Infractions—the NCAA's equivalent of judge and jury—which was all too happy to slap the offending parties with TV bans, bowl bans, probation, and the like. In its most famous case to date, the NCAA issued the first and only "death penalty" to SMU's football program in 1987, shutting down its operations for an entire season (the school canceled the following season as well) following its second ugly booster scandal within a five-year period (thirteen players were paid approximately $47,000, with several school personnel not only aware but involved). In its report, the committee said the intention of the severe penalty was to "eliminate a program that was built on a legacy of wrongdoing . . . [and] to permit a new beginning for football at the university." It hasn't exactly worked out that way, as the once-proud Mustangs have floundered in obscurity for nearly twenty years since, producing just two winning records. At this point, some desperate SMU fans might be willing to trade a couple more years in the slammer for just one sniff of the GMAC Bowl.

The NCAA hasn't administered the death penalty to another school since then, in large part because of the way it so permanently hindered SMU. In fact, in 1992 the organization overhauled its penalty structure entirely, eliminating television bans, among other things, because of the unfair consequence they placed on the guilty parties' innocent opponents. Additional factors have taken some of the teeth out of the NCAA enforcement process. For one, schools have changed their approach to handling such matters. Rather than fight potential sanctions like SMU did, most schools proactively cooperate with investigators, often handing out their own penalties before the infractions committee does to show they're serious. And many retain the law firm of Bond, Schoeneck & King, located in Overland Park, Kansas, site of the NCAA's previous headquarters, which specializes in aiding athletic departments embroiled in NCAA investigations.

Meanwhile, NCAA investigators are finding that they have to tread extremely delicately due to a recent rash of unfavorable litigation. In 1998, the organization was forced to cough up $2.5 million to settle a lawsuit filed by Jerry Tarkanian, the slippery basketball coach whom investigators had unsuccessfully hounded for more than twenty years. And in 2005, the NCAA and the University of Washington paid a $4.5 million wrongful termination settlement to former Huskies coach Rick Neuheisel, who was fired in 2003 for participating in a March Madness gambling pool. During the trial (which settled just before the closing arguments), NCAA enforcement director David Didion testified that others within the organization were trying to make an example of Neuheisel and had rushed to judgment during what was, by all accounts, a thoroughly sloppy investigation. That's right—the director testified *against* his employer. It's a smooth operation they've got going there.

The NCAA's most severe football sanctions since SMU were dealt to Alabama in 2002, when the revered Southern powerhouse was banned from participating in a bowl game for two seasons, stripped of twenty-one scholarships over three seasons, and placed on five years' probation for multiple recruiting violations involving payments by boosters. In one of the biggest bombshells ever to hit the sport, it was revealed that Logan Young, a wealthy Alabama booster in Memphis who for years had bragged to associates about his connections to Crimson Tide recruiting, paid $150,000 to Lynn Lang, a crooked Memphis high school coach, to assure the signature of the nation's top defensive line prospect in 2000, Albert Means. While the greasing of palms in the recruiting game occurs far more frequently than gets reported, $150,000 for one player is a downright staggering sum. Young's involvement was uncovered when Lang's bitter ex-assistant, Milton Kirk, blew the whistle on the scheme the two coaches had concocted to shop Means to the highest bidder, with Lang asking for as much as $200,000 and SUVs for both himself and Kirk. The plan hit a snag when Kirk never received his ride. Apparently, Lang must not have watched enough mafia movies to know what happens when you try to keep all the loot for yourself.

In all the annals of college football cheating, rarely has there been a case more cut-and-dried than this one. During the course of the NCAA's investigation, Kirk's version of events was corroborated by ten other individuals. Young (who died in April 2006 in what police described as an accident at his home) was eventually convicted of federal racketeering after both his and Lang's bank records confirmed many of the alleged transactions. Because Alabama was considered a "repeat violator," having been banned from the postseason in 1995 for another booster-related scandal, and because Means was not the only player involved in the latest go-round (another recruit, Kenny Smith, received $20,000 from Young and another booster, while linebacker Travis Carroll received a free SUV from a third booster), the Crimson Tide's sanctions could easily have been even worse. The transgressions were similar, and the amounts of money much larger than those in the SMU case. In fact, according to the infractions committee's report, "the death penalty . . . would have been imposed" if not for the school's "diligent effort to develop complete information regarding the violations" during the investigation. And yet to this day, Alabama fans wholeheartedly believe the NCAA screwed them over.

You see, part of being an Alabama fan is that you also despise

Tennessee. It comes with the deal. It just so happens that about the same time Young was alleged to have bought himself a very expensive defensive lineman, the Crimson Tide had lost to the hated Volunteers an unthinkable six straight times. According to witness testimony in the NCAA report, Young "rationalized his 'buying' of prospects as necessary to offset what he believed to be cheating by a Southeastern Conference rival, whose record of consecutive wins against the university he could explain in no other way."* Young was not alone in his obsession with the Vols, and in the years following the Means scandal—well after the Crimson Tide was already back playing in bowl games and trying to restore its good name—that obsession would manifest itself in the form of a conspiracy theory so colorful even Oliver Stone would have said, "C'mon, give me a break."

In 2003, Montgomery, Alabama–based attorney Tommy Gallion, a fourth-generation 'Bama grad and unabashed Crimson Tide die-hard, filed a $60 million defamation lawsuit against the NCAA on behalf of ex-'Bama assistant coaches Ronnie Cottrell and Ivy Williams, who had found themselves blackballed from coaching after being unofficially implicated in the Means scandal. It quickly became apparent, however, that the outspoken Gallion's true target wasn't the NCAA at all, but rather Phillip Fulmer, the portly head coach of the hated Tennessee Vols. "I'm getting ready to pop that fat bastard as hard as I can," Gallion told SI.com at the time. In the months and years to follow, Gallion told anyone who would listen that Fulmer had orchestrated 'Bama's entire undoing, spilling the dirt on the Crimson Tide in exchange for immunity for his own sins from SEC commissioner Roy Kramer (himself, conveniently, a Tennessee grad) and NCAA investigators determined to bring down 'Bama at any cost. Gallion even suggested that Young was set up for the fall by his Tennessee rivals, who baited him into bringing shame on his alma mater. The stranger-than-fiction case managed to galvanize an entire state into believing that Ten-

---

*I can think of at least one other explanation: Tennessee had Peyton Manning as its quarterback during much of the streak.

nessee, not Alabama, was the real villain in the whole ordeal. At its nastiest high point in 2004, Fulmer, who was never named as a defendant in the suit, skipped the SEC's annual preseason media event in Birmingham, Alabama, when Gallion threatened to serve him with a subpoena if he crossed state lines. It was at that event, in fact, that I truly learned the depth of interest in SEC football when I watched a horde of photographers and television cameramen swarm to get a shot of a speakerphone through which Fulmer's voice could be heard.

Proving that there is at least one sane person in the state of Alabama, a Montgomery judge dismissed nearly all the allegations in Gallion's lawsuit, presumably because they had no actual relevance to defamation against his clients. Interestingly, however, much of his conspiracy theory turned out to be true. Documents subpoenaed during the lawsuit and made public by the lawyers revealed that the NCAA did in fact use Fulmer as a "secret witness" in building its case against Alabama. Several prominent Tennessee boosters aided Fulmer in collecting dirt against Young and, according to one of them, convinced Kirk to spill the beans about Means. We learned that Fulmer, with knowledge gleaned from his assistants, had informed Kramer about Lang's bidding war for Means during its initial stages, yet the commissioner never warned Alabama. We also know that at one point Kramer hired a private investigator to tail Young. All of which helps explain why Gallion told SI.com way back in February 2003 he would only drop the suit under one of two conditions: "If the NCAA would immediately lift the sanctions against Alabama and offer a 'national apology.' Or slap the death penalty on Tennessee."

At this point, you might find it helpful to pause for a second, place your jaw back in its proper position, and say, "Wait a minute . . . which school was the one that cheated again?" That would be Alabama. Let's take a moment to review. In summary, one of the Crimson Tide's boosters paid $150,000 for one recruit and $20,000 and a car for the services of two others. There's a word for these kinds of actions: illegal. *Remind me again, what did Tennessee's coach do wrong in all this?* Nothing, other than he ratted them out. *So where exactly does this lawyer get off calling for the Vols to get the death penalty?* You mean, besides, spite and showmanship? Well, if you were to believe him, it would be for all the heinous crimes that Tennessee itself committed but was absolved of in exchange for delivering the goods on 'Bama. This is where Gallion's conspiracy theory breaks down and where the NCAA's enforcement powers come into question.

It's not as if Tennessee hasn't had its share of dirty laundry exposed over the years—the Vols have had at least two significant scandals under Fulmer's watch. The fact that they were never sanctioned for either demonstrates the fine line in college football between what constitutes cheating and what is indisputably shady yet, for the most part, unpunishable.

In the fall of 1999, less than a year after the Vols won their first national championship in forty-seven years,* ESPN.com obtained an internal memo written by a Tennessee academic administrator alleging that five members of the title team had schoolwork completed for them by athletic tutors. Complicating matters, the allegations had never been properly reported to the appropriate people or sent through the proper channels. The report caused quite an uproar at the time, but the school launched an internal probe and, a month later, proudly declared itself devoid of any impropriety. "We have no evidence that the student athletes or tutors acted improperly. There's no pattern," university president J. Wade Gilley told the *New York Times*. "We are confident we have a very sound system with seasoned people of integrity in place." The NCAA concurred, even though it never launched a full-blown investigation of its own.

Frustrated by the lack of response and appalled by what she called "a system tantamount to institutionalized slavery," UT English professor Linda Bensel-Myers decided to conduct her own personal investigation of the athletic department's academic practices. In reviewing thirty-nine football players' transcripts, she found what she considered

---

*One of the amazing "coincidences" of college football is how these things always seem to come to light after a team wins the national championship. Such was the case for Miami, Florida State, and Tennessee in the 1990s and Ohio State and USC in the 2000s.

an unmistakable pattern of academic abuse, including questionable grade changes, phantom majors, and athlete-friendly teachers. Once again, the charges were largely brushed under the rug, subject only to a cursory internal probe. In fact, the only party to suffer from the mess was the whistleblower herself, Bensel-Myers, who became the subject of hate mail, death threats, and a divorce. "Give it a rest," wrote the author of one e-mail Bensel-Myers shared with the *Florida Times-Union.* "The taxpayers of Tennessee like winning teams. The players pay your salary. Go to Harvard, Yale, Stanford or some private college and teach if you want a perfect institution." Wrote another: "'Do yourself a favor. Do the state of Tennessee a favor. Do the entire NCAA a favor and shut the hell up!!!!" You know the old cliché, "Don't shoot the messenger?" College football fans aren't big on the "don't" part.

Considering that college football players are, at least in theory, supposed to be students first and foremost, one could easily make the argument that manipulating a player's academic standing is no less a breach of ethics than handing him cash under the table. So why, then, did Alabama pay the price for its misdeeds while Tennessee skated? Because paying $150,000 for a recruit is a textbook violation of NCAA bylaws; steering players toward easy classes is not. Sure, NCAA president Myles Brand likes to talk tough when it comes to academic integrity, going so far as to adopt a new metric, the Academic Progress Rate (APR), in 2005, that takes away scholarships from schools that fail to graduate and retain their players at an acceptable standard. But the NCAA is still, at its core, a sports organization, one that lacks the authority to tell the University of Tennessee what its students should be majoring in or what criteria a teacher must follow before changing a student's grade. If Tennessee is willing to let half its football team major in urban studies, or if Ohio State, as was disclosed in the *ESPN the Magazine* articles, is willing to award credits for a course called "Officiating Tennis," well, that's up to the schools' own deans and provosts.

The reality is, these sorts of academic farces take place at nearly every school in the country with powerhouse football programs, and will continue to do so as long as the schools feel they're necessary to field winning teams. A 2006 *New York Times* exposé revealed that an Auburn sociology professor awarded high grades to eighteen members of Auburn's undefeated 2004 team (including star running back Carnell Williams) for directed-reading courses in which the players did not have to attend class and did little to no work. The professor wound up losing his title as department chair, but there were zero repercussions for the football program. There are in fact NCAA bylaws regarding academic fraud, under which the alleged writing of players' papers by tutors at Tennessee would certainly fall, but it's a tough charge to prove. In nearly all major cases where such violations have been found (Minnesota and Fresno State basketball come to mind), the people committing the fraud confessed to it; because no such volunteers were present at Tennessee or Auburn, it's not like the NCAA was going to send in homework experts to start examining the veracity of players' philosophy papers. Unfortunately, academic unseemliness will likely remain a largely overlooked staple of most major college football programs. But at least those Ohio State players who aced "Officiating Tennis" will be able to get a job one day as a line judge at the U.S. Open.

Besides academics, another big area the NCAA is seemingly powerless to legislate is player misbehavior. No matter how many millions of dollars they spend, no matter how many seminars they hold, no matter how many posters they plaster in dorm hallways, college administrators have yet to solve the age-old predicament of keeping college students from acting like . . . well, college students. To the continued astonishment of absolutely no one, the nation's eighteen-to-twenty-three-year-olds, most of them free from parental supervision for the first time in their lives, show no sign of losing interest in such illicit pastimes as drinking, smoking weed, and sleeping with one another anytime soon. College football players are not immune to such spates of debauchery, and in fact often find themselves the focal point of such festivities due to their celebrity status among classmates. Unfortunately, as is often the case when certain substances are involved, some players' behavior inevitably crosses the line from innocent fun into the realm of the police blotter. Nearly every week of the year, the nation's sports sections and Web sites contain at least one headline involving a lineman or tight end at some major program getting arrested for something. The transgressions range from the largely harmless (disorderly conduct, public intoxication) to the truly troubling (drug possession, DWIs, and DUIs) to the downright revolting (rape, assault).

Such stories have become so commonplace that it's hard for fans to be shocked by any of them. With the exception of violent crimes, most incidents are brushed off with something of a "boys will be boys" indifference. At a certain point, however, such indiscretions come to be viewed, fairly or unfairly, as a reflection of the players' football program and, in turn, its coach. If a team experiences a rash of player arrests within a certain time frame, or if a program happens to experience some particularly memorable incidents, questions inevitably arise as to the character of players the coach is recruiting, and whether or not he and his assistants are doing a proper job of disciplining and monitoring their players. Florida State's Bobby Bowden, the winningest coach in Division I-A history, has fielded as much criticism as anyone when it comes to this area. From star receiver Peter Warrick's infamous 1999 Dillard's heist, in which he conspired with a female employee to obtain $412.38 in merchandise for practically nothing, to kicker Sebastian Janikowski's multiple drug- and party-related arrests, to linebacker A.J. Nicholson's sexual assault arrest on the eve of the 2006 Orange Bowl, Bowden has dealt with no shortage of player misconduct, leading to the near-universal perception (at least outside of Tallahassee) that he runs a loose ship. Eleven FSU players were arrested during one span from 1997 to 1999.

Bowden, however, has consistently defended himself and his program, deriding such incidents as somewhat inevitable in today's society. "When these things occur, everyone blames the coach. They say, 'Why don't you recruit better boys?'" Bowden told the *Washington Post*. "Sometimes it's your better boys that do it." Citing the increasing number of players who come from broken homes, Bowden added, "We're dealing with some kids that haven't [previously] been disciplined. We're trying to teach them discipline."

During Bowden's thirty-plus years in Tallahassee, Florida State has been sanctioned by the NCAA just once, in 1996, for failing to properly monitor players' involvement with agents, and even then received just 1 year of probation. The punishment followed an incident reported by *Sports Illustrated* in which six members of FSU's 1993 national title team were treated by runners for an agent to a six-thousand-dollar shopping spree at a Tallahassee Foot Locker store. That indelible image (which prompted rival coach Steve Spurrier of Florida to infamously declare that FSU stood for "Free Shoes University"), along with the numerous player arrests over the years, have contributed to the enduring perception held by countless fans across the country of Florida State as "the Criminoles." In fact, if you were to ask the average unaffiliated fan which program is "dirtier," FSU or Alabama, I'm guessing eight out of ten would peg the 'Noles. Yet FSU has never endured any punishment remotely comparable to that of Alabama. Crimson Tide fans will presumably tell you it's because the NCAA has it out for them, or that it's protecting the revered Bowden, but the truth of the matter is, player misbehavior, much like academic abuse, is another area in which the NCAA has little sway. Obviously, assaulting someone at a frat party is against the law, but football-related punishments such as suspensions or dismissal from the team are left to the discretion of the schools themselves, each of which has its own unique set of policies and procedures.

In most cases, the sole disciplinarians are the coaches themselves, most of whom are genuinely concerned about setting the right example for their players—just not quite as much as they are about winning games and keeping their jobs. "You can think you did the right thing and these two [suspended] guys or five [suspended] guys aren't going to play," then–Miami coach Larry Coker told the *Palm Beach Post*. "Then you lose the game. That you suspended [players] and that you're a stand-up guy is forgotten pretty quickly." Coker and his program endured substantial criticism following a 2006 incident in which players from the 'Canes and Florida International engaged in a nasty, bench-clearing brawl during a game at the Orange Bowl. Despite video evidence that showed one Miami player use his helmet as a weapon and another stomp on a fallen opponent, the school's punishment for twelve of the thirteen disciplined players was a measly one-game suspension for the following week's trip to winless Duke. I'm sure the players were crushed to miss that one. In 2004, then–Florida coach Ron

Zook took no shortage of flak for his suspiciously convenient disciplinary treatment of star defenders Channing Crowder and Jarvis Herring. Following a summer incident outside a Gainesville nightclub, the pair was to be suspended for the Gators' season opener against Middle Tennessee State, but the game got postponed until October 16 due to a hurricane. Instead of making them sit out Florida's new opener against Eastern Michigan, which would have left the pair without a warm-up game prior to the Gators' crucial conference showdown with Tennessee, Zook instead shifted their suspension to the rescheduled Middle Tennessee game. "It's not their fault there was a hurricane," justified the coach. At least the players learned their lesson. Your behavior has consequences—unless those consequences affect our chance at a conference title.

It's one thing to poke fun at a coach when his players run amok; it's a much more serious matter, however, when a coach gets accused of playing a role in the indiscretions himself. Former Colorado coach Gary Barnett unwittingly found himself at the center of one of the nastiest scandals in recent college football history. In December 2001, three women alleged they were raped at an off campus party attended by Colorado players and recruits. No criminal charges were ever filed, but two of the alleged victims, both of them CU students at the time, filed a lawsuit against the university claiming it fostered a sexually hostile environment. In a deposition given during the case, Boulder district attorney Mary Keenan, a longtime critic of the CU athletic department who had investigated a similar rape case in 1997 (prior to Barnett's arrival), accused the football program of "using sex and alcohol as recruiting tools." Once made public, those explosive words set off a firestorm of accusations against Barnett and his program, with a total of nine women eventually alleging they had been raped by CU players or recruits (none of their cases were ever prosecuted). One of those, Katie Hnida, had been a kicker for the Buffaloes during Barnett's first season in 1999 and, in the pages of *Sports Illustrated*, accused the coach of ignoring repeated incidents of harassment against her by teammates. Former players interviewed by police spoke of other "sex parties" like the one in 2001, and the owner of a company called Hardbodies

Entertainment admitted to occasionally sending strippers to CU "recruiting parties." It got to the point where Barnett became petrified to open his newspaper in the morning.

As the weeks wore on and the venom mounted, Barnett steadfastly defended himself and his program. He spoke of the way he and his staff constantly preach the importance of appropriate moral conduct to their players, even distributing a thick handbook spelling out do's and don'ts for nearly any conceivable situation. "I've been an educator for 33 years and much of my teaching and emphasis is about character," he said. "Neither myself nor any of my coaches have ever encouraged or condoned sex as part of the recruiting process, period." Speaking of the infamous 2001 party, Barnett told an investigative panel: "There is no question in my mind that inappropriate behavior occurred. There is also no question in my mind that the behavior of the 10 young people involved was the result of their own poor decisions under the influence of alcohol." But in his pursuit of damage control, Barnett made one crucial mistake. While answering a reporter's question as to why Hnida had left the team, eventually transferring to New Mexico, Barnett replied a bit too candidly about her kicking ability, or lack thereof. "Katie was not only a girl, she was terrible. OK? There's no other way to say it."

That gigantic lapse in judgment got Barnett placed on three months' administrative leave. Most observers assumed the move was an unofficial precursor to his inevitable ouster—only it didn't happen. Comprehensive investigations into the program by both an independent university panel and the state attorney general's office failed to turn up any discernible evidence that Barnett or his assistants did anything wrong.* "I do not believe that coaches and administrators at this university knowingly used sex, alcohol, and drugs as recruiting tools for prospective football players," university president Betsy Hoffman said after reviewing the independent panel's report. "It is clear that in a few isolated instances, recruits attended parties where they consumed alco-

---

*One low-level recruiting aide, Nathan Maxcey, later pled guilty to soliciting a prostitute, but he was apparently obtaining her services for himself, not football recruits.

hol and had sexual encounters. That is unacceptable, and we are taking steps to see that this kind of behavior does not occur again." Barnett was reinstated that summer.

Needless to say, this seemingly tepid response was quite unsatisfying to the various political, media, and women's advocacy hounds that had been hovering around the program since the first lurid allegations had surfaced. Despite the seeming vindication, Barnett was never able to fully shake his newfound reputation as the leader of a gang of sex-crazed marauders. In the aftermath of the scandal, Hoffman, chancellor Richard Bynny, and athletic director Dick Tharp all exited Boulder. Barnett hung on until December 2005, when he was finally fired, not because of the allegations, but because his team lost 70–3 to Texas in the Big 12 championship game. Should Barnett have been ousted sooner? Maybe for the sake of the university's public relations office. But you'd have to be pretty cynical to think Barnett was calling up and ordering the strippers himself. Or that he told his players to make sure visiting recruits got laid. The sad reality of the Colorado scandal is that short of chaperoning their players around campus 24/7, there was probably very little the coaches could have done to stop what allegedly happened. The sort of tawdry behavior that supposedly happened at Colorado happens every week on campuses across the country, be it involving football players or frat boys, sorority girls or socialites. Alcohol, drugs, sex, and, sadly, rape are hardly limited to the Colorado football program. However, between CU's longstanding reputation as a hard-core party school and Boulder's highly charged political climate, Barnett's program happened to sit at the center of a perfect storm in what wound up becoming a highly overblown scandal.

In early 2004, about the same time the Colorado story took off, college football fans were exposed to a more innocent, yet also troubling side of the recruiting process. In an extremely candid and, at times, hilarious diary published by the *Miami Herald*, Willie Williams, the nation's most sought-after linebacker prospect that season, detailed the exorbitant star treatment he received during recruiting visits to Florida State, Auburn, Florida, and Miami. He spoke of steak-and-lobster dinners in Tallahassee, cheerleaders screaming his name at Auburn, and a ride to the Miami campus in Coker's brand-new Cadillac Escalade. Describing a party he attended at Auburn, Williams said, "I was kind of worried all Auburn had to offer was those farmer girls that talked funny. But the girls at the party weren't farmer girls at all." Auburn's admissions office immediately signed up Williams as its new campus spokesman. That eyebrow-raising series, along with the Colorado scandal, prompted the NCAA to convene an emergency committee to curb excessive campus visits.

The real shock waves, however, came when Williams was arrested for hugging a woman without her permission during his visit to Gainesville. Shortly after signing with Miami in early February, it was revealed that Williams had been on probation at the time of the arrest, stemming from a felony burglary charge in 2002. Furthermore, and apparently unbeknownst to Miami officials, he had been arrested ten times from 1999 to 2002. Much to the dismay of football followers everywhere, not to mention many Miami faculty and students, the school still elected to admit Williams and uphold his scholarship offer once it was determined he would not be facing jail time. "He has turned his life around," Coker told reporters. ". . . I think he deserves an opportunity." Coker declined to say whether the school would have offered the same opportunity to a chess player or debate champion with ten arrests on his résumé.* The Williams episode was admittedly shady, but it speaks yet again to the complexities of policing a sport where there is no ultimate arbiter of justice. While there are NCAA bylaws regarding everything from the length of practices to the length of jersey sleeves, there is no rule against suiting up a convicted felon. Those sorts of decisions are left to the schools themselves, many of which might have handled the Williams situation exactly the same way and others that might have acted quite differently.

Taking all this into account, it's hard to avoid the conclusion that the NCAA's stated goal of "ensuring fair play among its members" is an

---

*For all of Miami's trouble on his behalf, Williams wound up returning the favor by transferring prior to his sophomore season over lack of playing time.

inherently fruitless endeavor. It's possible to "cheat" in college football in any number of ways without actually breaking any rules. As long there are schools and football programs willing to bend the average standards of morality—be it by allowing convicted criminals to don uniforms, manipulating suspensions to avoid coinciding with key games, or devising laughable academic curriculums—there will never be a truly level playing field. The best the NCAA can hope to do is to continue sporadically catching the occasional brazen outlaw, like it did Alabama.

You can be assured that Alabama is hardly the only program with corrupt boosters; it just happened to be unlucky enough to get caught. If Clarett had decided to cooperate with investigators, Ohio State could have just as easily found itself banned from bowl games. And Colorado is hardly the only program where recruits wind up at sex- and drug-laced parties. Place an equally outspoken district attorney at an Oregon (where one-time recruit Lynell Hamilton said he was offered sex, alcohol, and pot during a 2002 visit) or Minnesota (where several recruits were taken to a strip club in 2004) and those schools could have had their own PR nightmares on their hands. Despite what the title of this chapter might indicate, I do not honestly believe that "everybody cheats." But I do believe there are a whole lot more offending schools than there are whistleblowers. In many cases, the dirty deeds involving agents, boosters, and other interested parties take place completely underground, unbeknownst to coaches and school officials, making it nearly impossible to police. When Oklahoma dismissed star quarterback Rhett Bomar in 2006 for receiving paychecks he didn't earn from a local auto dealership, it was the result of an investigation that began with an anonymous e-mail to school president David Boren. The dealership had recently undergone a change of ownership. If the offending parties had still been in place, what are the chances they would have voluntarily turned over crucial documents to the school? Zero. Which is why there are likely players from other schools receiving similar treatment as we speak, yet no one will ever find out about it.

So the next time one of your hated rivals shows up in the papers for something tawdry and embarrassing, don't be so quick to point fingers. The same thing could very easily be happening in your own backyard.

And if by chance your team is one of the unfortunate ones to get targeted, try to temper your defense instinct for just a second and remind yourself that no, you are not the innocent victim of a vengeful media. And no, the allegations were not made up out of thin air by some jealous, bitter rival. Chances are, someone associated with your program screwed up. They just happened to be one of the unlucky few that actually got caught.

Afterword

The 2006 college football season, which you've seen referenced throughout this book, contained more than its share of chaos and controversy, from the Oregon–Oklahoma replay debacle in mid-September to the hoopla and accompanying debate in mid-November over whether number 1 Ohio State and number 2 Michigan should be afforded a national championship rematch. The regular season ended, as it often does, under a cloud of complaints about the BCS as Florida passed the Wolverines for number 2 on the final weekend. Moments before Boise State scored its incredible 2-point conversion against Oklahoma to complete a 13–0 season, FOX game announcer Thom Brennaman went on a rant to his national audience that "it's calls like this, it's effort like this and guts like this which screams for a playoff in Division I-A football." A week later, Florida throttled season-long number 1 Ohio State in a national championship game that took place a full fifty-one days after the Buckeyes' previous game, leading many to wonder whether the game was in any way a true measuring stick of the season preceding it.

One of those making the latter argument was bestselling author and sportswriter Mitch Albom, who, on January 14, 2007—nearly a week removed from that title game—penned a column in the *Detroit Free Press* entitled "College Football: The Ends Junk the Means." Albom is one of the many prominent newspaper columnists around the country who pay little to no attention to college football during the regular season, then swoop in at the end and tell those of us who do follow the sport closely everything that's wrong with it. "College football is a mess," wrote Albom. "Of all our major sports, it is the most confused and the most hypocritical." Albom's points about the championship game—that the system is flawed, that it fails to reward momentum, that the teams are forced to play a different style than they would during the regular season—were all perfectly reasonable. But then he closed with this thought: "College football has more unhappy fans than any sport. The bowls are a joke. The polls are one big argument. And the championship game comes in the middle of the NFL playoffs."

I see college football fans every week, and I've got to tell you, they don't seem unhappy to me. Quite the contrary, actually. When I walk through the parking lot at Jordan-Hare Stadium in Auburn or the Coliseum in L.A. on a Saturday, I see thousands and thousands of smiling, happy people drinking beer, grilling brats, and generally looking like I've happened upon them on the happiest day of their lives. When I walk into Blondie's, the popular sports bar on New York's Upper West Side where alumni of numerous prominent college teams gather to watch games on Saturdays, I see a bunch of supposedly jaded New Yorkers decked out in school colors whooping it up while glued to the action on the TVs. When I turn on the car radio in Columbus, Ohio, on a random Monday in July, I hear a series of callers voicing their giddy anticipation for the upcoming season. And when I log on to nearly any major team's Scout.com or Rivals.com site the first week of February, I see thousands of anonymous fans celebrating their latest recruits and dreaming of all the future glory they will surely deliver.

Do these people seem unhappy to you?

No question, there's a lot about college football I'd like to see changed. I agree with Big East commissioner Mike Tranghese, who told the *New York Times* that the annual BCS controversy has become "debilitating and wearing." Please, guys, do something—anything—to appease your detractors. A plus-one game would be a nice start. I agree with the many coaches who have thrown up their hands in frustration over the increasingly circuslike recruiting business. An early signing day in August or September might help alleviate some of the madness. I'd certainly like to see some of the sanctity of bowl season restored by cutting the number of games in half (while still ensuring that at least the champion of every conference gets a berth), banning teams with 6–6 records and sub.-500 conference records and playing the most meaningful nonchampionship games on New Year's Day. This would require the NCAA stepping in and implementing some stricter standards for bowl certification. And I think I made it abundantly clear in "FireMy Coach.com" how I feel about the coaching market, both the salaries that are being paid and the utterly unreasonable expectations being placed on the men making those salaries. It'd be nice to see someone take a proactive step toward reining in both.

But there's also something to be said for the fact that college football would not be college football without the chaos and the controversy. Mitch Albom and other prominent media voices would have you believe that if college football would simply conform to the norms of all the other sports they cover, implement a playoff and rid itself once and for all of all that "appalling" ambiguity all would be right with the world. Maybe. Maybe not. While making the sport more orderly might reduce some of that unwanted criticism, it might also do another, more troubling thing: it might make college football boring.

What if someone stepped in tomorrow and brought some oft-demanded uniformity to the proceedings—gave every conference the same number of teams, made them play by the same rules, schedule the same opponents? What if that same person installed a sixteen-team playoff? Did away with the polls? Seeded the bowl games? Gave everyone—Notre Dame included—the same TV deal? Would college football run more smoothly? Absolutely. But would it still *be* college football, or would it be a shameless knockoff of the NFL? I'd say the latter. And to be honest, I'm not sure I'd feel as passionately about that sport. I wonder how many others would feel the same way?

If college football fans were truly unhappy, wouldn't it stand to reason that they would stop going to the games? Stop watching them on television? Stop following the sport so intently? Instead, it seems to be the exact opposite. NCAA schools set new records for both total (47.9 million) and average (46,249) attendance in 2006. An estimated 28.7 million viewers watched the purportedly "unsatisfying" Florida–Ohio State championship game, third-highest of the BCS era. And the number of daily page views generated by college football articles on SI.com, Rivals.com, Scout.com, and any number of other Web sites continues to grow exponentially by the year. "I see don't see [fans] walking away from anything," said Big Ten commissioner Jim Delany.

Don't get too cocky, commissioner. Something tells me we've yet to see the all-out, Armageddon-type BCS controversy that truly pushes the public over the edge. The commissioners know that, and that's why an increasing number of them are pushing for some sort of change the next time the contract comes up for renewal. They also recognize, however, that chaos and controversy have been a part of college football since its inception, and that yet, perhaps implausibly, the sport not only remains standing, but is thriving. College football, therefore, is in no hurry to conform. No one would ever want to infringe on the rivalries, the pageantry, the tradition, and the passion that make the sport so unique. None of these will go away anytime soon. But neither will the cheating, the bickering, the politicking, and the power struggles. Those are here to stay as well.

My advice: don't run from the chaos. Embrace it. Appreciate that it's an integral component of the sport you hold so dear. And whatever you do, try not to let it affect your livelihood. Your friends, your family, your coworkers, your neighbors—they don't want to hear you bitch and moan about how badly your team got screwed. That's what I'm here for.

Update

More Chaos, More Controversy in the 2007 Season

Something tells me we've yet to see the all-out, Armageddon-type BCS controversy that truly pushes the public over the edge.

—Stewart Mandel, preceding page

When the hardcover edition of *Bowls, Polls & Tattered Souls* was released on August 24, 2007, I was excited to see the finished product finally hit the stores. I was also somewhat concerned, however, due to the "current" nature of many of the issues discussed herein, that some of the content might become outdated as soon as the new football season commenced six days later.

Therefore, it was with considerable relief and unexpected fascination that the 2007 season turned out to be more chaotic and controversial than any before it. In fact, the themes contained throughout nearly every chapter of this book managed to become even more relevant with each twist and turn. There were many occasions, while doing one of numerous radio interviews to promote the book, when the host would jokingly ask whether I intended to write a sequel based solely on the season at hand. It wasn't a bad idea, actually, but considering that it took two and a half years to write the first one, it would have been 2011 by the time said sequel arrived in your hands. I figured that an additional chapter would be best.

On the very first Saturday of this highly unusual season, defending I-AA national champion Appalachian State pulled off arguably the biggest upset in the history of the sport when it went into the Big House in Ann Arbor and stunned fifth-ranked Michigan. While a handful of I-AA teams have knocked off lower-level I-A teams over the years, never before had a I-AA team beaten a ranked I-A team, and certainly never a team anywhere near as prestigious as the Wolverines—college football's all-time winningest program. To any remaining fans who had been living in a cave the previous decade and failed to notice the increasing wave of parity to hit the sport, this result served as the ultimate slap across the face. It also set the tone for a staggeringly turbulent season where, week after week, one team after another—USC, LSU, Ohio State, Oregon—would rise to one of the coveted top-two spots in the BCS standings only to be blindsided by some unheralded underdog. As SEC commissioner and BCS coordinator Mike Slive put it, the teams "just couldn't grab the brass ring when they needed to." It was only fitting, then, that when all was said and done, the season produced the first-ever national champion, LSU, to have lost two regular-season games.

Armageddon officially struck on the final night of the regular season, December 1. The day began with 11–1 Missouri and 10–1 West Virginia sitting number 1 and number 2 in both the polls and the BCS standings. Assuming the Mountaineers took care of business at home against 4–7 Pittsburgh, the national championship game would presumably pit West Virginia against either Missouri or, if the Tigers lost to 10–2 Oklahoma in that night's Big 12 championship game, 11–1 Ohio State, whose season had concluded two weeks earlier but, thanks to the continued rash of upsets elsewhere, had managed to rise back up to number 3 without lifting a finger, or even snapping the ball.

Both the Big 12 game and the Pittsburgh–West Virginia game kicked off around the same time that Saturday night. With a couch and a clicker, you could watch both games simultaneously—and watch the ensuing mammoth BCS controversy evolve in front of your eyes. Oklahoma routed the Tigers 38–17, not an entirely surprising result considering that the Sooners had handed Missouri its lone previous loss earlier in the season. The real drama unfolded in Morgantown, West Virginia, however, where, from the opening minutes, 28-point underdog Pittsburgh held the Mountaineers' normally prolific offense in check. And it certainly didn't help West Virginia when star quarterback Pat White went out with a hand injury late in the first half. The outcome came right down to the final minutes, with Pittsburgh prevailing 13–9 and, in turn, sending the college football world into absolute upheaval. Ohio State was a lock to move up to number 1 and play for the national championship, but less than twenty-four hours before the official pairings would be announced, the question of who the Buckeyes would face had deteriorated into a wide-open debate between a hodgepodge of similarly flawed, two-loss teams—LSU, Georgia, USC, Oklahoma—all of whom could make a legitimate argument, and did. In those chaotic moments following the conclusion of the two upsets, LSU coach Les Miles, Georgia coach Mark Richt, and USC coach Pete Carroll made unsolicited calls into *SportsCenter,* where anchor Scott Van Pelt found himself playing the unexpected role of moderator in college football's equivalent of a presidential debate. In actuality, it was more like a job interview, with each coach trumping his team's résumé and making the case why the voters should elevate his team above the others. (Oklahoma's Bob Stoops made his own case during a postgame press conference in San Antonio.)

In the end, the consensus among the AP, coaches, and Harris voters was to elevate LSU—which had won the SEC championship game earlier that same day—to number 2. Of the bunch, the Tigers were in fact the most deserving team (as I argued in an SI.com column that night), but it also meant that a team that just eight days earlier had lost at home to unranked Arkansas would be playing for the national championship. This decision evoked the loudest cries yet for a playoff in college football. But then, what else is new?

The following is a chapter-by-chapter update of the topics discussed in this book, one year later.

1. One Nation, Under the BCS

Once the hubbub died down, LSU beat Ohio State 38–24 in the national championship game, the Tigers hoisted the crystal football, and Earth continued to orbit on its axis. It was no coincidence, however, that Georgia president Michael Adams—whose 11–2 team finished second to the Tigers in the polls—chose the morning after the game to announce his intention to use his position as chairman of the NCAA executive committee to bring an eight-team playoff to college football.* Adams told the *Atlanta Journal-Constitution* that he believed his proposal had "at least a 50-50 chance" of passing, and that his goal was to implement the system "within a year or two." Later, he pledged to eliminate hangovers within six to eight months and solve global warming by 2010.

As discussed in chapter 1, the playoff issue is far too complex and involves far too many divergent parties for one idealistic president to suddenly step in and resolve it. Within three days of his announcement, the *Journal-Constitution* surveyed thirty Division I-A presidents, out of which five supported Adams's proposal. It was formally discussed a week later at the NCAA's annual convention in Nashville, where his colleagues basically said: "Yeah . . . thanks for that." On the other hand, Adams did raise one legitimate issue pertaining to the 2007–08 BCS bowls in general, which was, quite simply, that they stunk. In a year when so many teams finished so closely bunched together, fans were overwhelmingly disappointed by the four nonchampionship matchups, which, due to the selection order of the bowls and their various conference tie-ins, failed to match any of the other top-seven teams against each other. Not surprisingly, three of them (Georgia-Hawaii, USC-Illinois, and West Virginia–Oklahoma) resulted in anticlimactic blowouts. Adams's friends in the state legislature called the BCS bowls "the greatest disappointment of the 2007 college football season."

---

*The Georgia state legislature later approved a resolution supporting his proposal, despite the fact the Georgia state legislature's jurisdiction would seem to be limited to a playoff between Georgia, Georgia Tech, Georgia Southern, and Valdosta State.

Judging by my in-box, most fans' biggest gripe was with the grandest bowl of them all, the Rose Bowl, for its selection of lowly ranked 9–3 Illinois to replace Big Ten champion Ohio State, which it lost to the championship game. For decades, nary a soul questioned the Pasadena game's loyalty to its two longtime conference partners, the Big Ten and Pac-10; however, in the BCS era, that tradition has already been significantly dampened, what with five teams from other conferences playing there since 2002. As a result, fans made it clear that they would have preferred the Rose Bowl to eschew tradition and select a higher-ranked opponent rather than automatically tabbing the first three-loss at-large team in BCS history, especially one that most observers figured (correctly) to be overmatched against the Trojans. The fact that the ABC/ESPN monolith spent three weeks beating everybody's brains with promotions for the game (the only BCS bowl on its airwaves) did nothing to soften the criticism.

Both the Rose Bowl's unpopular choice and the overall backlash created by the 2007–08 pairings (which resulted in decreased TV ratings for four of the five games) came at an interesting time in the BCS's history. Both *Sports Illustrated* and SI.com published lengthy pieces in December 2007 in which officials across the sport expressed their increased interest in exploring a "plus-one" game (the previously mentioned "mini-playoff" where the BCS bowls would serve as de facto semifinals for a new national championship game) when the current BCS contract expires in 2010. "A plus-one [would be] helpful because it gives every major bowl the opportunity to have the winner of that game mean something," said Fiesta Bowl CEO John Junker.

At the BCS's annual meetings in April 2008, Slive, the most adamant proponent of a plus-one, presented a formal proposal for a new system that would seed the top four teams at the end of the regular season and pit them against each other in two bowl games. Following a roughly five-hour discussion, the proposal was promptly shot down by not only the Big Ten and Pac-10 but Big 12, Big East, and Notre Dame as well. The current system will remain in place through at least 2014.

Feel free to begin pulling your hair out ahead of time.

2. Pulling Rank

Toward the end of chapter 2, I discussed a noticeable and encouraging shift in philosophy among pollsters when it came to filling out their final ballots of the 2006 regular season, elevating eventual national champ Florida over Michigan to number 2 based on the Gators' superior overall résumé. That trend continued in 2007, albeit out of necessity, as voters were charged with the unenviable eleventh-hour task of sifting through a pile of similarly bunched, inherently flawed two-loss teams for that all-important number 2 spot. Under the old-school approach, where voters automatically moved up the next team on the ladder, that choice would have been 10–2 Georgia, which had completed its season a week earlier and entered that final weekend ranked fourth, behind Missouri, West Virginia, and Ohio State. When both the Tigers and Mountaineers lost, however, voters had some understandable reservations about allowing the Bulldogs to play for the national championship when they had not even earned a spot in their own conference's title game. Georgia had lost the SEC East tiebreaker to Tennessee, which had pummeled the Bulldogs 35–14 on October 6. Georgia improved dramatically after that, winning its final six regular-season games to soar back up in the polls. But there was no escaping the fact that fellow two-loss team LSU, not Georgia, was the SEC champion, having beaten those same Volunteers in the title game to earn that distinction. Meanwhile, the Tigers had defeated another team perched above them in the previous poll—11–2 Virginia Tech—48–7.

Considering those circumstances, plus the fact that LSU had defeated four ranked foes while suffering both its defeats in triple overtime, voters took the unprecedented step of bumping the Tigers from number 7 to number 2 in the final BCS standings. While their decision caused outrage among fans of the other contenders, most notably Georgia,* more detached observers realized that LSU had a better argument than not only the Dawgs and Hokies but also 10–2 USC (which inexplicably lost

---

*What a coincidence that Georgia's president decided around the same time to unveil his grand playoff plan.

to 4–8 Stanford), 11–2 Oklahoma (lost to 6–6 Colorado), and 11–1 Kansas (lost to Missouri in its final regular season game and did not play any of the top three teams from the Big 12 South).

While I felt comfortable with my own decision in the final poll, as a whole, the 2007 season was not my finest as a pollster. In the course of navigating such an upset-heavy regular season—one in which both the number 1 and number 2 teams lost on three different weekends and six different squads were defeated immediately upon reaching the number 2 spot—I was guilty of playing the "most deserving" card a little too early. For example, the night of October 13, I, like most of the country, found myself completely flustered when both number 1 LSU and number 2 Cal stumbled; unlike most of the country, I had an AP ballot to fill out. Not comfortable with elevating Ohio State—which had yet to face even a semidecent opponent—to number 1, I went with . . . South Florida. Yep, that's right—South Florida. In my defense, the Bulls had previously knocked off ranked foes Auburn and West Virginia. Looking back, however, that early in the season, one should probably trust his own instinct over a set of numbers. By no means did I truly believe USF was the best team in the country, and the Bulls bore that out soon enough, losing four of their last seven games. But at least I could take heart in knowing mine was a slightly more informed decision than that of Harris Poll voter Eddie Crowder, a long-since retired coach at Colorado. Crowder admitted to CBSSports.com that "I haven't even seen a brief highlight of [USF]," and that he couldn't name a single Bulls player. Yes, he's one of the people helping determine your favorite sport's national champion.

3. *He* Won the Heisman?

Clearly, the Heisman electorate must have read *Bowls, Polls & Tattered Souls* before casting their ballots in 2007. After spending an entire chapter imploring voters to shed their outdated, unwritten restrictions regarding the Heisman (that is, only junior or senior quarterbacks, running backs, and receivers from prestigious, national-title-contending programs could win it), the electorate tabbed a player, Florida quarterback

Tim Tebow, who defied two of those previously supposed criteria. For one, Tebow was a sophomore, becoming the first underclassman in the Heisman's 73-year history to capture the trophy. Nor did voters seem to mind that Tebow's 9–3 team was eliminated from the national-title race by the end of October. His staggering 51 touchdowns—29 passing, 22 running—were simply too impressive to deny.

The bigger question that remains—albeit one we won't be able to answer for at least another two years—is whether Tebow will ultimately defy the larger theory of this chapter, that the Heisman's image becomes further tarnished each time another winner fails to succeed in the NFL. By the time he graduates, Tebow could be one of the most decorated college players in history. With both a national title ring and a Heisman already under his belt, there's no telling how many more accolades he'll achieve in the two years to follow. Yet Tebow doesn't exactly fit the prototype of what NFL teams look for in a quarterback. They don't care whether their quarterback can run, which Tebow does quite often, and while he's certainly an accurate passer, he's not going to wow anybody physically. It's entirely possible he'll never throw a pass on Sundays, while the player he beat out in the voting, two-time Heisman runner-up Darren McFadden, has been widely pegged as a likely superstar NFL running back. If both projections hold true, will Heisman revisionists crucify voters for having slighted McFadden, or will Tebow's college accomplishments be so great as to assure a proper legacy regardless of what he does or doesn't do at the next level?

Only you, Tim Tebow, hold the power to one day render this entire chapter moot.

4. FireMyCoach.com

As you may recall, chapter 4 opened with a cyber-rant from some UCLA fans expressing their displeasure with head coach Karl Dorrell. In 2007, following a 6–6 regular season, Dorrell was fired.* Later in that

---

*At one point, the proprietors of a Web site entitled DumpDorrell.com took out an ad in UCLA's student newspaper calling for such.

chapter, I excerpted some Internet tirades directed by Michigan fans toward longtime coach Lloyd Carr. You should have seen some of them after the Wolverines opened their subsequent season with losses to Appalachian State and Oregon. Carr retired at the conclusion of the regular season. In addition, one of the more bizarre recent coaching changes I discussed was that of Nebraska, where in 2004 egomaniacal athletic director Steve Pederson hired the completely miscast Bill Callahan. In Callahan's fourth season, the Huskers imploded, finishing 5–7, and subsequently both Pederson and Callahan were dismissed. And Ole Miss added yet another chapter to my self-dubbed "Ole Miss/Clemson Syndrome," canning coach Ed Orgeron—the same guy who was hired to rescue the program from the "ashes" of its winningest coach in 30 years, David Cutcliffe—after just three seasons. Granted, Orgeron's teams failed to crack the four-win plateau during his time there, but you have to scratch your head in light of the school's uninspired replacement: Arkansas retread Houston Nutt, whom Razorbacks fans all but ran out of town and who in ten seasons at the school won exactly as many SEC championships as Cutcliffe and Orgeron did: none. Best of luck to Ole Miss in its continued quest for whatever it is they're looking for, because I sure as heck can't figure out what it is.

The biggest coaching stories of 2007, however, did not involve those who were fired as much as those who were hired. Following Nutt's resignation at Arkansas, the university shelled out nearly $3 million a year to land Bobby Petrino—the same coach who less than a year earlier walked out on Louisville mere months after signing a ten-year, $25 million contract and who, in bolting for Fayetteville, left his new team, the Atlanta Falcons, with three games remaining in his first and only season there. UCLA made the controversial decision to bring back former star quarterback Rick Neuheisel, exiled from college coaching since 2003 after incurring NCAA sanctions at both Colorado and Washington.

Without question, however, the most bizarre coaching change occurred at West Virginia, when highly successful coach and native son Rich Rodriguez left for the more glamorous post as head coach of Michigan. Never in my time covering this sport had I witnessed such virulent backlash toward a departing coach as that in West Virginia toward Rodriguez, who weeks earlier was universally regarded as a statewide hero. The governor of the Mountain State, Joe Manchin, a longtime friend of Rodriguez's, decried him for abandoning his "dream" job due to the influence of "high-priced agents." Rodriguez was immediately branded a traitor by fans across the state, including a deplorable few who reportedly harassed family members of both him and his assistants. And rather than negotiating the terms of his exit behind closed doors, as most parties are wont to do, West Virginia officials wasted no time suing Rodriguez for the $4 million buyout owed them in his contract. Someone within the school even leaked allegations to the local media that an apparently vengeful Rodriguez shredded vital documents on his way out of town. (It turned out he was literally "cleaning out his office," and that the documents were largely inconsequential. Maybe next time hire a cleaning staff.) All of which prompted me to dub West Virginia a "psychotic ex-girlfriend" in an SI.com column. I meant it in the nicest way possible.

In its quest to move on post-Rodriguez, the school conducted arguably the strangest coaching search in recent memory. Prior to the Mountaineers' Fiesta Bowl date with Oklahoma, the school interviewed one qualified candidate after another only to pass, usually because the governor himself—a former West Virginia football player and, apparently, part-time athletic director—didn't approve. However, when interim coach Bill Stewart led the Mountaineers to a rousing 48–28 upset of the Sooners, the school practically offered him the job right there on the sideline. And thus, thanks to an entirely emotional decision made during the heat of the moment, one of the nation's most prominent programs these past few years was handed over to a man whose only previous head-coaching experience was a three-year stint at Virginia Military Institute, where he went 8–25. Raise your hand if you think this will end well.

5. What's the Deal with Notre Dame?

Another season, another nationally chronicled soap opera involving the Irish, only this one took on epically embarrassing proportions. After attaining savior status in South Bend during his first two seasons, both of which ended with BCS bowl berths, third-year coach Charlie Weis saw his popularity plummet to Tyrone Willingham territory while producing the most losses in a single season (9) in the program's 120-year history. Notre Dame was fully expected to endure a "rebuilding" season after losing senior stars like quarterback Brady Quinn, but when the Irish got drubbed in their first few games out of the gate, Domers chose to place the blame at the feet of the long-departed Willingham for leaving Weis with such an empty cupboard of upper-class talent. (Never mind that he also recruited Quinn and Co.) However, as the lopsided losses piled up and with the Irish failing to show any tangible signs of improvement, even the biggest Weis loyalists couldn't help but wonder whether maybe, just maybe, the coach's self-professed X's and O's mastery wasn't everything it was cracked up to be.

The tipping point came in the ninth game of the season when Notre Dame saw its NCAA-record forty-three-year winning streak over Navy snapped thanks in no small part to Weis's mind-numbing decision to go for it on fourth and 8 late in regulation rather than attempt a potential game-winning 41-yard field goal. Navy went on to win in triple overtime, dropping the Irish's record at the time to 1–8. They went on to lose to Air Force the following week before beating 1–11 Duke and 4–8 Stanford to finish the season 3–9. Afterward, a notably humbled Weis sought advice from his former New England Patriots mentor Bill Belichick, reevaluated his entire approach, and even handed over his trademark role as play-caller to offensive coordinator Mike Haywood. "I was probably too high a percentage offensive coordinator and not a high-percentage enough head coach," he told CBSSports.com. Despite the Irish's on-the-field woes, Weis managed to land a consensus top-five recruiting class in 2008, his third straight haul ranked in the top 10, which means lack of talent will no longer be a valid excuse if his teams continue to struggle.

Notre Dame's ever-demanding faithful will expect nothing less than at least a four-game improvement (back to above .500) in 2008, and, be it realistic or not, national prominence the year after. At the conclusion of chapter 5 I wrote, "It remains to be seen whether Weis will be able to deliver the national championship Irish fans have been craving for nearly twenty years. If he does, Notre Dame will be able to officially reassert itself as one of the sport's reigning powers. If he doesn't, the Irish will continue to be just one in an army of good-but-not-great programs that litter the national landscape." It would seem that put-up-or-shut-up time is fast approaching for Weis and the Irish. If you believe the recruiting rankings, Notre Dame has assembled more talent the past few years than all but a handful of elite programs (USC, LSU, Florida, et al.). If he keeps up his current pace, yet fails to deliver on the field, you've got to wonder whether it's ever going to happen for the Irish. (Though I'm sure not too many of you will feel sorry for them.)

6. Invasion of the Recruiting Geeks

In chapter 6, you read about the ever-spiraling hype machine surrounding football recruiting. Nothing chronicled in that chapter could possibly compare to the phenomenon surrounding 2008 hotshot Terrelle Pryor, a gifted athlete from Jeannette, Pennsylvania, who excelled as both a basketball player and a combo run/pass quarterback. Recruiting analysts dubbed him "the next Vince Young" early on during his recruitment, and thus he soon became the most coveted prospect I've seen in nearly a decade of following recruiting. Cryptically vague early on about his potential college destination, the message boards truly lit up once it became apparent by late December that the race to procure Pryor's services would likely come down to Big Ten enemies Ohio State and Michigan. Fans of whichever team signed him would not only be able to envision future glory but rub it in the face of their hated rival. When Pryor attended a Wolverines basketball game during a visit there in mid-January, the *Detroit Free Press* and other media outlets chronicled it and photographed him. When the two teams' head coaches, Ohio State's Jim Tressel and Rich Rodriguez, as well as half their staffs, attended one of Pryor's games the weekend before Signing Day, it made national news.

However, in the most surreal moment of not only Pryor's recruitment, but perhaps the entire history of the annual spectacle, media members from around the country descended on Jeannette for Pryor's nationally televised (by both ESPN and CSTV) Signing Day press conference, only to find out . . . that Pryor hadn't yet made up his mind. "I really haven't had that much time to really get involved in the recruiting process," said Pryor, whose basketball season began within days of his football state-title game, "and I'd like to just take some time and be fair to all the coaches who recruited me." (While 99 percent of prospects sign letters of intent on Signing Day, it is actually the first day of a signing period that lasts through April 1.) Pryor's unusual nondecision drew a barrage of criticism on the message boards as well as from mainstream media pundits like ESPN's Mark May.* In their minds, the quiet eighteen-year-old must obviously be an attention-seeking prima donna who enjoyed goading fans and media. In the weeks leading up to Signing Day, however, Pryor did not seem to seek out attention as much as the attention sought him. He repeatedly dogged interview requests from the gazillion Internet reporters out there, but on those rare occasions when he did offer commentary, his words instantly cascaded across the Internet. He seemed to me to be a truly confused kid who exercised his right to take a little extra time, ultimately choosing the Buckeyes. The real mystery was why his decision attracted such paparazzi-like attention in the first place.

While Pryor's press conference may have been unsatisfying, at least the schools he was deciding upon were actually recruiting him. A week earlier, Fenley (Nevada) High offensive lineman Kevin Hart participated in the rite of so many blue-chippers. At a packed gymnasium filled with his classmates, and with the school's cheerleaders in uniform, Hart sat at a table with baseball caps of "finalists" Cal and Oregon and announced his intention to play for the Golden Bears. Only one problem: It would soon be revealed that neither Cal, nor any of the other schools on Hart's list, had offered him a scholarship. In fact, none had even recruited him. He made the whole thing up. The story made national headlines for days. While incredibly embarrassing for both Hart and Fenley officials, including his coach, who came across as

---

*May played for Pittsburgh. Pryor is from a town 30 miles outside Pittsburgh but never seriously considered playing for the Panthers. You do the math.

downright negligent in the whole deal (shouldn't he have found it suspicious that none of the coaches of said schools had contacted him about Hart?), it also said something about just how ludicrous the recruiting business has become that a player would go to such lengths to enjoy its celebrity, if only for a day.

7. How Boston College and Clemson Became Neighbors

No Division I-A conferences expanded, realigned, or even thought about expanding or realigning in 2007. Sorry.

8. Tonight, It's the MPC Motor City Car Care Credit Union Bowl

While the 2007–08 BCS games did not fare so well in the ratings, it was another banner year (relatively speaking) for the twenty-seven less glamorous bowls. The January 1 Michigan-Florida Capital One Bowl sold out within thirteen hours and drew a 9.1 Nielsen rating, the highest for a non-BCS bowl since 1998. The Auburn-Clemson Chick-fil-A Bowl, played on New Year's Eve, drew ESPN's second-highest bowl rating (since 1998). The Motor City, Music City, Champs Sports, Las Vegas, and Meineke Car Care bowls garnered their highest ratings in five years or more. Even the second-year PapaJohns.com Bowl, played ten days before New Year's and pitting relatively unheralded squads Cincinnati and Southern Miss, became the second-highest-rated bowl ever on ESPN2.

The names may be clunky. There may still be far too many of them. But football-hungry Americans continue to show an undeniable interest in even the most obscure bowl games, no matter what day they are played. Which is why, in April 2008, the NCAA certified two more of them, to be played in St. Petersburg, Florida, and Washington D.C. Suddenly the PapaJohns.com game is *so* 2006.

9. That's Great, Now Run a 40

The 2008 NFL Scouting Combine took place just a few days before I sat down to write this chapter, and lo and behold, the consensus star of the event was former Arkansas running back Darren McFadden, who dazzled the coaches and GMs in attendance by running a 4.33 in the 40. This apparently confirmed that McFadden is really, really good. Personally, I would have thought that was fairly obvious when he, oh, ran for 1,830 yards and 16 touchdowns as a junior, including a staggering 321 against South Carolina and 206 against eventual national champion LSU, but apparently it took those 4.33 seconds for all parties to be absolutely sure.

10. Everybody Cheats, Just Not My School

If there was a lesson to be learned from the NCAA's enforcement brass in 2007, it was: Don't turn yourself in. Seriously. In July, the organization slapped Oklahoma with two years' probation, docked it four scholarships, and forced it to vacate its eight wins from the 2005 season* as punishment for the phony car-dealership jobs of two players mentioned on page 251. Mind you, the infractions never would have come to light if not for an internal investigation by the school, and the players in question were dismissed as soon as they confessed to the crime. (A school official later told me the players lied the first two times they were interviewed, but the school kept investigating until it could prove the allegations true.) Elsewhere, Colorado was slapped with probation as a result of its own highly egregious, self-reported crimes: walk-on athletes had been inadvertently allowed to eat the same discounted meals as scholarship players. No word whether the punishment would have been lighter had they simply provided them with a few of those ubiquitous Arby's coupons from the Sunday paper.

While all this was going on, the Pac-10 and NCAA reached the two-

---

*The NCAA later redacted this part of the punishment upon an appeal by the university.

year mark of their "investigation" into allegations that former USC star Reggie Bush and family accepted nearly $300,000 in benefits from a pair of wannabe sports marketers during his final season at the school. The details of the allegations have been reported at length, and one of the individuals, ex-con Lloyd Lake, even spilled the beans in a tell-all book. Yet, as of this writing, it appeared that investigators were no closer to levying any sanctions than they were when the allegations first surfaced in April 2006, mainly because they involved outside sources, not the school itself, and the main figure, Bush, has refused to cooperate. So USC will likely endure no ramifications for letting a de facto professional athlete line up in its backfield, but Colorado remains in the doghouse for all those half-price lunches.

Afterword

While the historically unpredictable 2007 season may have caused headaches for those of us who cover the sport* and fill out weekly AP ballots, it proved undeniably exciting for the fans and, in turn, great for business. CBS, benefiting from a slew of highly entertaining games in the ever-rugged SEC, recorded its highest average rating for a season (3.7) since 1999, while ESPN averaged 2 million households per game, its third-highest total ever. In perhaps the most telling sign of the interest created by such unprecedented parity, a Thanksgiving weekend showdown between second-ranked Kansas and fourth-ranked Missouri—two age-old rivals who had never before staged such a nationally significant matchup—drew the seventh-largest audience in ABC history (nearly 11 million viewers). *ESPN GameDay*'s live broadcast from Kansas City that morning drew the biggest audience in the show's history.

All of which provided ample fodder for officials across the sport whose primary reason for continually defending the highly unpopular BCS is that it would devalue the regular season. "The BCS has created

---

*On at least three different occasions, I had to cancel a planned trip to an anticipated big game because one or both participants unexpectedly lost the week before.

what I call cross-watching," said Big East commissioner Mike Tranghese. Citing the dramatic, season-ending Pittsburgh–West Virginia upset, Tranghese noted, "An LSU fan had interest in that game, an Ohio State fan had interest in that game. Most of that would go away if we had a football playoff—that is one thing I'm certain of."

After witnessing the drama unfold all season, I'm inclined to agree with him. There's no questioning the unmatched excitement that unfolds annually during college football's regular season, a fact that usually gets overlooked come the end of said season when we all start hemming and hawing yet again about the sport's unsatisfying postseason. The BCS is still in drastic need of an overhaul (count me among the many who was disappointed by the plus-one's rejection), but unlike many of my colleagues, the 2007 season only further validated in my mind that while a playoff may work in other sports*, it's not necessarily the best fit for college football, where the regular season truly does matter.

As you've now seen, most of the topics in the book ring even more true today than they did a year earlier, and that applies to the very last thing I wrote as well. Chaos is and will always remain as integral a part of the sport as helmets and face masks. Not to mention that without it, I might not have a job.

---

*No one seemed to mind that the 14–6 New York Giants were deemed NFL champions over the 18–1 New England Patriots.

ACKNOWLEDGMENTS

After years of writing for the Internet, where the articles I write are often published within hours of penning the first word, the experience of writing a book has been one heck of a culture shock. The idea for *Bowls, Polls & Tattered Souls*—once known as *Three Yards and a Cloud of Nuts*—dates back to the spring of 2005 and was inspired by, of all things, a sci-fi satire. The movie version of Douglas Adams's classic *Hitchhiker's Guide to the Galaxy* was about to be released and I was rereading and admiring the entire series. In the books, the Hitchhiker's Guide is like an electronic, early 1980s-vision of Wikipedia, where the customer can look up any planet, culture, or hotspot in the galaxy and find an informational but also completely sardonic entry. (Example: "Earth—mostly harmless.") I thought to myself, What if there was a version of the Hitchhiker's Guide for college football? I imagined what the entry for "BCS" would sound like. Instead of, "The BCS is a coalition of five major bowl games that determine the national championship," it would probably say something like, "The BCS is really screwed up. I mean, *really* screwed up. You just can't imagine how screwed up it is."

Somehow, the book you hold in your hands is the end result of that initial daydreaming. And to think, it only took two and a half years to make it happen! The initial material was written in the spring and summer of 2005, while the majority of the chapters were written in the spring and summer of 2006 and the entire thing was completed and updated following the 2006 football season. This book would never have become a reality if not for the shared vision and passion of my editor, Stephen S. Power, and my agent, Jeremy Katz. Many thanks to both of them for their belief and support throughout this project. Dan Listwa deserves major credit for helping me formulate the idea back in its earliest stages. And the unsung hero of this project was my tireless research assistant/proofreader/all-around lifesaver Lesley McCullough McCallister. Lesley: thank you, thank you, thank you.

For the past 9 years, I have been blessed to have the support of numerous amazing editors and colleagues at *Sports Illustrated* and SI.com. I am grateful to them for giving me the opportunity to espouse my views on college football to a national audience while conveniently overlooking the fact that I'm making most of it up. Thanks to Paul Fichtenbaum, Terry McDonell, Mark Godich, B. J. Schecter, Adam Levine, Ryan Hunt, Gennaro Filice, and Mark Mravic. Thanks to my fellow writers on the beat, Luke Winn, Austin Murphy, and Mark Beech, with whom I've endured so many "treacherous" bowl weeks. And thanks to two former bosses and a former colleague, Phil Green, Mitch Gelman, and Marc Connolly, to whom I'm forever indebted for getting me started on this path.

Life on the college football beat wouldn't be nearly as rewarding without the friendship and wisdom of numerous valued colleagues, many of whom contributed to the material in this book. Thanks to Bruce Feldman, Pete Thamel, Dennis Dodd, Wendell Barnhouse, Teddy Greenstein, Andy Bagnato, Ivan Maisel, Pat Forde, Joe Schad, Ralph Russo, Tim Griffin, Heather Dinich, Emily Badger, Dave Curtis, and many, many others. Thanks to Allen Wallace and Jamie Newberg for their insight into the recruiting scene, and John Junker at the Fiesta Bowl for giving me a valuable history lesson on the bowl business. Thanks as well to all the coaches and players whom I've interviewed over the years and all the hard-working sports information directors who made it possible.

ACKNOWLEDGMENTS

Finally, thanks to my wonderful friends and family for their constant encouragement throughout this experience. You know who you are, but since you'll never let me hear the end of it if I don't mention you by name, many thanks to Brett Kurland, Hank Bullock, David Clark, Adam Rosner, Howard Rothbaum, Randi Stanley, Marla Trilling, Rachel Weinstein, Sasha Lyutse, Risa Katz, the members of my league champion New York City softball team, Brian Crane, and Jonathan Ganz. My most important supporter by far, however, will always be my mom, Karen Mandel. Thanks to her, Jamie, Amanda, Noah, and Deborah.

Index

INDEX

INDEX

INDEX